# BEYOND
# BLACK
# AND
# WHITE

# BEYOND BLACK AND WHITE

James P. Comer, M.D.

QUADRANGLE BOOKS

A New York Times Company

11-25-74

Second Printing

*Slavery Defended: The Views of the Old South,* 1963, edited by
Eric L. McKitrick, published by Prentice-Hall, Inc., Englewood
Cliffs, New Jersey. Used by permission.

*Lay My Burden Down,* 1958, by B. A. Botkin, published by Phoenix
Books, University of Chicago Press. Used by permission.

"An Indignation Dinner" by James David Corrother in *The Poetry
of the Negro,* 1949, edited by Langston Hughes and Arna Bontemps,
published by Doubleday & Co. Used by permission of Appleton-
Century-Crofts.

Library of Congress Card Number: 76–162812

*To my mother and father,*
*brothers and sisters,*
*wife and children,*
*and a better America.*

# Acknowledgments

My special thanks to my friend and colleague, Dr. David Musto, who encouraged me to write this book and who read, evaluated and discussed the manuscript. My thanks to Mrs. Miriam Abramovitz, Dr. Albert Solnit, the late Dr. Seymour Lustman, Mrs. Lottie Newman, Mr. Merrill Martin, Mrs. Karen Fortney, Ms. Zinaida Alexi, Mrs. Ethel Strainchamps, Mrs. Laura Kemper, Mrs. Joan Logan, Mrs. Katherine Raboteau, Miss Alba Borsoi, Mrs. Janice Gore, and other colleagues and friends who helped in the development of this book.

# Table
# of
# Contents

# Introduction
# by
# Robert Coles

Freud knew that his own life—his dreams and day-dreams, the rebuffs he went through while still a boy, the affections and resentments he long ago held or as a grown man continued to feel—counted a great deal in the life of a psychiatrist. *The Interpretation of Dreams* is in one sense Freud's long and hard look at his own life—as a child born to a certain family at a particular moment in Europe's history. Apart from the brilliance and originality of his mind, the founder of psychoanalysis had to have the gall to think that his experience would be thoroughly edifying to others; and he had to summon up the courage to talk openly about painful things, which he knew would arouse the anger and scorn of his many self-satisfied and insistently "proper" colleagues. He persisted because he believed he had something important to say; and again, what he said was never far removed from his own life's experiences.

Not all psychiatrists and psychoanalysts have been anxious to follow Freud's lead. Between ourselves and our readers—and yes, even our patients—we manage often enough to throw up the barrier of unalleviated abstractions. We build our theories, make our categorizations, turn them into sweeping formulations, and dare anyone to disagree. We build up for ourselves a stock of labels, and without much hesitation (let alone shame) we throw them around: this is *that,* he is *it,* what bothers her can all be included in one or another *word* or *term* we happen to have. And if our psychiatric terminology gets exhausted, we can always call upon other disciplines; there are the sociologists or the anthropologists or the political scientists with all their ways of explaining so very much—sometimes too much. Meanwhile individuals, particular men, women and children cry for a kind of understanding (and if need be, description) which takes into account what is shared, what is handed down by history and determined by a given society, but which also tries to evoke the precious and often defiant distinctiveness each of us never quite loses, however grim and controlling (or slyly seductive) the world around us has become.

Nor in America is one's race such a straitjacket that the bigots among us are in a perverse fashion proven right: to be black is of such overriding significance that all else means virtually nothing. At the very start of this book Dr. Comer lets us know that he is indeed black, has indeed been looked down upon, insulted, gently and not so gently ignored or treated with that condescension so many of us who are "educated" and well-off have learned to demonstrate. Still, as a boy he was also an American, and as one reads his reminiscences one can at times almost (never fully, granted) forget his skin color; because his parents, like millions of other mothers and fathers, had taken in and made their own certain values and ideals that characterize most of this nation's citizens. Work, study, sacrifice today's pleasures and moments of indulgence in the interest of a more secure and settled (if not happy) tomorrow; such admonitions have been handed down over the generations in this country—and if some social critics now scorn such advice, such a philosophy, such near religious injunctions, as a collection of pieties, some harmless, some thoroughly corrupting, there can be no doubt that the United States of America, as others have seen it from de Toqueville's time to our own, has been an extraordinary and in certain respects an enviable nation.

All along, of course, as we have grown to be number one, the world's richest and mightiest people, black families like the Comers of Alabama have worked and slaved (alas, in all the senses of the word) to keep us going, provide us with a substantial part of our productivity. All along, too, we who are white have had to contend with the singular and awful failing that slavery and its successors (the South's sharecropping system, the North's ghetto life) have amounted to—a mark upon our political system, a burden upon our integrity as a people, a symptom of a social disease of sorts we have not apparently been able to shake off. In this book Dr. Comer wants us to stop and consider the costs, to each and every one of us, whether black or white. He wants to remind us that many of his people for generations have tried scrupulously to behave themselves, mind their manners, spend their time being serious, conscientious and law-abiding —only to find themselves, in a way, made fools of. For doing so, for taking seriously what our Declaration of Independence and our Constitution (including the Bill of Rights) declare and promise, black families like Dr. Comer's have been laughed at by their kin and neighbors as well as by the white people across the tracks and over on the other side of town. Even so, they have persisted; by the thousands and thousands, in each generation, young black boys and girls have heard their parents, responded to their ministers, heeded the advice of a teacher, or of an aunt or uncle or grandparent, and stayed in school, studied, tried to find a job, made every effort to work hard, save money, move on up in the world, as we are all told to do in school, in church, on radio and television and in the newspapers. Even when the family is headed by black sharecroppers or tenant farmers in Clay County, Mississippi—as was no doubt the case with some of Dr. Comer's maternal ancestors; even then the loyalty to this country's social and economic values can be heard repeatedly—to the point that I have heard many an activist youth, bent on doing what he or she can to change the South, change the United States, just about cry (or scream) in mixed surprise and resignation and confusion.

Certainly a good case can be made by those who call Dr. Comer and his parents betrayed if not brainwashed; in the first part of this book the author himself virtually says as much. But as Dr. Comer keeps insisting, the mind is full of contradictions and ambiguities; the mind lives more comfortably with ironies and riddles than it can often bear to admit—to itself, let alone others. And for the black man those ironies and ambiguities are especially abundant, and at times taxing beyond description. If blacks have been thwarted, they also have been challenged. If they have been particularly hard-pressed, they have had to develop especially resilient ways of dealing with a cruelly exploitive world. If they have feared for their lives, and felt time and time again the futility of their situation, they have stirred themselves and their children as only the desperate can do—with tenacity and persistence and sly determination, and with a blandness or meekness or ingratiating humor that masks (and measures) the fierce pride and rage of people down and out, but not at all overcome.

Throughout this book Dr. Comer struggles with such paradoxes; nor does he try to resolve them into easy conclusions buttressed by his position as a child psychiatrist associated with one of the nation's leading universities. In fact this book lacks much that is familiar these days: no rhetoric, no hysterical denunciation, no apocalyptic announcements, no outbursts of hate, no calls to vengeance. Dr. Comer does indeed want to go "beyond black and white." He wants his own people to live fuller, better lives— free of demeaning and weakening poverty. He wants jobs for black men and women who seek them, decent homes and schools for black children. More than anything else, though, he wants his people to achieve for themselves the measure of dignity they have never stopped hoping for, praying for, dreaming of; and in wanting that he wants something very important for us, the "bossmen" of Clay County, Mississippi, or the "ordinary" Americans who live by the millions in the all-white suburbs that circle our cities so tightly. He knows, he ends his book saying, that the oppressor and the victim are together caught up in the "dilemma" Gunnar Myrdal wrote about many years ago and still lives to see unresolved. Blacks suffer hardest and most concretely, but whites, however rich and powerful and sure of themselves, pay a price, a high one indeed, for the meanness and brutishness they offer their children as a heritage—a dubious one indeed.

For years I have talked with some of those children, white Southerners or white Northerners, and heard the apprehensions and doubts they have learned, often before entering school. True, they do not go hungry, as many black children do in counties like Clay County, Mississippi; nor do they live under the awful circumstances that writers like Richard Wright and James Baldwin have described. But our white children are afraid, they feel confused and troubled, they shake their heads and ask and ask questions—until one day (it has to be acknowledged) they stop asking. Then it is that the mind gives up and the heart dies a little. Then it is that boys and girls become scarred with the kind of narrowness and fearfulness Christ spent His life on this earth trying to subdue. "I used to think I could be friends with a lot of kids, but now I'm not sure you can trust anyone except the people you know from your own street." So spoke a nine-year-old white boy I have known these recent years. Dr. Comer would not want to start comparing such a boy's tragedy with that of the many black children he knows; but on every page to follow he lets us know how sad it is for all of us when a child, any child, loses faith in his or her capacity to trust and enjoy other human beings. We can of course express easy thanks for the presence among us of a man like Dr. James Comer; but one suspects he has not written his book in order to earn our gratitude, but rather for another reason—in response to the doctor's sense of alarm and chagrin at the sight of needless, hence utterly outrageous human suffering.

R. C.

*Cambridge, Mass.*
*Oct. 1971*

# Foreword by Mayor Richard Gordon Hatcher

In direct contact with the consequences on racism, machine politics and mixed-up national priorities, I am sometimes moved to ask, "Does anyone understand?"

Does anyone understand that the jobless father often destroys himself, his family and his community? Does anyone understand the frustration of a mother who knows that her children will need the best education possible, but she can't afford it and the national community won't help pay for it? Does anyone understand that the young men who make city streets dangerous and destroy themselves with drugs could have been proud, productive citizens? Does anybody understand that these problems can destroy this country?

In *Beyond Black and White,* my friend Jim Comer has shown that he not only understands but that he cares deeply. He should, for he is a "son of the city" and from a low income black family, who went around, over and under every barrier, and made his way to a respected position in one of the most prestigious universities in the world. Fortunately for all of us, he did not turn his back on his beginnings or the problems of black people and America.

In this unique and important book, he has laid it on the line as only a black man with his unusual background, training and experience could have done. This is not a detached analysis written from a distance by a sympathetic observer. This is an objective but passionate quiet scream written by a man who has "stood the storm" and knows that the American Dream is going to be blown sky high unless its black dreamers can have more than a nightmare. But he does not just tell us that is the case . . . he shows us how and why.

He has substituted research for rhetoric, and energy for anger. He works on the reader's mind and heart. He has used his public health and psychiatric training with restraint; to inform and interpret rather than to overwhelm us. The readers are addressed as people rather than as blacks, whites, psychiatrists, social workers or politicians. Most important, he shared himself with us.

As a black person, I could walk in his shoes. The book awakened memories, hopes and fears which all black people must have. It will provide whites a vantage point which has not yet been available. The intermingling of the personal, the historical, the social and psychological perspectives provide us with the sense of immersion one must have to understand where we are as people and where we must go as a nation.

He did not simply lay out the problem, probe deeply into the minds of blacks and whites and then walk away from the dissection table. He outlined an action course which could lead us out of our present dilemma. The moves suggested are not glib or unreasonable. They do not pit business against government against labor against people. In fact, throughout the book, he does not see "bad people" but ordinary human beings caught in a web of complicated circumstances, destroying themselves and their country as they attempt to survive real and imagined dangers.

He does not assure us that it's going to be okay. In fact, he tells us that it may be too late. But he suggests that if the people who really care about America begin to pull together, we can still make it.

I hope that everyone who cares will hear the message of this book. It is a good place to start.

R. G. H.

*Gary, Indiana*
*Dec. 1971*

# BEYOND
# BLACK
# AND
# WHITE

# Free,
# Black
# and
# Twenty-Seven

One day in 1960, during my medical internship, I got an emergency call while I was on duty. When I reached the hospital ward to which I had been directed, I was greeted by a woman who had been anxiously awaiting someone to attend her mother, who seemed to be at the point of death. I recognized the younger woman. The sight of her face instantly and vividly took me back to a moment long ago that she had either forgotten or did not associate with the young black doctor who had responded to her call.

Nineteen years earlier, my mother had arranged a party in my classroom to celebrate my seventh birthday. I was the only black child in the class. The next day, one of my classmates insisted that I walk past his house with him on the way home from school. When we walked into his backyard, we saw his mother, the anxious woman who was now confronting me, on the back porch of their second-story apartment, hanging out laundry. Johnny called out triumphantly, "Ma, this is the boy that had the party in school yesterday!"

The woman walked over to the railing and peered down at me skeptically. "You didn't really have a *birthday* party, did you?" Puzzled as to why she would doubt it—birthday parties had become a tradition in our school—I nodded affirmatively.

"Well!" she said. "It's the first time I ever heard of a nigger having any kind of a party but a drunken brawl!" With that, she turned and walked into the house.

I remember feeling as if I had been struck by lightning. I walked away feeling hurt and confused. I was not only innocent but had no idea what she was talking about. That was my first encounter with overt racism.

By the time my patient was out of danger, several relatives, including my former second-grade classmate, had congregated outside her door. When he introduced me, his mother was quite surprised to learn that she had met me before. "So many of you kids have done so well," she said warmly. But obviously she had forgotten that she had once, in effect, predicted for me a life that would be a succession of drunken brawls. But I remembered, and I felt a surge of vindication; I had shown her. Them. White folks. With their ignorant stereotypes.

Once I was back in my apartment, I began to reflect on the curious occurrence. What an unlikely coincidence! How strange that I should see that unforgettable face again, with all the spiteful arrogance replaced by meek anxiety. I regretted that I hadn't reminded her, after the crisis was over, of the circumstances of our earlier meeting. But I dismissed that impulse; it might have added a little to my feeling of satisfaction, but I knew by then that it would not have changed her. Everybody knows one or two blacks who are, superficially, almost as good as white folks.

I remembered what my father had always said about racial bigotry: "Don't worry about it. Prepare yourself and your time will come." This meant, "Get a good education, then you will be accepted on your merits. The color of your skin won't matter." I believed that, and the belief was the mainspring of all my conduct up to then. I had gone through college and medical school sustained by faith in my father's little truism. For all my twenty-six years, I had worn a pair of blinders that permitted me to see only one thing: the best and shortest path toward making it as a physician. The weird encounter with the nemesis from my childhood made me feel I had completed the circle. She now accepted me; I was her mother's doctor. I was okay—race and all. I was soon to learn differently.

The following year I made a trip to Atlanta in my capacity as a (staff) member of the United States Public Health Service, based in the Washington headquarters. I was not allowed to stay in the downtown hotel with the other officers in the group, so I stayed at the Walla Hage hotel in the black section of Atlanta. The next morning I boarded a bus for the hour-long ride across town to a meeting. It was on that bus that the first of a series of incidents occurred which were to make me realize that the achievement-acceptance maxim was a myth.

Public transportation had recently been desegregated, and, without realizing that I was doing anything unusual, I took a seat directly behind the driver. I noticed that he was fitfully glaring at me in the mirror, but I thought maybe he just didn't like the way I tied my tie. But then I saw that the white people across the aisle were giving me dirty looks. That gave me a clue and I looked around. All the blacks were sitting in the back of the bus. There I was, with my neat business suit, my buttoned-down shirt, my properly tied tie and my fine leather attaché case. And nobody would sit next to me.

The bus emptied and filled several times as we rode across town. All the blacks who got on looked straight ahead, aiming for the rear. An occasional absent-minded white moved toward the empty seat by me, then noticed me and hurriedly moved on. At one stop, a young white woman carrying a small child got on. She walked toward the seat, then noticed me, and in her haste to get away, tripped and almost fell. She looked around desperately, but there were no other empty seats. The situation was tense. Everybody on the bus was watching her with commiseration. I looked around to see how her plight was to be resolved, and, as if to dampen the slight amusement my glance must have betrayed, a white man gave me a chilling look, got up and gave her his seat, and stood in the aisle.

My amusement at the gyrations of the bus riders was not undiluted. Beneath the irony of the trivial dumb show I had been watching, there were implications of tragedy. I had seen a small demonstration of the fact that whites would rather deny themselves comfort and convenience than violate even the smallest racial taboo, regardless of whether the laws that supported the taboo have been wiped from the books. And—more frighteningly—that blacks can still be coerced by social pressures into playing the whites' game.

After a few similar demonstrations of that fact, I began to realize that whites were never going to let me forget that I was black, and therefore, in their opinion, inferior. Often the best-intentioned whites, men and women who were my friends, said things to me that caused me to despair for their souls. "Just forget about your race and be a good doctor," they would say to me affectionately. Translation: "We all know you have a serious congenital defect there, man, but you can work hard and compensate." I also began to recognize the fact that I had been functioning from that very view myself. I had made myself into a successful professional man just to prove that blackness and inadequacy were not synonymous. So I faced the real truth: I did not like being black.

Now, at twenty-seven, with the achievement-acceptance theory debunked, I saw that I had to get busy and establish a positive black identity. Quickly. This realization was a crucial step toward psychological freedom—the freedom to be me, not a physician, or a middle-class Negro, or a college graduate, or an imitation white. Just me. Free, black and twenty-seven. The next steps were harder.

Shortly after the Atlanta trip there was another incident that sharpened my need and gave initial direction to its fulfillment. One Sunday I took my family to a plush officers' club in Washington, D.C. I was enjoying the atmosphere, the meal and my status, but then my pleasure began to distress me. Several of the white officers and their families entered the club, accompanied by ten or twelve children from Junior Village, a center for dependent children in the city. About two-thirds of the children were black. Watching them I began to feel very guilty that I had not done the same. But I was also aware of the fact that the presence of the black children embarrassed me.

Was it their conduct, which was no different from that of the white children in the group? Was it their black dependency? Inadequacy? At the time I was not sure about the cause of my uneasiness, but in retrospect, I think the dependent children implied black inadequacy, even immorality. How could I have a positive black identity if a disproportionate number of black people were dependent and judged inadequate? I had to do something. I do not deny that my desire to be involved in changing that situation was as much for me as for the people whom I had wanted to help. The most driving force for action was the realization that my previous inaction showed me up as a fraud. The fact that I had begun to read and talk about racial problems right after my "re-union" with my childhood tormentor had so far proved nothing; I had not yet lifted a corrective finger.

Seeing those children and recognizing my uneasiness galvanized me. I became a volunteer at Hospitality House, a helping agency which was founded by a middle-income black woman, Mrs. Nadine Winters, and sponsored by middle-income whites and blacks. None of the books I had been reading had prepared me for what I observed and experienced at Hospitality House. In fact, I had never met the part of the black community that came through the doors of Hospitality House.

A youngster whose fatherless family had been evicted and was then in temporary shelter at Hospitality House left for school asking, "Mama, where will I find you tonight?" One afternoon I found a woman experiencing an acute anxiety reaction. She had come to the House two months earlier after a serious suicide attempt provoked by the fact that she was expecting her fifth child and had been purged from the District of Columbia welfare rolls for allegedly having "a man in the house." After great effort, we got her back on the rolls, but she informed me that her check was being held up because of a clerical oversight.

The temperature was ninety-eight degrees. The overwhelmed mother had spent the entire morning in the clinic where her three sons were receiving treatment for seizures. The infant in her arms was hungry and crying loudly. There was no food in the house. She said to me, "My baby is not going to starve, even if I have to . . ." I knew the alternatives she had, which could lead to the next unwanted pregnancy. Often a laborer, a busboy or someone else who is earning a wage gets called in in situations like this. In fact, that is often why the man is in the house.

Many months later, when she was working, she repaid the small loan made to her during the period of stress. At that time, several congressmen were pressuring the District of Columbia Welfare Board to purge their rolls of immoral, lazy, cheating women, who did not want to do anything but draw a check. I was then a full-time physician in a city clinic used primarily by welfare applicants and I knew from my encounters there and at Hospitality House that, for the most part, these were not lazy or immoral women. Most were honest, well-meaning women, trapped and overwhelmed by a complex set of circumstances.

I also saw well-meaning men desert their families. It was clear that it would only be a matter of time before some of the children would repeat the cycle or be in trouble with the law. To me, it did not make sense. People were in trouble, yet a few congressmen waged irresponsible war on them.

These circumstances were as confusing as some of the things I had observed during my internship a year or two earlier, when I had an opportunity to work for a colleague in my hometown, East Chicago, Indiana. He had a large, mostly black practice and many of the patients were on public welfare. During the first day in the office, I saw forty-five patients, delivered two babies and made four house calls. The most striking aspect was the large number of seriously depressed patients he saw in his practice. The sense of hopelessness, helplessness and despair was all-pervasive. An unusual number of people had questionable physical illnesses; most of their illnesses were psychosomatic. (I have now seen this phenomenon in many institutionalized patients; it occurs in a disproportionate number of oppressed, low-income black patients, particularly among those over the age of forty. I have come to classify this as social depression—a result of overwhelmingly adverse social circumstances.)

My colleague's office was diagonally across the street from a bar called the Frat. It was the place where I used to hang out as a teenager and young adult. At the end of my first day in the office, I stood at the window and looked at some of my old friends who were standing on the corner. Just a few years before, I had stood with them on the same corner. For a fleeting moment I wondered why I had bothered to go to medical school; they were having a good time and I had just come to the end of an exhausting, upsetting day.

After I left the office, I made a house call to a family living over the Frat. As I walked through the crowd, my friends greeted me, "Hey, Doc, my man! . . . Look at that cat with his bag! . . . What's happening, man? . . . Hey Doc, save me! . . . Doc,

I'm dyin'!" After I made the house call, I had a drink with Tim Sams. Tim was a bright fellow who had dropped out of high school in his junior year and had been working in the steel mill ever since. He could make everybody laugh. Many times during the years I was going to college, he had told me that he was going back to finish high school and see me down on the campus. During our conversation, he said, "Doc, don't let them kid you. Them cats talk, and laugh, and look like they're having a ball, but there's not one man out there that wouldn't trade places with you if he could." Thinking of our foredoomed friends outside, we were silent; Tim stared morosely down at his glass. When he shrugged off his gloom and turned to pick up the conversation, I could see that his eyes were glistening with tears. The sight of Tim—the funny man—crying had a tremendous effect on me. But laughter, masking hopelessness, is a common defense when the cards are stacked against you.

One night shortly afterward I made a house call to a basement apartment "across the tracks." The patient was the mother of a fellow I had known in high school and college. I knocked on the door and a weak voice asked me to come in. I was a little hesitant because it was dark and this was a rough area. I opened the door and turned on the light switch. The walls, floors and furniture were dark with cockroaches. I shuddered. Three small children were asleep in orange crates and they began to stir when I turned on the light. I was shaken; I could not believe anybody lived like this. I had passed this house many times; I had played basketball in the empty lot down the street. This could not be. But it was. *She* was. The children in the orange crates were.

I examined the woman and I found no physical disorders. She was suffering from chronic depression. I suspect that the depression accounted, in part, for the fact that she had had six children out of wedlock and for the condition of her home.

I had other experiences that year that defied understanding: A black man scarred for life in a fight with a friend over a cheap bottle of wine. A white doctor who gave all his black patients penicillin because he felt that "they all have a little venereal disease." A white patient who could not believe there were any black doctors.

After I completed my internship, I joined the Public Health

Service to give myself time to figure it all out. I was assigned to a District of Columbia health clinic and my experience there raised more questions for me than it answered. A majority of the people I met at the clinic had worked regularly all their lives for less than an adequate wage. The first accident or illness they incurred forced them to go on welfare because they had no savings. But they were abused by congressmen and clinic personnel alike.

Most of the D.C. health clinic's personnel were not overtly antagonistic toward the patients; but there was an indifference, a coldness, a covert disrespect that the more perceptive patients sensed. Even the nurses' aides, who were black people from the community, often demonstrated an inflexibility and a knack for making things more difficult than they had to be for the patients. Unnecessary delays, fussing about bureaucratic details and other forms of direct and inadvertent harassment were common because the aides had the same attitude toward the people who required their services as did the complaining congressmen on the Hill.

Something was radically wrong and I didn't know what it was. People were suffering, and instead of being helped they were being criticized and abused. I sensed that the root cause was the way the whole social system functioned—or malfunctioned. How could I go out and treat people for symptoms of a condition my medical training had not taught me to diagnose? Nothing in my little black bag did any good at all.

What I had not acknowledged was that the problems of the people who came to the clinic were my problems too. Then the most stunning confrontation of all made me realize that while my economic life was less shaky than most black people's, my social and psychological plight was identical.

Then a group of black professional men invited a Muslim minister to explain his beliefs and practices to us. We met in the plush apartment of a colleague. There was wall-to-wall carpeting, twelve-year-old Scotch whiskey, stereophonic sound and thick T-bone steaks. When I walked into the meeting, everything in that apartment represented what I wanted and was prepared to get. When I left, I was flying high—not on the whiskey but on the minister's message. Later, when I examined his arguments, I knew I didn't agree with all of them, but he had made me realize that steaks and stereo were not enough to make me whole.

His presentation had been designed to instill a pride in black-ness—my blackness. He talked about the origin of black people, the meaning of the black experience, the importance of self-respect and group respect, and the role of family life. But why should this discussion touch me? By the standards of many, all the black professionals at that meeting had "made it." We were achievers. We should not have needed the psychological support he offered us. But we did. The reason we needed it is wrapped up in the damaging effect of white racism on every aspect of black life.

Reflecting on my own experience, which was comparatively placid, I could see that the reality is that black America has been, and is, subjected to a continuous bombardment of irrational threats to the self-concept that are above and beyond the threats experienced by other Americans. It was the need of our social and psychological souls that education, good jobs, prestige and opportunity did not meet. It was this need in me that the Muslim minister stirred. It is this need for a positive concept of self and group which is at the root of the black consciousness and black power movements. It is because of this unfulfilled need that not even the elimination of poverty will cure the ills of black Ameri-cans.

Atlanta, the clinic, Hospitality House and now the minister gave me a look at the source of my own pain. There was obvi-ously something radically wrong with the notion that all you have to do is to work hard, get ahead and be accepted to feel comfort-able and adequate as a black man in America.

I decided to study public health and psychiatry. Then I could help individuals, learn more about the confusing behavior around me—including my own—and learn more about the nature of the social system in which I sensed that many problems were rooted. But my formal training was only one source of insight. The other was my own experience of growing up black in a white-controlled America.

The analyses of the black experience presented by blacks and whites in the past few years do not give a composite picture. The view of blacks as totally overwhelmed, poverty-stricken, suffering, hostile, disorganized, sick people is only partly accurate. Black people are many people: some angry and active; some angry and passive; some not so angry; many poor and suffering; a few rich; some religious and pious; some religious and fun-loving; some rejecting religion; some trying to make a place in the total society; some tuned in largely to the black community; some ready to go against the total society; some in stable families; some in unstable families. There is, and always has been, a social, cultural and political center majority—not too poor, religious but practical, tuned in to the black community and to the larger society. I grew up in a kind of cultural short centerfield. (In a world series game, the umpire stands there because it gives him a good view of all the action.) While I was busy playing the game, I could not see it all. Reflection explains a lot of things. It was to my experience that I turned for enlightenment.

My mother, who was born in rural Clay County, Mississippi, experienced extreme hardship and poverty while growing to young adulthood in Memphis, Tennessee. All her days of formal education did not equal two school years. My father was born in Comer, Alabama. Comer was the name of the white family for which my family were first slaves and later servants, and which gave my ancestors the surname I bear. Braxton Bragg Comer, Governor of Alabama from 1907 to 1911, was the "grand patriarch" of the area during the period my father was growing up.

Both my parents' families were large and relatively close-knit. During my childhood in Indiana, Southern cousins periodically came north to "earn a little summer money" or to "stay with Uncle Hugh for a few months" until they found a job and got established in the north. Aunts, uncles and home folk (unrelated friends from the same local Southern community) visited often. I listened intently to a variety of tales and direct and indirect accounts of life "down home," told from the vantage point of the sharecropper, the house servant and the "kept" professionals who are selected by and responsible to the white power structure.

Such information from relatives and friends later helped me challenge the textbook account of the experience of black folks. I knew that many of them shared goods and services and helped each other when politicians and social scientists were saying that was not the case. At times of church conventions we would sleep on the floor and visitors from out of town would use our beds. Giving one's last dollar to an uncle or a friend rather than putting it in the bank puzzled the social scientist, but made sense when one knew that friends would help in an emergency and the bank would not. I also learned that a lot of the happy, faithful servants were not so happy or faithful but were doing what they had to do to hold on and survive.

Growing up in a middle-sized, multi-ethnic community rather than in a large urban area or a segregated Southern community also helped in getting a full picture. We lived in East Chicago, a city of approximately 50,000 in the northwest corner of Indiana between Gary and Chicago. This situation afforded direct contact with a wide socio-economic range of whites. The myth of good whiteness and bad blackness could not stand the weight of experience which came from my relatively intimate contact with white people. I almost—but never completely—bought the myth that has long been the basic justification for the exploitation of black people in America. It is difficult to convince a black person who has done well academically in a racially mixed school that his race is of innately lower intelligence than the white race.

My neighborhood was typical of the black community's complexity. The house on one side of ours had broken stairs, weeds growing in the yard instead of grass, and a sagging fence. One of the youngsters living there was a delinquent but was "saved" when he became a remarkable high school athlete. Another eventually had nine children, began to drink heavily and finally spent a great deal of time in a mental institution. Another was an outstanding athlete but did not go to college and eventually worked in the steel mills, drove a flashy car and wore fancy clothes. He died in his thirties from the complications of alcohol. Next door to that family lived the Browns. They had a long yard with a manicured lawn, a neat, well-cared-for home and a white picket fence. Mr. Brown worked all day in the mill and worked all evening caring for his home.

My father and mother built our house themselves. My mother helped haul bricks and carry lumber to build most of it. A "jack-leg" carpenter helped them finish up the back porch and steps. Apparently he did a poor job because I remember my folks complaining about the stairs and the fact that "Negroes just don't do business right."

The fellow across the street earned a Phi Beta Kappa key and graduated with top honors from a professional school. Next door to his house was a truck barn—it was quite possible to rezone black communities for such structures. On the other side of our house was a family of ten children. Five became college graduates. Down the street lived Mr. Thomas. He had a lot of money which, I am told, he earned from charging 100 per cent interest to fellow blacks who "threw away their money the day after payday." He once tried to get a franchise to operate a taxi service in our city, but city officials would not even accept his application.

In another house lived the Carters. Mr. Carter was a tall handsome man with "good hair" (straight, like white hair), who could have passed for white. In the steel mill he did pass for white and as a result had a better job than most of the other black men. His son, Bobby, was killed while training as a pilot in the Army Air Force Training Center for Negroes at Tuskegee, Alabama. My cousin, Larry, said that if *he* had to die, it was not going to be in a segregated army. Mr. Brown told Larry that he would either go where "they" (the Establishment) told him or to jail. This powerlessness in the face of racism explains why Muhammad Ali, who refused the draft, is a hero to so many blacks.

But to me all these were racial realities far off someplace. "Too bad . . . it's hard to be black" must have been my reaction. But I was too busy going to school and playing football in the street and basketball in the alley to be much concerned. And besides, "My parents won't let anybody bother me!" Then, too, I knew white people and they were not so hot.

Not far from us was the Lakota Hotel—a white bar and flophouse. The drunks frequently staggered past our house and we were warned to stay away from them. There were many fights at the hotel and the police were always there, although sometimes they were there having a drink. Thus, the first fighting and drinking people I knew were white. That is probably why I was so confused by the attack on blacks that I heard after my seventh birthday party.

Our neighborhood slum landlord was Jake Sacage. Jake was a Hungarian who barely spoke English. He owned a dirty apartment building and a little store. The rumor was that he cheated the kids when they came in to buy candy. I never knew for sure because we always shopped at Huffs, a neighborhood store around the corner. I always heard that the Huffs were not like "regular Jews" because they did not cheat blacks and always tried to help some of the people in need. In fact, Mrs. Huff was always scolding Mrs. Slaughter, a black woman, for allowing her children to run in the street all day while she was drinking beer in her dirty house. Most of the women agreed that Mrs. Slaughter ought to do better, but did not think Mrs. Huff should "butt into her business."

(This neighborhood situation was an example of the conditions that have led to the ambivalence which many blacks feel toward Jews. On the one hand is the Jewish helper who is a step above on the status ladder looking down. On the other is the "regular Jew," who, according to the neighborhood gospel, cheated and exploited blacks for his own profit. Of Jews who helped, the question is asked, "Should they?" What does it mean to black adequacy if blacks *need* help? Nobody in a competitive society can *need* help and be a man, an adequate person.)

Not far from my family, two black brothers pooled their funds and bought a house when the last white family moved out. It fell into a state of disrepair and I heard a few of the black men on the block complain about "colored people straight out of the South." Obviously I picked up "white racist teaching" from blacks in this and other incidents. There was no understanding of or explanation for the unfortunate condition of blacks. Some whites said it was because they were black. Blacks read and heard that explanation, and developed negative feelings about themselves. They even passed these feelings along to their children. But there was also a kind of respect passed on—a respect for old folks and ministers, particularly, which eventually generalized into a respect for others.

The church played a big role in the development of the black man's self-respect and dignity. Because of the church's dominant role, Sunday was always a big day at our house. We awoke to the smell of bacon and the sound of gospel music. Every house down the street seemed to be tuned in to the same station. Our favorite vocal group was the "Wings over Jordan." My father was a deacon, a position of great importance in the black church, and a deeply religious man. He said a very long grace and we often got a little restless around the table. Sometimes my two brothers and I would make faces and I could hardly keep from laughing—my younger sister would get mad at us and we would look up and find our mother giving us a withering glance. All eyes closed and there was silence again. She would not tolerate any disrespect for our father. The black woman often zealously protected the dignity of the black man, because his dignity was under such constant assault outside the home.

The major roots of our family were in the church; ours was the Zion Baptist. Some of the ministers could touch the congregation deeply. One approach always caused people to shout and cry: these were the sermons that were full of assurances that conditions would be better in the hereafter. They were also designed to help a rejected and abused people feel good about themselves and enjoy a sense of purpose and worth.

During such sermons, the minister would gradually build to a high emotional pitch and then in a repetitive fashion cry out, "He's a Rock in a weary land! He's a Shelter in a mighty storm! He rescued Daniel from the lion's den! He's a Father to the fatherless! He's a Light in the darkness! He's Eyes to the blind and a Cane to the cripple! He brought the children of Israel out of bondage and He'll take care of you!" With each assertion, the "Amens," "Yes, Reverends," and "Yes, Lords" would become more frequent and the excitement would grow. When he reached "He'll take care of you," the shouting and crying would start.

Some of the women would lurch back in the pews, as if having a fit, their arms flailing back and forth. I often thought the force against the pews would pull them from their moorings. Two or three ushers would rush up to control them. One man in our church shouted and others would occasionally weep quietly with one hand over their eyes. I often wondered why grown men would cry. As a child, I never did quite understand the shouting and crying and the explanations I received always left me more curious: "Well, Negroes have had it hard"; "Some people have to let it all out." Later, when I met many of these people in the steel mills and in the world beyond the church, I began to understand what the shouting and weeping were all about. While an element of African and even Southern black and white religious culture was involved, the intensity of the response reflected the sense of frustration and helplessness the people felt. The church was the place to discharge frustration and hostility so that one could face injustice and hardship the rest of the week.

The black church had another important function: it was a place for participation and belonging. The deacons, trustees and ushers were ten feet tall on Sunday. This was not Inland Steel, Miss Ann's kitchen nor the bank. This—the church—was theirs. In retrospect, the trustees were like the city board of finance and the deacons were like the city council. There was a little bit of respect for everybody.

One Sunday I visited a storefront church with a friend of mine. Several of the choir members and ushers were people I knew from school. It seemed to me odd that some of these people were quite withdrawn in school and were hardly known to the teachers and staff, but in their church they were lively, active participants. At the storefront church that day, I found at least part of the answer. The choir gave a rousing rendition of a spiritual. The soloist responded to the audience's enthusiasm with these words, "One thing I like about this church is that if you have a speck of talent you can use it, and the people will love you and respect you for it." I had noticed this in my own church as well. In the Baptist Young People's Training Union Bible Drill, girls who barely participated in school could quickly find the chapter and verse. Many black children were not respected in school even when they attempted to use their talent. I still observe that many black children who are turned off in school and considered dull are turned on in church and in other less alien places.

The biblical and hereafter sermons bothered my mother. "What's he talking about David, John, Moses and Paul and all those people for? . . . Why does he talk about golden streets and rewards in Heaven? . . . I'm worried about these cement sidewalks I have to walk down every day. He ought to be teaching our people about saving their money and buying homes and taking care of their families."

Occasionally a minister would come to town who could preach two sermons—one spiritual and one intellectual. Then many of the educated people, old and young, who had abandoned church would come back. But it would never last. Soon the people who wanted to hear the spiritual sermon would complain that he "wasn't preaching." These people were the backbone of the church: the church was their major investment and they were the major contributors. They did not want the church branching out and getting into areas like business, education, or even recreation. I recall that one of the major debates in my church was over a plan to have a youth night. The officers would not have any dancing in our church! Some members argued that it would be better to have the youth dancing in the church than in some "smoke-filled den of iniquity." Others countered that if young people are going to sin, they should not sin in the House of the Lord. The church was for listening to the Word of God!

Divisions of this sort were usually between the group who turned toward the values and interests of the total society and those who remained primarily tied to the substitute culture—the black church. Education and opportunities in the "outside world" enabled some to keep their feet in two cultures—the church and the total society. Others, for various reasons, remained enmeshed in the culture of the church alone.

One Sunday, a sixteen-year-old girl brought her born-out-of–wedlock baby to church and created quite a stir. A few women fussed over the baby. The minister talked about forgiveness and understanding. Most of the women did not see it that way—they grumbled about "people carrying on over the baby like it had a daddy." Some of the women who complained were of the "black puritan" background. This "better class of Negroes," as some have referred to themselves, attempted to "out-middle-class" or "out-decent" the white middle and upper classes in vain efforts to win respectability. Because of the stereotype of the immoral Negro, sexual morality was an issue of special concern. In the academy my father had attended as a youngster, girls were always accompanied by a matron in front of the line and at the rear. Until very recently, supervision of female students was much stricter at black colleges than at white.

Because the minister and the church could gratify so many social and psychological needs, he and the institution were very powerful.

My parents occasionally disagreed about the church. I sometimes thought my mother was less religious than my father. I asked her about it once. She replied that it was not that she was less religious, just that she did not trust all the people who claimed they were called to spread the gospel. Gradually I came to understand what she meant. One Sunday the minister was preaching a "race sermon." This is a sermon in which the minister "gives white folks the business." The congregation responds with loud and enthusiastic "Amens," as the sins and wrongs of white America are spelled out. Just as the minister was warming up to the subject, the head user rushed down the aisle and onto the pulpit and whispered something in the minister's ear. This was highly unusual; nobody ever disturbed the minister after he started his sermon. The usher returned to the vestibule and brought two white visitors to the rostrum. They were given the honored seats of the assistant pastors and the minister continued his sermon. But there was an abrupt change in his tone. He began to preach about love and brotherhood and how white folks and colored folks could get along together.

The visitors were from the Inland Steel Company. As I recall, Inland Steel gave a large check to the church every Christmas. (Some say it was as much as $1,000.)

My mother's distrust of certain ministers was again vindicated when I was in the seventh grade. The older black students asked me to talk with a minister I knew to get his support for our side in a disagreement in our school. There was a black Paul Robeson Glee Club and a white glee club. The black students did not think we needed both. When I explained the argument to the minister, he paused thoughtfully and said, "Well you see there's a difference in our voices. We have richer, stronger voices and that's the reason for separate glee clubs." Although I had been taught to respect my elders, particularly ministers, I argued that if our voices were stronger and richer it would appear that the white glee club could use our help. He did not appreciate my point of view and told me that some day I would understand. I understood at the end of the year when I saw him on the school stage giving the benediction at the high-school graduation. He was the only Negro on the stage; in fact, I am told it was a black first for East Chicago. He had had to "go along with 'the Man's' program" to appear on the program —to take one step forward.

In the recent flurry of major studies of the black experience, only E. Franklin Frazier and Carter Woodson, both blacks, have given more than a passing glance at the role of the black church. The director of a black-studies program told me that he could not find collections of church sermons in the libraries of major universities. Some young students would like to ignore it all together. But how can we? The root, heart and soul of black culture in America are in the black church—whether we blacks like it or not.

The school was, for many of my black churchmates, "the white man's world." I was aware of that very early. I can remember thinking that if Marshall Long can do so well in the Baptist Young People's Union Bible Drill, why could he not do the same in school? All the B.Y.P.U. crowd hung out on the corner of Carey and 140th Streets. I knew many other kids who could think fast, talk fast and act fast in the playground, in church and on the corner, who seemed to be immobilized in the classroom. I now recognize this as a complex syndrome, but one aspect of it was the sense of rejection and lowered esteem black youngsters felt in school. The message they got was subtle and not so subtle, direct and indirect, sometimes unintentional, other times deliberate.

There were only five or six black children in the elementary school that I attended. Until the third grade, I was the only one in my class. In fourth grade there were two others. One day, the fourth grade teacher urged us all to join the book club at the library. A few weeks later she asked how many gold stars we had earned for reading books. I had accumulated more stars than any of my classmates, but, the other black youngsters had not joined the reading club. The teacher was angered and told them, "If you colored boys don't want to be like the rest of us you should not come to our school." She had ignored my reading habits and the fact that I was "colored." But I remember wishing, as she yelled, that I was not "colored."

When I was in the fifth grade, there was a major uproar over school integration. The following year many more black students came to the school than in previous years. Some of the white students didn't like the new students and some of the blacks didn't like the whites. I was in the middle. The white students had been my friends, but I knew that the black students were my people. I had been taught that. In fact, my older sister had been one of the teachers at the predominantly black school from which they had come. It was not long before we had a problem. In my sixth-grade class we had class officers and the existing officer appointed a successor every week. I was the only black appointed. One day, before I realized it, I was on the floor complaining about the practice of passing over other blacks for class office. The white students were surprised. They had appointed me because I was one of the old gang; now why was I complaining? After a heated discussion we agreed not to appoint by race anymore.

I stole a quick glance at the teacher, whom I liked very much. I was afraid she would be irritated with me, but she was quietly knitting away. As I left the class, she winked at me. I was relieved and grateful that she understood. But if my teacher had not approved of my stand, and if my white classmates had not gone along with it, I would have been crushed.

I realize now that anxiety about pleasing a white authority or a white majority can prevent blacks from speaking out for black rights, and can lead black social activists into settling for watered-down compromises. This is one of the reasons blacks in predominantly white political and professional groups often form their own caucuses—black students, black teachers, black psychiatrists, black congressmen.

One day a white girl in my class told me that she knew my mother, but would not tell me how or why she knew her. I asked my mother and she acknowledged that she had once worked for the white girl's mother. Seeing that I had some troubled feelings about that, she assured me, "You are just as bright and clean and good as she is and you can learn just like she can. You had better!" Time and time again, when my self-esteem was threatened, my parents provided such support and incentive.

One of my mother's lessons startled me. One Saturday as the fruit peddler passed through our street, a peach basket fell off the back of his truck. All the kids on the block grabbed as many peaches as they could and ran before the driver could stop. Because it was dishonest, I refused to join them. When the kids started eating their fruit, I went to my mother and asked for one of the peaches she had bought. She said, "If you don't know how to get when the getting's good, you can do without." A while later she gave me a peach and said, "Let that be a lesson to you." I was very confused. My mother had always stressed honesty and fairness; she would even use a ruler to divide a candy bar four ways so that none of the four children would be cheated. Years later

I realized that she had used the peach episode to give me a survival lesson.

The message went like this: "Look, black boy, it's tough to be black and poor in America. You try to play by the rules, but sometimes you can't. You may have to do what you have to do to make it." It was a confusing message; however, I understood it by the time I needed to utilize it. When I was about to fail an eye test in the steel mill, the tester fortuitously dropped his pencil. While he was picking it up, I sneaked a peek at the chart with my already tested good eye and I got the job. My entire career was at stake. I needed money to go to school. Sure, whites do it too. But blacks, with fewer resources, no second chance and fewer alternatives, have to be deceptive to get by more often. That kind of getting by can become a habit that will eventually be self-defeating.

Throughout my childhood, I received enough input and protection to feel fairly good about myself, so that one part of me assumed that it was the white man who had the problem. When I was ten, we moved to another neighborhood. The first Sunday in the new house I remember being surprised when I saw a lot of white people all dressed up and going to church. I had figured a few things out. Now I was confused again. I did not know that so many white people ever went to church. I could not understand how they could go to church and treat blacks the way they did. My father explained that the white man hid from the truth, but that some day he would have to change or face up to the fact that he is not a good Christian. That was when I started asking myself, "What is there in the white mind that anaesthetizes it to the cruelty inflicted on blacks and its inevitable consequences?"

I had a great deal of respect for my father. Not only did he help me with the racial rough spots but he was also totally reliable. You could set your watch by the time he got home from work. If he promised you a baseball bat for next week, you could start preparing for the game. When we were in public, particularly the white public—schools, grocery stores, etc.—he said very little. He left most of the "out-front" operating to my mother, but behind the scenes he was the boss and made the big decisions. This was a carry-over from the South. It was safer for black women to be assertive in the outside world than it was for black men. Sociologists discovering mother-centered black families miss the fact that within the family environment, it was often different in real and important ways.

The age of innocence for a black male is before puberty. Around thirteen years of age, relationships with white students become more complicated. When I was thirteen, I received a telephone call from one of the white girls in my class who was then at a party given by a mutual friend. I could not tell whether she was calling me because the friends felt guilty about not having invited me or because they had made her call as a punishment in a game. Either way, I was very hurt. My mother was sitting nearby and figured out what was going on, although she said nothing that night. The next day, as she was washing the collard greens, she brought the subject up. She explained to me that as black and white children grow older, they usually grow apart. She said that it was mainly because of the fear white people have that black men will want to marry white girls. But she emphasized, "For the eleventh time, don't you worry about that. You're just as clean and bright and smart as they are, and you learn! Don't worry about all that other stuff."

Constant daily reminders that it's tough to be black caused many youngsters enough discomfort to turn off or turn away. But my parents had a foot firmly planted in both cultures, and going to school and getting ahead were not to be questioned—hurt feelings or no hurt feelings. When my self-esteem was battered, it was patched up and I was sent back into the battle. My parents' main concern was to keep my attention riveted on the goal. I was so busy getting gold stars and the best grades, singing, playing ball and running for office, that I hardly noticed a racial slur here and there. My parents always said, "You never let race stop you from doing what you want to do. The only time you stop to fight a racial injustice is when it stands squarely in your path. Otherwise you'll be fighting all the time."

This formula worked, but the results were a mixed blessing. Unlike black students only a few years before me in the same school, I usually got full recognition for achievement from the teachers—all of whom were white. I was elected and appointed to school positions with the support of the son of my part-time employer, and of schoolmates for whose families my mother had worked as a domestic. These were tangible demonstrations that if you work hard you can make it and will be accepted. However, they made me particularly vulnerable to the pervasive rejection I was soon to encounter in the real world.

One more "school" provided lessons for the real world. That was the school of the street. Just as one must know the church to know an important segment of black life, one must also know the street and its people. My street days started on the corner in front of the Frat. There I met jive cats, illiterate geniuses, pimps, prostitutes, philosophers and ordinary people, including some of the church people.

The Frat was exciting. The first night I went in I was greeted by Ray Dodson, one of my former "street brothers."

"Hey man, what are you doing here?"

"Looking for the happenings like you, man."

"Well, skin then brother."

We did the black salute (a sliding of the palms in a near handshake).

He said, "Let me buy you a drink and initiate you right, man."

That was a strange thing about the crowd at the Frat. In the middle of a long steel strike and no paydays, my friends there would be almost broke but would still buy me a drink. Later, when I had more money than they did, they would still insist on buying. Trying to feel adequate in a society that demands and then limits one's opportunity to be adequate takes unusual forms. Buying the drinks is one of them.

On Friday and Saturday nights the Frat was full of men and women, all having a good time—laughing, "wolfing" and talking. One night Joe Johnson started reciting "The Signifying Monkey" (a well-known off-beat verse which has to do with aggressive provocation and reprisal). He went on for what seemed to me to be more than thirty minutes. I don't believe I could have memorized a verse that long. (Joe probably did poorly in school and I'm not sure he ever graduated.)

Joe Johnson was also a barber-shop philosopher. The black barber shop was a place where brilliant illiterates speculated about fascinating subjects of all kinds, from the nature of life to the probability of playing the correct policy number. The language and style were different, but the thoughts were often as profound as those I have heard in professional circles.

Summarizing the black community's handicaps, one of these wise men said some fifteen years ago, "If the grass ain't growing too well, don't ask what's wrong with the grass! Say, how come it ain't been no rain? And what's wrong with the soil?" Only within the past couple of years have most social scientists begun to study the problems created by the social system rather than the victims of the system.

One night my college roommate and I went to a real dive, Joe's Place, in my hometown. A black policeman had warned me against going there. Someone there was usually knifed or shot or beaten up. I had to see it. We entered through a door on the side of a storefront. The main door was barred shut and two or three pool tables filled the room. Two bare light bulbs lighted the entire place. Several tough looking cats played pool, hardly saying a word. This place was different from the Frat; there was not the gaiety and richness, nor the sense of oneness. There was something sad, hopeless and frightening about it. A man who had been sick earlier was lying in the store display window. No one paid any attention to him. Only a dog stood over the vomitus and flies buzzed around it. I felt sick. As we walked by, my roommate asked, "Remember Roy Beck, Jr.?" "Yeah," I replied. Without looking back, he cocked his finger toward the man in the window and said. "That's him." Roy was a nice guy in school—he got average grades and had never bothered anyone. I learned that he eventually died from an overdose of heroin.

Later, when I thought about the scene at Joe's Place, it occurred to me that most of the people in that room had been under the influence of one drug or another, including the son of one of our church deacons. At the time, I had felt, "Too bad about Roy Beck lying in his own vomit attended only by a dog and flies." I thought "Too bad!" when I heard he had died. It was not until after Hospitality House and years of study that I understood that he had been murdered—by prejudice, by an unjust social process. And it took a few more years before I was outraged at the fate of a thousand other foredoomed Roy Becks.

Some of the most interesting people on the street corner were the jive cats. A jive cat talked about what he had told "the Man" (the white boss) in the steel mill; about how many women he had laid; about how much money he had gotten from his woman; about how fast he had run the 100-yard dash in high school on the day they were not keeping official records; about what he was going to do to any policeman who bugged him. And so his story goes. He was often articulate, had big plans and was totally unreliable. His tales were enjoyable but not to be taken seriously. If you didn't know what was happening, he would touch you for a five spot until payday—just after he had told you how well he was doing. If he got it, forget it.

Insecurity, dependency, self-indulgence, inadequacy? Yes, all those things. Worse, it is a life style that sacrifices credibility and trust for a moment of center-stage spotlight and small gains. The jive cat is often labeled a sociopath, but the psychosocial dynamics are different. The jive cat, unlike the sociopath, has often had a relatively good developmental experience. His traits are the product of meager opportunity in the real world as a result of oppressive conditions; fixed over time and transmitted by a few people from generation to generation . . . a kind of permanent playacting. If it didn't sound like a racist pun, I would call it a kind of shadowboxing at life. It is a life that is too threatening and overwhelming to be dealt with realistically.

The jive cat, articulate and convincing, appears to be very bright and sometimes he is. But often he cannot produce anything in the long run because he spends too much time winning points and losing the total game—talking when he ought to be working. If you know the street you can recognize a jive cat from the "git go."

The street corner provided a distorted consensual validation that was very necessary, but crippling if one was doing more than temporarily playing the game. All groups—unions, bankers' associations, street gangs—provide this for their members. For the high school dropout, the man cheated at work, frustrated at love and rejected at the bank, the corner crowd said, "Everything is cool, you're making it. The problem is with the world, not you." Because that is so true, it is accepted uncritically. Because attaining the power to bring change is so unlikely, it is fortunate that such a rationalization is available. Because making it at work, love and play is possible only with massive effort, support and luck, the rationalization is supportive, though damaging.

Oscar Brown, Jr., the entertainer, has a tune about a man who suffers one overwhelming trauma after another and is carried away screaming, "Be cool, be cool, be cool." That's the message of one's buddies on the corner.

I learned most about the street world on Chicago's Southside scene, which I always made with my college roommate. Chicago was an exciting world. In the basement of the Partisan Hotel, I saw some of the most beautiful girls I had ever seen, black, brown, golden. Many were prostitutes. Good looking, stable-looking women—what had happened to them? When we went through the street-walking area, we were asked, "Want some lovin' baby for five and one?" (five for the body, one for the room).

We stood and watched for a long while. Long Cadillacs driven by pimps passed. Most of the white prostitutes plied the black district in cars. A few stood on the corner. One day as we stood watching, a prostitute who had approached us earlier came back and said angrily, "Look, this ain't no research project! You boys don't want nothing. Ya'll go on home." We moved on. Several of the girls had been college students.

The most striking fact about the street-corner society was that it was just that, a society. There was a warmth and a sense of well–being that paralleled the Baptist black church society. I often felt much as I had in church at the end of the service when we would all clasp hands and sing "Lord Be With You Till We Meet Again." Each hangout had its own core of people and its own style. There was a spectrum of night-life places and people—from the good fellowship of Kitty Kat, where street men and Roosevelt College students mixed, to the danger of Joe's Place. I recently heard a businessman referring to a night-life section of Harlem he had once known as now "gone." What he meant was that it had passed from the club-like atmosphere to a dangerous dive for addicts and a variety of other tormented people.

A second impression of the street-corner society, one that should give caution to the romantic, was "what a waste." Here, as in the storefront church, the District of Columbia health clinic, and Hospitality House, I found numerous people under-producing—that is fine for those who don't want to do more. If it could be demonstrated that a majority of the affected people never had other aspirations, my impression could be labeled middle-class and dismissed. That is not the case. For many, the odds were too great and the street was a retreat and a refuge. Few who romanticize the street have been willing to live under the conditions it imposes.

I was warned that it was tough for black folks in the real world, beyond school and play. But you cannot really be prepared by words. When I had finished high school I needed a higher-paying job to go to college, but I was only seventeen years old. My mother called the steel foundry where my father had worked for twenty-six years. He had hardly missed a day and was never late. They said I could not get a job until I was eighteen. Talking with the son of a plant foreman, a white classmate, I discovered that he was employed there as were several other white classmates, all under eighteen. My mother called back and was told again that I was too young. She told him that she knew about my classmates; that my dad had worked there more than twenty-six years; that I was trying to go to college; that white people were always claiming that blacks didn't want to do anything; and, finally, she asked, "Do you want me to name the boys who are working there?"

"Never mind, never mind, send your son out Monday morning," he said.

My first day in the steel mill was the beginning of understanding for me. The first black man I met in the foundry was Deacon McKegney, from my church. He greeted me warmly but I was so shocked I could hardly respond. He was dirty from head to toe. When I saw that he worked in a big dust-bowl I could understand. I later found out that that was the type of work my father had done for many years. He was a grinder. I was so accustomed to seeing Deacon McKegney sitting at the front of the church with a white shirt and tie on, looking important on Sunday, that I could not imagine him in that job. No wonder he was ten feet tall on Sunday; he was important in church—in spite of his job. I soon found that black men had all the dirtiest, hardest jobs in the steel mill.

I was a small kid and on the first day they gave me a broom to sweep the yard, like most of the other college kids. In the afternoon there was a truck of bricks to be unloaded. I was given the assignment. The sun was blazing and the truck was standing in the open. The work was fast, back-breaking and difficult. At 3 P.M. the truck was not yet completely unloaded but the foreman came by and reached up and put his hand on my leg and said, "Okay, you have to stop. Teenagers can't work overtime." I was near the point of collapse. At the same time, some of the white teenagers, carrying clipboards, were passing by to check out. They had been making a stock inventory. I couldn't think about it. I was glad to have a job. I remained with the labor gang and later got the hang of throwing those bricks.

The bricklayers' gang was an interesting one. The foreman, who began to work in the foundry about the same time as my father, was born in Scotland. He had no special talents but made a very high salary, had a summer home and was about ready for a very secure retirement. My father had worked just as hard, just as long and just as diligently, but didn't really make enough to support his family. In his best year he earned $3,800, and he was forced to retire at fifty-three because of an industrial illness. He received compensation which, I was told, was relatively good compared to what most blacks got; but it was not enough to send four children to college and afford retirement in the dry climate of Arizona he needed for medical reasons. My older sister bought a small duplex in Arizona, which enabled my father to live there and the four of us to remain in school. Such acts are common in struggling black families, even when they mean changing the life plans of the one who makes the sacrifice. In many black families, the future of the oldest male child is sacrificed when he has to stop school to earn a living for the family. That could have been me!

The two chief bricklayers were white men in their mid-thirties. The one full-time bricklayer's helper was a Negro, Benny Brown, of the same age. Benny was a bright, North Carolina-born fellow from Gary, Indiana. He enjoyed teasing and "fooling around." He had great manual dexterity, and he worked hard and laughed hard. But sometimes he didn't show up for work, particularly on the day after payday.

Al and Dick, the white bricklayers, often wanted to talk to me about Benny. "He's a good boy, but why does he miss work and not pay his bills?" Or, "I like Benny, but, you know, if all Negroes were like *you* . . . " I must admit I didn't quite understand him either, but it did occur to me that Benny could probably lay bricks as well as they but could never expect to get into their union or to earn more than a common laborer's wage or to hold a job like theirs.

The difference between the black and white locker rooms at the mill was noticeable. In the black locker room there was a lot of bantering and kidding. It was warm and alive. The white locker room was different. There was joking and some kidding, but it was different in a way I really didn't understand but that I could feel. The few white students who were in the black locker room also felt it. One became a college classmate of mine and described it to me several years later, but neither of us could explain what the difference was. It is probably what blacks today call "soul," which is part of the black adaptive effort.

After my first two working summers, I transferred to a job at the Youngstown Sheet and Tool Company, where my Dad was not so well known. This time I really got the test. I was in a labor gang that lined up in the morning in a fashion similar to long-shoreman gangs. A squat, rugged foreman gave out the job assignments. He wore a big hat, had a huge wad of tobacco in his mouth, drove a Cadillac and did not work. He rarely said a word to anybody, and I never saw him display any emotion. He had an assistant who did most of the talking and supervised the jobs. There were a few blacks in the gang, but it was made up primarily of young high school graduates and college students working for the summer. I recall one day when it was 95 degrees in the shade, and some of us were assigned to clean out the grease pit underneath a steel roller. We wore hip boots and raincoats. A spray of water from a machine above peppered us. Water mixed with thick grease oozed up and slapped over the boots and down into our shoes. The footing was slippery, and I was afraid I would fall into that sticky two-and-a-half feet of muck and never be heard from again. We had shovels and we were supposed to dip up the grease and put it in a huge barrel. It was so hot down there we could work for only a few minutes at a time. Since there were no whites in the pit, I suspected that this was a "black job," but I was not sure at the time. It was not long before it was clear that there were certain jobs for black laborers and other less demanding ones for whites.

One Sunday my suspicion was confirmed. Usually, heavy work was not done on that day. Overtime pay and easy work were the rule for a Sunday. We lined up in the usual fashion. The foreman said he had a job for two big men. Since I weighed about 125 pounds then, I knew I would not be selected. He looked over the gang and pointed to a husky black fellow who had been a fullback on the high school football team. He looked slowly around the group. There was a husky tackle from Gary Tolleston High School, a fullback from Hammond Clark High School, two freshmen football players from Indiana University—all white. He finally pointed his finger in my direction as his second choice. I looked around to see who was standing behind me. I was sure he didn't mean me. I was wrong. He hadn't meant he had a job for two big men, he meant he had a "nigger job." Only two black laborers were present that day. For two days I used a pneumatic hammer to break cement. It jarred every bone in my body. But the aching of my body could not equal the silent fury and rage in my mind.

While I was in the plant, Emmett Till, a fourteen-year-old black youngster from Chicago, was murdered in Mississippi for allegedly whistling at a white woman. On the morning that news was announced, the black workers were furious. A young black born in Mississippi yelled, "The white man ain't no good, he ain't no good!" He slammed his shoe against the wall and sat down hard on a bench, trembling. The tension was great in the locker room. The few whites dressed quickly and went out to the job. Nothing happened. The fury and rage must have been turned inward. I have wondered since how many got drunk and beat their wives that night. The real world was tough, but I shook it off. I was preparing myself.


College, too, was the real world. There my self-esteem props were knocked out from under me. Achievement and recognition in high school had been my way of dealing with the fact of being black. There were dozens of people with records like mine and better at Indiana University. Now my blackness became evident. For the first time I really got the feeling of being an outsider. I was overwhelmed by the huge fraternity houses and the many flashy cars of the wealthy students, almost all of whom were white. In my hometown I had known many wealthy youngsters and had been to their houses, but I was excluded here. To make matters worse, some "public" accommodations were closed to blacks.

After registration, I was exhausted and stopped at a malt shop two blocks from campus to get a cool drink. Without any idea that I would not be served, I flopped in a seat and looked up at the owner to give my order. I was shocked. He was glaring at me and his finger was pointing toward the door. For a moment, I couldn't comprehend what he was saying. In a heavy Greek accent, he ordered me to get out. I finally got the message. *Now it had happened to me.* Only twice before had I been refused service, but in those cases the refusals were apologetic. I was young and I could deny what was happening. But not anymore. I got up from the counter, enraged, shaking, standing there helpless. I looked around for somebody to help. A hush had fallen over the place. A white man next to me kept his eyes glued to his own soda, sucking furiously on the straw. I wanted to say, "Look at me, look at what's happening and you're not doing a thing!" I wanted to yell at the whole room. Everybody looked away. Nobody moved. I backed toward the door and threatened to tell my father, tell the legislator from my district, tell somebody, but it didn't matter. No one left, no one moved, no one cared. Desperately hating my helplessness, I wanted to do something. For an instant I wanted to break his window. I knew better. I had always been told that a black man has only one chance. Trembling with rage, I went home. For days I moped around and every new car, every laughing voice at the fraternity house and every classroom full of white students reminded me that I was black, poor and unwanted. The loneliness and estrangement got to me; I almost went down.

The dormitories had been racially integrated a few years before, but it was still the custom to put blacks together in an otherwise integrated dormitory. Relationships were relatively good, but generally superficial. Toward the end of my first year, many of the white students became more friendly and wanted to find out what blacks were really like. I have often wondered why the blacks didn't want to find out what the whites were really like. But maybe we had had so much experience with them we didn't have to ask.

At dusk one evening, my roommate, who looked like a black Ichabod Crane, started toward the central part of the campus. As he was going down the hill, he saw a white coed coming up the same narrow path. She faltered, stopped, then ran away across the grass screaming. He was stunned, unable to comprehend what had happened. He stood there on the pathway, yelling, "Come back, little girl, I'm not going to hurt you." He was defensive when he hadn't done a thing, and he was shaken and hurt when he got back to the room. Later we teased him and called him a black rapist brute. That evening, two black fellows in the dorm put a KKK sign under our door and told us we had better be out of the building by 9 P.M. We laughed about that, but later, several of us spontaneously gathered in my room and began to talk about what had happened and what it meant. We gradually grew quiet. Finally, somebody said angrily, "You know, just a few years ago we might have all been hanged for what was in that white bitch's mind." A few minutes later we left the room to get a snack. As we filed out, looking miserable, Bobby Bannister, one of the friendlier white fellows in the dorm, saw us and said quizzically, "What's the matter with you guys?" We said nothing, but we were feeling, "Man, leave us alone." Sometimes it's very painful to be with whites.

One of the things wrong at Indiana was that, officially, all activities were open to all students. Some of us felt in our hearts that we were sometimes just being tolerated, but that couldn't be proved. There was nobody to be angry with for sure, except on the rare occasions when overt racist attitudes were revealed. But the subtle, the covert and inadvertent slights were ever present. One night our fraternity reserved a room and its balcony for a dance. It was a warm night and some of the white students wandered in, even though the dance was closed. A few joined in the dancing, but most went out on the balcony. As one white coed was passing through, she looked at the black students and shuddered like someone who had touched something nasty, slimy and dirty. Those of us who saw her gesture were furious and wanted to close the dance to outsiders. But one fraternity member said, "Why, man? It's integrated, that's what we want, isn't it?" But even then many of us knew that that was not what we wanted, not on those terms, with the attitude so many whites had toward blacks.

Indiana University is a beautiful campus and I had many fine experiences there, but the uncalled for, ludicrous and senseless acts of racism are the memories that gnaw at my gut. There were a few hundred black students on a campus of some ten thousand. That is why the black fraternities and sororities were terribly important to us and it is also why most black students spoke to each other as we crossed the campus, even to those who were strangers. We needed group support. When somebody didn't speak or preferred "not to identify," he was a marked man, scorned for trying to be white. The other thing we had in common was that most of us were poor, from struggling families. Many of us held part-time jobs and had to maneuver cleverly to stay in school. One fellow from Indianapolis was in school for four years without ever living in the dormitory; he slept from place to place. Blacks from this type of background are infuriated by the cliché that blacks don't try as hard as other people.

My first semester at Indiana was disastrous: I made all C's. For many others it was even worse. Many good black students just didn't make it; their dropout rate was much higher than the whites'. The white faculty's explanation was the blacks were poorly prepared for college, but many of the flunk-outs were adequately prepared; they were defeated by the social situation. Nor were social difficulties confined to problems outside the classroom. My own academic record was punctuated with peculiar events which, I realize in retrospect, were related to the racial situation.

I recall that in three different courses I flunked the first examinations. These were given in huge classrooms with many students and I was either the only black student or one of two or three. In two of the classes the laboratory assistants talked with me and let me know that they knew I could do the work and that they expected more of me. In both cases, I made top grades in the next exam. In the only course where the instructor was indifferent, I eventually flunked. My unconscious question had been, "Who cares?" This is a function of personality. But, the point is, the question of acceptance or rejection on the basis of race confused and complicated what is a very natural and common problem for all sensitive young people who need group acceptance. Black people have a right to want to be liked. This is a basic human need. Without it, there cannot be healthy personality development and social order. Needing to belong creates despair for a black man in a white-controlled, racist society.

Indiana had a program in which students could enter medical school at the end of their third year if their grades were high enough. While I had had a difficult first year, my grades picked up and I applied for medical school in my third year. When I was standing in the hallway waiting for my interview, I looked over the large crowd of applicants, measuring my competition. But I was not measuring the entire group. I was only looking at the number of blacks and thinking back on their performances compared to mine. It was strongly rumored that there was a quota system for black students. This has been said about most medical schools. I had checked the records, and found that there was a fairly consistent number of black students per class. In the present group of applicants, there were several black seniors and I was a junior, which meant I had another year. Whether there was a quota system or not is relatively unimportant—I believed it. I entered the interview with the fear that the board might not be looking at my performance, but rather at the number of blacks to be accepted. I was not accepted.

The interview in my senior year was more intimidating than the first one had been. In a huge room, two medical school faculty members sat behind a large oak table. Everything in the room was heavy with tradition. But not my tradition. One of the interviewers was short and appeared friendly. The other was tall with bright red hair and red freckles on his face, neck and arms. "Be careful of this redneck," I thought to myself. The friendly fellow opened the interview with some questions about why I wanted to be a physician. I answered these easily and then it was the other interviewer's turn.

He asked me to give the name of the Attorney General of the United States. This was a very common approach used by medical school interviewers to determine how well-rounded the applicant is. Already frightened and anxious about a number of things that may or may not have been true, I became defensive and angry. I could not think of the Attorney General's name. Meanwhile the friendly interviewer had been thumbing through my record without looking up or noting the interaction going on. He said spontaneously, "This young man came as close as you can come without making it last year." Then he looked more carefully and said, "You know, I don't know why this boy didn't make it last year." He pushed the folder toward the other interviewer who gave it a superficial glance, appeared irritated and snapped at me. "You don't know the name of the Attorney General of the United States?"

Having learned that I probably should have been accepted in medical school the year before, I was more furious. With four youngsters from my family in college at this point, we needed the money I had had to use for the extra year. My dad, who had sacrificed his own health to see us through college, had died the summer before. Now I was being arbitrarily and self-righteously asked an irrelevant question. I could feel myself losing control. The friendly interviewer could see that something was going on between me and his colleague. To save the day, he asked me to tell something of the activities in which the Attorney General was now involved. Glaring at the "redneck," I snapped, "He's investigating the Emmett Till case." My adversary looked confused, and turned to the other interviewer, "Who is Emmett Till?"

"Why," I wondered disgustedly, "don't you know about something as important as the murder of Emmett Till?" The other interviewer informed him in a hurried and embarrassed fashion. The interview continued, but I was hardly there. A million times I had been warned, "Keep your cool," "Don't get angry," "Be careful," "White people don't want to be told that they are prejudiced or unfair," "Don't be arrogant and you can survive." Now, at the most important time of my life, I had blown it all in a few short minutes.

When I left the room, my head was swimming, my legs were weak, I wanted to cry. Back in the dormitory one of the fellows said, "How did it go?" I shook my head and threw up my hands. Alone in my room, I cried the tears of the men I had seen in my church on Sunday mornings. I then knew what their tears were all about.

A few months later I received notice that I had been accepted to the Indiana Medical School. In the months that had intervened, a number of things had happened. At the beginning of the year I had led a protest against a dormitory group that had extended an invitation to a black sorority and then withdrawn it. On Alumni Weekend I was walking with a black girl who could have passed for white and a white middle-aged woman stuck her tongue out at me. Later that same year, the baseball team had planned to leave their black members at home while they toured the South. That was another fight. The bombardment of slights and indignities over the four years were beginning to get to me, so much so that when "The Star-Spangled Banner" was played at one of the basketball games at Indiana, I could not stand. I had had enough. I had to go where I was wanted, not where I was merely tolerated. I chose to go to Howard University, a predominantly black school.

(It is only fair to acknowledge that Indiana has changed a great deal since 1956. In 1968, it had the greatest percentage of black students of all the Big Ten schools. Like many predominantly white medical schools of today, it is actively seeking black students.)

Howard was an important corrective experience for me. I began to establish my real identity. I found the frame of reference I had needed. But most important, I came to realize how terribly complicated the race problem is; that, in fact, it is one part—albeit critically important—of the larger problem of human organization and function.

At Howard I discovered that I did not want to be a leader. I did not have to lead. There were plenty of good black leaders in my class. I gradually became aware of the bind I had been in on the predominantly white campus. I had been trying to "carry the race." The burden of the black student in the past was to prove by his conduct and performance that the myths and stereotypes—they laugh too loud, they are poor in math, they are emotional, they are inarticulate, they are not smart—were not true of all blacks. Thus, if one missed an answer in the classroom, one had failed the group. That proved blacks were not smart. One hushed blacks in a mixed audience. One flinched when a black man made a grammatical error.

I realize now that much of the motivation for learning under these circumstances is negative. The motivation is "I'll show them." One is very vulnerable here. It creates a great deal of stress. Once, in junior high school, I got a "C" in math and cried hysterically. Nobody could understand that. I was not able to explain my grief to my classmates because I didn't understand it myself. Now I know I cried because I had not shown "them." So was it true what they said about Negroes and math? A youngster does not thrive under such stress.

It was at Howard that I began to discover what the real me was like. I began to throw off the stiffness and inflexibility I had developed in becoming the "acceptable Negro." I began to relax and swing with a group of fellows who were fairly comfortable with being black. Class parties would swing like none I had ever been to before. There was indeed a real sense of belonging.

Occasionally bull sessions would turn to the race problem. Although the anger was not expressed as directly as it is today, it was certainly there. The issues ranged from slavery to sex, from sin to integration. One fellow succinctly summed up the general feeling, "I can understand why the white man would cheat me, abuse me, and exploit me, but I can't understand why he expects me to like it!" The trait that seemed to provoke the most anger was white duplicity. Two fellows who had worked as bellhops in white hotels prior to and during their undergraduate days scornfully described what they had observed of white sexual immorality and we all marvelled at white obsessions with black sexual mores.

At Howard I met many teachers who had a special dedication to black education and a sensitivity born of shared experience. But sometimes I found just the opposite. Some of the professors were bright, aggressive people who had never achieved the recognition they were due—because they were black. Their choice of employment had been limited; professional societies had barred them; professional organizations had failed to recognize important work. Perhaps as a result, the spark had gone out of several once dynamic teachers. Their frustration was taken out on the students— perhaps a bit more than at predominantly white universities.

On one occasion, the AMA distributed a questionnaire to determine how many students needed financial aid. Most of my class responded positively. One professor teased us a bit, pointing out that many of us had scholarships or loans. He told us that when he was going to medical school he had a job and sent half his earnings home to support his impoverished family in Baltimore. I was amazed to learn how many black professionals had worked, often fulltime, while going to graduate school. I was amazed because, when I was growing up, I had read that Abraham Lincoln walked miles to school each day—an example of the will to succeed for which he and other "builders of our nation" have received recognition—while I was taught in many subtle and not so subtle ways that black people were too lazy to expend any energy to improve themselves.

I was introduced to some of the serious consequences of overt racism while I was at Howard. My first patient in pediatrics during my clinical assignment was a seven-year-old black girl who had been injured in a car accident. She and her mother had been put on a porch because the Negro ward in a Maryland hospital was crowded. As a result, she received poor medical attention. A relative finally had them transferred to Freedman's Hospital. The accompanying medical report indicated that there was no serious medical injury; so she was transferred to the pediatrics ward rather than the emergency room. A routine examination indicated internal bleeding. She was rushed to surgery but died. I went with the intern to tell the mother about the death. The mother only said, "The Lord knows what's best." I wanted to scream that the Lord had nothing to do with it, but I could see that she needed to believe that. It was so wasteful, so unnecessary, so cruel—a little girl dead, not because there were no medical services, but because she was black and could not have them. Yes, many white people also receive inadequate or incompetent medical care from time to time—but not because of their race.

Atlanta, Hospitality House and jarring confrontations elsewhere awakened a lot of sleeping dogs. Instead of feeling "I've made it," I began to ask myself, "Who am I? Where am I going and why? Why are so many people *not* making it? Is it the people or the system?" While I was asking myself these questions, I met Walter Stoner. He was the other side of my own experience. We could have been each other. He helped me begin to put it all together.

# Me,
# Walter
# and
# America

In 1968, Walter Stoner walked into the clinic where I was finishing my child-psychiatry training and asked for help. He was assigned to a white female colleague who, after the first interview, decided that he needed a black male therapist. Walter's chances of being treated by a black male therapist were negligible. At that time, there were approximately six black male child psychiatrists in the country. (Today there are only about a dozen.)

I had a full patient load and didn't want to hear about another case. But my colleague was determined. She described a seventeen-year-old black youth who had terrorized several students and struck his male teacher. She felt that he was terrified by the ordeal of passing from adolescence into adulthood and could be served best by a therapist who could also be a model. As she explained her patient, a voice said to me, "That's exactly what you need, a ghetto tough to take up all the free time you don't have." But I was moved by her concern for Walter. It was clear that he did need help, although I thought from the beginning that he probably did not need a psychiatrist, that he was victimized by circumstances and conditions.

I came to our first interview expecting a mean, sullen, angry, tough guy. A very pleasant, round-faced, smiling youngster extended his hand and said, "Good morning, sir. I'm Walter Stoner." Walter was short and stocky, and alert to the point of being threatening. I could feel him reading me. But we took to each other immediately. He had a winning innocence and determination.

At seventeen, Walter was two years behind in school, although he had an IQ of 108, and his true intelligence was estimated by a psychologist to be at least ten points better than his score reflected. Despite his intelligence, he had been having difficulty in school from the beginning. He got into arguments and fights daily. He was the class clown, was good at turning the students against the teacher and was popular with many of his classmates for this skill. He did some of the things that they were tempted to do but wouldn't. Of his own conduct, he would say, "I don't want to make nobody—the teacher or nobody—mad, but I just can't help it. I guess I'm just a born clown." As he spoke, he didn't look funny or happy. The tone sounded more like doom.

Occasionally the intelligent, warm and appealing side of Walter showed through. This aspect of his personality had attracted many helpers. He had tutors, and he voluntarily participated in special programs designed to help "underprivileged children." He had heard all the media propaganda urging youngsters to "Stay in school or you won't get a good job!" In spite of the personal help and the propaganda, Walter was not making it in school and he knew it. Because of societal and family pressure, he couldn't just quit. He had to set up a situation that would get him thrown out. When that didn't work, he finally did quit, with the rationale, "They were gonna get me anyway."

Leaving school caused another conflict. He had been completely taken in by the American Dream–Horatio Alger ideal, and was convinced that any American who worked hard enough would eventually be rich. Besides, he strongly adhered to the essential American-manhood values. Referring to a man living off the income of a woman in his neighborhood, he said, "A man ain't s'pozed to depend on no lady. Lady s'pozed to depend on him! That's why I'm gonna be a football player and make a lot of money." We weighed less than 150 pounds and his grades were too low to permit him to try out for the school team. When I asked about his actual chances, he brushed me off with, "Look at Jimmy Brown, he made it!" He had a remarkable capacity for ignoring all the steps that would have to be taken to get from where he was to where he wanted to go. Walter harbored a magical notion that his hope would be realized without any change in his circumstances.

Magical thinking is an adaptive mechanism called forth when realistic opportunities for control of one's environment and destiny are few. Young children, slaves, prisoners of war, and non-scientific, non-technological societies engage in a great deal of it. Even in a technological society, when a reasonable control by the individual of his own life seems unattainable, there is a rise in magical thinking. This phenomenon probably accounts for the increasing interest in astrology in American society.

Though only seventeen, Walter was the father of a nine-month-old son by his fourteen-year-old girlfriend. Determined not to be like his own father, he wanted to spend time every day playing with his youngster. On the other hand, he found it difficult to "be the man" while his mother was supporting him and the baby, and while his girlfriend still lived with her mother. After he quit school, he held three different jobs in two months and talked longingly of going back to school. Had he gone back, he probably would not have remained, although he wanted to "be somebody."

Walter viewed himself as defective, unwanted and vulnerable to attack by a host of more powerful, exploiting people, male and female. He lived among people who, overwhelmed by life's problems, cheated one another, lied, deceived and occasionally violently attacked one another. Walter desperately wanted a different kind of life, but as he indicated, directly and indirectly, he felt that he was doomed to a similar fate. Most of the adults he had known well—parents, teachers, shopkeepers, policemen—had deserted, disappointed or exploited him. Even the over-indulgence and over-protectiveness of his mother and his grandmother were forms of exploitation, a way of gratifying their own needs. Over-indulgence does not promote adequate personal control or a sense of security in any child. The attention and concern Walter got did permit him to develop some strengths, such as concern for others, sensitiveness and determination. He sought, on the other hand, to be "the little man"—to protect himself and to control his mother, teachers and friends. On the other hand, he wanted to be dependent, cared-for and secure.

He knew fear, but he had to deny it in order to feel like a man. Acknowledging his fear would have disorganized and paralyzed him. He constantly avoided the truth of his situation—leaving school, changing jobs—to avoid self-shattering personal confrontations. His dominant, yet least apparent, response was pro-found rage—so all-consuming it frightened him. He laughed uneasily about the conscious murder wishes he had once ex-pressed toward his father. "Now I know better," he said. He handled his anger by playing a good-natured role in reality and fantasy: the helper of abused people, even the would-be philan-thropist: "If I ever get rich, I'm gonna help all the poor children in Washington." He wanted to be loved, respected and well-known. During one session, he told me hesitantly that he had to become famous "even if I have to kill somebody." Only the week before, another psychiatrist suggested that Walter was the kind of youngster who, without a change in fortune, could lose his de-fenses and become a killer. Even if the outcome is less serious than that, it is likely to be unfortunate.

Walter initially had the basic biological endowment necessary to develop into a well-educated, productive citizen, and he still had the desire. But his gradually accumulated deficiencies in personal and educational skills, the rising performance demands from so-ciety, and racism past and present reduced his chances of becom-ing "the man."

His father deserted the family a few days before Walter was born. He had a rural North Carolina sixth-grade education and was ill-prepared to provide for his large family. Three or four times after Walter's birth he attempted to come back to the family, but it never worked out. Each time there were constant arguments, primarily about his income, which was inadequate. Nevertheless, the father had to believe in his own manhood and deny his feelings of inadequacy. To do so, he drank heavily and became sexually promiscuous. This behavior, in turn, caused more family argu-ments.

Walter's mother was born in Washington, D.C. Her parents were from rural Virginia and were under–educated and unpre-pared for urban Washington life. They were hard-working but under-employed—a domestic worker and a government messen-ger. Mrs. Stoner had attended one of Washington's "custodial" schools—racially segregated, overcrowded and badly neglected. She dropped out in the ninth grade. Within a year, her first child was born; within six years, Walter, her fourth and youngest child, was born. After the third child, the relatively satisfactory marriage had begun to disintegrate. Walter's most critical developmental years coincided with the most tumultuous events associated with the breakup of the marriage.

In a series of interviews, Mrs. Stoner described the conditions that led to Walter's difficulties:

> I stayed in the hospital four or five days after Walter went home. I was just so upset and nervous; it was the fourth baby and my husband was gone. I didn't know how I was going to take care of them. When I got home, I was in bed for three or four months before I could begin to take care of Walter. By then, he hardly knew me. He was spoiled good. He was an ornery little boy and just as irritable as he could be. Cried all the time. He had a lot of colic too. His grandma spoiled him. She'd sit up all night holding him . . . I used to cry a lot back then and worry about my husband. He was tied to his mamma. One while there, it looked like he was gonna come home and stay. But he couldn't get away from his mamma. She had all four of them boys, Walter's uncles, you know, tied to her apron strings. He wouldn't send me a dime. I know he didn't make much till he started hackin' [driving a cab], but looked like he would have taken care of his son. But he didn't.

Mrs. Stoner described Walter's early development:

> Soon as Walter was able to walk around he was into somethin' all of the time. He'd tear up everything he got his hands on. Sometimes he'd get on my nerves so bad I know I didn't do right by him. I'd just get so mad I'd beat him too much. Mamma would scold me and that would make it worse. He was a smart little rascal and he knew just how to get us arguing, to get his own way. Funny thing about him, bad as he was, he was still scary. He'd walk 'round right under my dress tail, mine or mamma's, sucking his thumb or carrying his bottle or teddy bear, 'till he was three, four years. I think he was still doing it when he went to school . . .

When Walter was four years old, his father came home and stayed with the family about a year. When he was sober, Mr. Stoner was very gentle and gave Walter much attention. However, during his drunken spells, he was threatening and violent toward his wife and children. Naturally, Walter was frightened during those periods and would run to his mother or grandmother for protection. By the time Mr. Stoner left the family, his drinking had gotten heavier and more continuous. When he left, the family went on public welfare. Mrs. Stoner reported that the first welfare worker assigned to her case was very understanding, but the second one kept confronting her with the suspicion that Mr. Stoner was still coming to the house and that Mrs. Stoner drove him away just to get on public welfare. Thus, aside from being overwhelmed by very serious personal problems, she was accused of wrongdoing by society's helping agent. This is not the way it's "s'pozed" to be.

The first year of life, like the first act of a complicated play, is the most important. The stars of the first act are the mother and the child. The plot involves the former helping the latter move from a helpless bundle to a one-year-old child, with rudiments of all the tools—relationship capacities, body control, speech, the ability and desire to explore, inquire, think, understand and learn —necessary to take on the world. The mother must have certain skills and must receive specific kinds of support. In the optimum situation, the mother herself is mature and enjoys a reasonable degree of security—psychological, social and economic. The mother's security is critical, because the most important thing she can give her child in the first year is a sense of trust and confidence. Depending on her own level of confidence, development and security, she either succeeds or fails to impart this sense to her child.

The father's primary function is to provide the mother with the economic and emotional security that makes it possible for her to give the child the nurturing it needs. To do this, he obviously needs a reasonably well-paying job that also offers some degree of job security. He cannot attempt even to look for such a job if he has not had adequate developmental experiences.

During the second and third years of life, the growing child has a number of important tasks to accomplish. He must come to appreciate himself as an individual and strive for self-expression and pleasure, but at the same time he must learn to appreciate the needs and feelings of others. However, there is a pull to remain dependent, cared-for, without restraint, unrealistic in thought and action. Against this is a developmental push toward independence, achievement and recognition. Numerous tasks—self-care, sharing a toy, talking in turn—become projects around which children assert their independence by taking a positive initiative, or by being negative and uncooperative; but they come to some agreement with their parents (to gain their approval and recognition) and thereby experience achievement and security. At the same time, they learn the rules of the world they live in. These many parent–child interactions help the child learn the realities of his environment, to reason and to understand cause-and-effect relationships. For example, the toddler learns that if he perisists in demanding a glass of water at 2 A.M., he eventually incurs the wrath of important loved ones, the major source of his sense of well-being and security. He learns to drink at other times.

Parents and adult caretakers, through firm but flexible and reasonable external control, help the child move toward greater inner control and self-expression without snuffing out initiative and curiosity. If the job is adequately handled, children enter the next phase with a fairly firm grip on reality, a positive self-concept and a moderate degree of self-control, with less need for control by their parents or by society.

The period of life from three to six years of age is a time of intense relationship with the parent or caretaker. It is the time when a child begins to become like the parents, particularly the one of the same sex. Parents, teachers or other important adults mold the child—usually without conscious awareness—toward the standards, values and ideals of their own culture. Some children celebrate Chanukah and others Christmas Mass with little understanding of the meaning, but all are impressed and sensitized by the effect these events have on important family members. They will first imitate the others and then, usually, accept the event as meaningful for themselves. Through give-and-take with important adults and other children, impulsive behavior, raw hostility and unrestrained self-gratification are brought under a greater degree of internal personal control.

During the period from six to twelve, children begin to develop the capacity for sustained work. Consequently, it is the time when most societies get involved in the planned and systematic instruction of their children. Even in non-industrialized societies, it is at approximately this time that the parents begin seriously to train their children for adult tasks. Identification with dependable adults who can stay with a job and complete it is important if children are to develop such adult skills.

Long before entering school, many youngsters from stable families (which may contain either one parent or two) have been developing styles and skills necessary to acquiring a sense of industry and the desire to work. Simply being in a household where people are regularly getting up, organizing to be on time and preparing for work transmits the notion that work and constancy are important and rewarding. Many youngsters at their play type or teach like mommy or carry a stethoscope or a wrench like daddy, practicing to become workers. Various aspects of middle-income living, such as goal setting, time orientation and expectation of stability, give a direction and discipline to living that develop goal–directed and problem-solving behavior.

The capacity for sustained work in our society is, for better or for worse, also developed through mastering the basic academic skills and maneuvering through the social system of a public school. The child who can maneuver with relative success wins praise, develops a sense of adequacy and a need to be involved in productive activities. Failure in school may do just the opposite. Erik Erikson wrote: "Many a child's development is disrupted when family life has failed to prepare him for school life . . ." [1] As the child begins to move beyond the confines of the family and neighborhood and into the larger society, the things his family life have taught him are put to the test.

Obviously, Walter's experience did not prepare him for the test. Though he got inadequate over-all care, he did receive a great deal of strict moral training, particularly from his grandmother. Walter's grandmother often scolded him and threatened him with the devil or hell because of his bad behavior: his tantrums, impatience, aggressiveness, and so forth. Walter described his grandmother's approach angrily: "I love her and all that, but sometimes she's hard to take. She'll say, 'Speak up if you disagree with me,' and if you do speak up, she'll say, 'You ain't got no respect for your poor old grandma.' " Respect for elders was important in Walter's home. Walter, Mrs. Stoner and his grandmother went to a sin-conscious Baptist church every Sunday, but Walter quit at twelve or thirteen " 'cause some of my men [friends] laughed at me." His grandmother cried for weeks afterward. In large part, the church and the values of the church talked about at home—work hard, be good, respect your elders and meet your responsibilities—formed the basis of Walter's demanding value system.

In spite of his charge from home to achieve and be good, and his desire to do so, he could not do well in school. He was unable to sit still and work; his memory was short. Mrs. Stoner recalled, "He'd go from one thing to another; couldn't concentrate on nothing." In the early grades, he was often punished and forced to stand in the corner or in the hall. By the third grade, he began to take lunch money, clothing and other things that belonged to his classmates. At this point he underwent psychiatric treatment for about a year. His school performance was slightly better but he was never able to overcome the stigma of being the "bad boy." When he was in the sixth grade, he and several other disruptive boys formed a little gang. Walter said proudly of this period, "Everybody in school knew our gang. We didn't hurt nobody . . . 'cept sometimes, but you got to look out for yourself in this world. Ain't nobody gonna look out for you. That's why I feel sorry for Benny [a friend who was not a good fighter] 'cause everybody mess over him."

Mrs. Stoner complained that the school was always requesting conferences with her about Walter. Because she worked as a housekeeper in the suburban community of Chevy Chase, she was tired from work and travel at the end of the day; having to go to talk about Walter was wearing and annoying. She said, "I couldn't do anything with him no way . . . Course I know it wasn't all his fault. Things at home weren't always the best."

One of Walter's most torturous periods was when he was ten. His mother and father were again having severe marital difficulties. Walter distinctly recalled what it was like:

> I was so glad he came home but before it was over with I
> was glad he left. I tried. I gave him my bedroom and I gave

him my key and everything. Looked like he was glad to be home and looked like he liked us, but it just didn't work out . . . he was sick! But back then I used to think he was just mean, but he was sick. He used to go down the street and tell people, "This is my son." I liked that. But then you never could depend on him. He was always making promises he never kept. After he left again, we used to see him on the street and he'd say, "I'll be by the house next week, Tuesday." But he'd never come. We might not see him again for a month, two months. When he was with us, he was happy and looked like he liked us, but you just couldn't depend on him!

As he talked about his father, the anger in his voice was unmistakable.

As a result of Walter's chaotic childhood, he passed into adolescence with massive academic and social deficiencies. He read poorly, he could not spell, and he received more reward for teasing his classmates and teachers than for doing his school work. Occasionally he liked a teacher and would apply himself but that would never last. He liked his tutor and saw him sporadically for two and a half years, but he did not make much progress. Special projects and books about Africa and Afro-Americans held only initial appeal for him; the only things that did interest him were action-packed comic books and football. However, Walter enjoyed school more than he realized. After he quit, he complained, "I miss the place bad!" The relationships he had with teachers and classmates, though fraught with conflict, were more fulfilling than his unsuccessful work experiences.

Mrs. Stoner said that during his adolescence Walter was not dependable, that he was always looking for fun. She pointed out that sometimes he was in good humor and polite and at other times he was sulking and angry. During our sessions, Walter talked of the aspirations he had for himself as an adult. But he was unequipped and not able to concentrate long enough to make even minimal dreams come true. Mrs. Stoner noted:

He was always hanging out with the boys. I'd ask him why didn't he stay at home. He'd say, "There ain't nobody here to stay home with." I couldn't keep up with him. 'Course I couldn't blame him, he didn't have no daddy to take him places or nothing. He had a "big brother" once who was very good but he left town. Another big brother was just like his daddy, always making promises but he'd never keep them. Walter started hanging out in the streets so much I warned him about getting into trouble, 'specially about bringing a baby home he couldn't take care of. But he was such a big man he finally brought the baby home.

When she spoke of the baby, her voice and manner reflected anger. Mrs. Stoner declared that she loved the baby, but worked hard and had no time to take care of it. She complained that the baby's fourteen-year-old mother was immature and irresponsible and treated the baby like a doll. "Both of them's like two children rather than parents. Sometimes I say to the baby, 'Poor child, you ain't got no mamma and pappa. You got a brother and sister.' " She felt that Walter tried hard at times to be a father but at other times forgot about the baby. "It doesn't look right to see him running down the street chasing four or five boys like somebody ten or twelve years old when he's got a baby upstairs to take care of."

Walter's background of failure and disappointment in school pushed him toward success on the street. The street—full of people trying to meet their relationship and achievement needs—beckoned to him. On the street he fought well, bought a car and made a baby. But his efforts to achieve brought him man-sized responsibilities before he had the social and emotional tools to meet them.

Adolescence in the scientific and technological age is a time for further development of academic, vocational and social skills. It is a time for trying on, not taking on, adult roles. It is a time when adolescents say to parents, "Go away and leave me alone until I find out who I am . . . but don't go too far." They will even ask a couple of questions to make sure the parents are still there. It is, in short, the time to establish an organizing, stabilizing, direction-giving, personal identity. It is a time of ambivalence: adulthood, freedom and uncertainty; childhood, dependency and security. The anxiety adolescence engenders was greater for Walter because his desperate urge to be "a man" was thwarted as long as his mother had to take care of him and his baby.

While I was working with Walter, I often thought about how similar and yet how dissimilar we were. We resembled one another in appearance and in basic disposition; we were reasonably close in intelligence and aspirations. Our parents (except his mother) were under–educated rural folk, and we were from low-income families. But, my developmental experience was the way it was supposed to be—except for the racial incidents. I did not know that we were poor. My parents were not part of the problem, but my dependable support. A promise was always kept. A chocolate bar was divided evenly to make sure that nobody was cheated.

Before I went to Hospitality House I was still convinced that hard work brought success, that it was largely a matter of just deciding to work hard. I still believe it is important to perform to the best of one's ability. But getting to know Walter—and thereby getting to know more about myself—made it abundantly clear that good performance depends on more than individual effort. I was a product of a relatively good family, community and educational experience, plus a little luck. From Walter, I got a partial answer to the important question, "Who am I?" I am, in large part, more than me. I am what my family and society enabled me to be. He also helped me realize that there are too many people who are not making it because society prevents them from doing so.

Walter had been denied what a child needs to develop basic trust, regularity, security and a sense of his own worth and value. As a result, he did not develop the ability to relate well to others and to accomplish his goals. Failure at work and play made it even harder for him to feel good about himself. He responded to failure and disapproval by aggressive teasing, fighting and frustration. This in turn made his life even more difficult. Obviously one can be rich or poor and be disadvantaged in the same way.

Although Walter worked hard in therapy it was difficult to help him. His life was full of shattering social conditions and crises and limited in alternatives. His girlfriend was hit in the head with an electric iron by her mother. He quit his unrewarding job and had trouble getting another. Finally he found a new job, but his car broke down and he had no way to get to work. It went on and on. His dreams of job success, returning to school and eventually playing professional football collapsed under the pressure of heartless reality. He denied that his girlfriend's second baby was his (though it most likely was) so he escaped to the comfort of the United States Air Force.

Walter was not "sick" in the sense that he could not function. He might be classified as having an "impulse control disorder" or "ego deficits." Even a paranoid flavor was present. His situation was what child development and behavior experts call minimal psychopathology.[2] But the label is not very useful. Walter had many more strengths than weaknesses. In fact, he was basically quite healthy; he had healthy desires; he had not completely given up and he was a nice person. His primary difficulty stemmed from distorted, uneven and maladaptive psychological, social and intellectual development, as a result of social and family conditions. One outcome was a lack of academic and vocational skill, and a poorly established work pattern. At the same time, his experience created in him all the hopes, aspirations, beliefs and dreams of other Americans. Beneath all his defenses, he was perceptive, and bright enough to know that he was in trouble.

Walter is like too many other American youngsters, black and white. In fact, he was luckier than many. He was spared more serious psychological problems and intellectual impairment because of the care provided by his mother and grandmother. Many youngsters are even less fortunate because they have suffered even more complete neglect.

In a 1961 study of almost 400,000 children served by public agencies, one of every three was receiving attention because of neglect, abuse or exploitation by parents or others responsible for their care. Approximately 50 per cent of these children were in foster care. About 100,000 had had two or more foster-care placements.[3] Many—no one knows how many—are shuttled between relatives and friends and never come to the attention of public or private agencies. Many move from place to place with their parents, often under disorganizing circumstances which in no way resemble those entailed in job promotion moves for middle-income people. Look in the record files of any poor urban school and you will find children who have been in four or five schools by the time they have reached the second grade. In some schools, there is a 100 per cent turnover of students in a single year. There is also evidence that the low-income family has a higher level of conflict than higher-income groups, a situation that often interferes with the development of relationship skills.

Children born to very young or immature mothers frequently have a difficult childhood. There is growing evidence that the quality of early mothering among the socially overwhelmed leads to inadequate intellectual stimulation, and that the effects may sometimes be irreversible. The lack can also lead to patterns of behavior that will be disruptive throughout life.

One of the most troubled youngsters I have ever worked with was a seven-year-old Afro-American girl who had been shuttled around during the first three years of her life. Her mother was a prostitute in New York City and her father was a narcotics addict. The unstable situation continued until she was adopted and received adequate care at three years of age. But it was already too late to overcome the damage that had been done. She was of average or better intelligence, but extremely difficult to live with. She manipulated adults, pitting them against each other in pursuit of her own personal pleasure. She was provocative, testing and damned annoying, yet she was appealing and highly desirous of adult interest, concern and care. Before I was able to establish a satisfactory relationship with her, she drenched me with water, rubbed clay on my clothes, threatened to throw paint on me and ran out of the therapy room repeatedly. Elaborate efforts were made to keep her in public schools, but she was just too impulsive and destructive to make it. Her adoptive parents, though quite good, could not manage her. Psychiatric treatment on an out-patient basis was not enough. She needed to be placed in a residential treatment center but adequate facilities were not available. At seven years of age she gave every indication that, short of a miracle, she would not perform adequately as an adult.

There are people who point to the independence and aggressiveness of such children as evidence that they are not as seriously damaged as some claim. This is wishful thinking.

Children who do not enjoy the opportunity to establish good relationships between the ages of three and six may never develop the internal controls, the sense of right and wrong or of responsibility necessary to modulate and channel the expression of aggression and sexuality. These drives, unchanneled into depth relationships, curiosity and intellectual pursuits, are manifested in excessive anger and hostility and appear to go into what could be called survival energy: doing whatever must be done to survive in a frightening world without the care and protection of a reliable adult. This may be bullying, bluffing, manipulating, exploiting, provoking others, and so on. Such behavior may not produce a negative feedback in the home, neighborhood or subculture where it is common and even needed for survival—"you got to look out for yourself in this world. Ain't nobody gonna look out for you." But it is troublesome in school, in work, in love, and even in play. These are the children the teachers and the whole outside world call "bad." This was Walter Stoner.

The outcome for many such youngsters is tragic—especially if they are black. For many whites such anti-social characteristics lead to minor crime. Because whites have more access to legal aid, they often receive minor or suspended sentences, or they may be referred to psychiatric facilities. Such histories are much less a barrier to good future employment for whites than for blacks. I recall a white executive who left a psychiatric ward with suspended criminal charges and got a $30,000-a-year job. Some whites thrive in illegal rackets from which most blacks are closed out except for the "fall-guy" role—the one who goes to jail during a crime crackdown. Indeed some white youngsters with undesirable characteristics—those of a bully, a manipulator, an exploiter—eventually do well in politics and business where such traits are all too often an asset.

For the black and the poor—without money for good lawyers, with poor education and training and with extremely limited job opportunities after a minor offense—a jail sentence is much more likely than a psychiatric referral or a rehabilitation program. Jails across the country are filled with black youngsters who need residential-treatment services, guidance and direction rather than the higher education in bitterness, alienation and crime that they acquire in prison. Black men are on death row for rape in this "civilized" age. Though rape is a serious crime, the death sentence is an excessive, cruel and inhumane punishment. Few whites incur it.

But the extreme cases distort some issues, hide others and even cast doubt on whether anything can be done. Children and families like the Stoners, extreme examples, are not the rule. It is my impression that most poor children, black and white, have an early developmental experience that could prepare them for the world of today. Even the Walter Stoners of America could make it in spite of the home conditions. Most do not need therapists; they need good schools. Many of our schools are not good; most of them serving the black and the poor are not good. But we are too quick in pointing the finger of blame.

Too many educators blame the children and their parents for the schools' failures. Too many parents and youngsters blame the teachers. Too many critics, who are not in the midst of the problem, cry for the children and assassinate the characters of the educators. What is wrong with the school is what is wrong with the family is what is wrong with the society. We are a society that has failed to gear itself to enable people to meet their basic needs. The failing public school system is only a by-product of this larger failure.

With the traditional American flair for ignoring behavioral complexities, the failure of our schools has been reduced to racism, classism and lack of concern. Some researchers have even demonstrated with facts and figures that when teachers care, problem children can learn. On the other side, a group of scientists have facts and figures which prove that there is just something inherently wrong with poor, black children and their families. Would that life were so simple, it would be so sweet. But it is not. Teachers who do not care are the end products of a long process that is as destructive of them as of the children.

In the first place, intellectual and academic achievement is only one part of the school mission and only one part of what the student will need for adult living. The school also has an important role in promoting socialization and psychological development. Tests and measurements of academic achievement should not be the only indicators of the child's school success. Second, and more important, public education cannot be reduced merely to a classroom, a pupil and a teacher. Education is a complex process that reaches beyond the classroom and into the chambers where social policy is formulated and financed. Unfortunately, it is not the social policy of today alone that impinges on today's education, but the social policy of yesterday and the day before that. To say if a child is not doing well that it's because the teacher is middle–class, racist, or does not care grossly oversimplifies a very complex problem. Teachers and schools have also been accused of programming children, dulling their senses, "turning them off," destroying their sense of worth and a number of other high crimes. I have known many young teachers and have not met one yet who entered a classroom determined to limit or destroy the development of any student. It is poor teaching conditions and techniques, and our present system of teacher preparation that cause many teachers to do harm unwittingly.

The training of teachers is simply not on a par with the training of other professionals. Too many teachers are inadequately prepared for the classroom job. Most have been in college for three to three and a half years before they ever enter a classroom in a teacher's role as part of their formal training. This is unlike England, where teachers are in the classroom during every year of training. (Some of our student teachers discover at a late date that they do not like children or teaching; but, having little alternative, they may choose to stay with their profession.) After a few weeks of student teaching, Americans can become "certified" and sent out as teachers to influence the intellectual, social and psychological development of children. Young teachers from stable and middle-income homes are not likely to be able to cope with the sort of child who, not because she is bad, but as a reflection of her socialization, says to her dolly, "Shut up, you black bitch!"

Few teachers have had courses in individual, group and classroom psychodynamics. They have learned educational theories and methods, but the application of these in real-life settings is often delayed until the "baptism by fire" on their first jobs. Theories are fine, but application is what it is all about. Some teachers regard impulsive children moving destructively around a classroom as curious scholars in search of knowledge. It is an easy mistake to make if you have never had an opportunity to study impulsivity in children. Opportunities for ongoing, supervised observation and analysis of successful teachers dealing with such problems are rare. Closed-circuit television and other technology are freely supplied for space and medical exploration, but too expensive for those charged with the responsibility of developing the next generation.

Unlike most occupational roles in business and industry, the teacher's is not simple and clear cut. Children indicate their problems and request help in subtle ways. Walter Stoner was bright, had a difficult life experience and desperately wanted help. In pursuit of this, he sought a relationship with one teacher in the only way he knew—a provocative, testing, teasing manner. He disturbed and disrupted the class in spite of himself—"I don't want to make nobody, the teacher or nobody mad, but I just can't help it." The teacher, poorly prepared to understand and manage such children, perceived a personal attack and fought back. After one of Walter's provocations, the teacher read to the class a letter that Mrs. Stoner had sent him and laughed at the misspelled words. He warned Walter that he was going to be just like his mother if he didn't settle down and work. Needless to say, that approach only elicited more disruptive behavior. Yet disruptive, testing behavior is often a sign of health in children who have been abused and neglected. The task of the teacher or any caretaker is to help the child learn better ways to deal with his problems. Some teachers are intuitive and sensitive and can handle the most difficult situations. Most teachers, given adequate training, could handle them.

Teacher preparation also suffers from "advocacy training." The latest and most successful method being used, say, in Norway, that catches the eye of the visiting professor from the United States, can become *the* answer to the problems in Harlem, without being given critical evaluation. Some people with the answers for Harlem have never been in any community like it. In fact, many college professors preparing their students to teach in public schools have never worked a day in public schools themselves. When a professor with a pet method is popular and powerful and publishes prolifically, his method often catches on whether or not it is applicable to a given child or community.

Too few teachers are trained to ask, "But will it work with some, all or any of my students? Will it work in this community? Is it what the parents want for their children? Is it what the children need to learn how to handle their present and future environment? Will it facilitate their growth and development or does it fail to meet them where they are?" A commitment to a given approach makes for personal security, but if the approach is the wrong one for a given child at a specific time, using it is a disservice. The children who suffer most from the inadequacies of teacher preparation are those who have had bad home experiences and come to school with developmental lags, and these include a disproportionate number of black children. But the inadequacy of teacher preparation is again only part of the problem.

Across the country, as blacks moved into communities and whites moved out, school systems were allowed to deteriorate. Even good administrations found themselves understaffed and forced to do some shabby planning. Alan Campbell, an educator, has pointed out that as economic activity became decentralized, business and industry began moving from the core city to surrounding areas, weakening the tax base of the city. This is a process that has accelerated rapidly over the past twenty-five years. For the thirty-seven largest population areas in the U.S., the average education expenditure per capita in 1968 of the central cities was $82 vs. $113 in the suburbs. The expenditure per student was $449 in the cities and $573 in the suburbs.[4]

Blacks are people who have had only two non-contiguous decades, 1920–1930 and 1940–1950, of even minimal opportunity on the job market in their 100 years of "freedom" and their more than 350 years in America. The consequences of this to family and community stability are well known. To prepare youngsters from a deprived community to cope as adults, the schools in the central cities should have been maintained at the economic and community support levels that existed before the whites moved out. In fact, an even higher level of support was indicated. Both compensation and reparation have been and still are indicated.

But even well-financed schools and school systems are very complex social entities. People with different professional backgrounds must work together as a team—teacher, paraprofessional, social worker, psychologist, psychiatrist, nurse and administrator. In low-income areas, people of different income levels, races, religions and political persuasions are working together, and the potential for conflict under these circumstances is high. The admixture of people and factors can be chaos or a symphony, depending on the management or orchestration the system receives.

Most of us who boast of caring more about people than about objects or money would like to ignore the fact that the school system is a business—with a human product. In fact, it is now big business, and it needs good management. It must be able to attract good personnel and serve their needs in ways that permit them, in turn, to serve the needs of the consumers—the students and families. School systems, because of politics and finances, must sit and wait, then accept whatever crosses their thresholds, while the personnel officer of a chewing-gum company can traverse the nation in search of talent, and wine, dine and woo the prospects into his business on a comparatively limitless expense account. A good business has the support staff necessary to keep its service staff operating at maximum efficiency. Few schools are able to do the same. A good business knows its market demands several years in advance and tools up to meet them. Most schools do not have the manpower or equipment necessary to mobilize for the year just ahead. New schools often start out over-crowded and chaotic because systems analysis and adequate planning are not available.

It has been traditional for school administrators to pick a teacher who has been successful in the classroom for ten or twenty years and make him or her an administrator. Often the choice is political and has nothing to do with ability. Although some so selected become excellent administrators, few of them are well prepared. Many fail. To strengthen school administrations, states are now requiring that administrators take a handful of courses but these are likely to be theoretical and inapplicable to real-life conditions. Such is the training of the people who run America's most important business—the school.

Even if their preparation and training were adequate, many principals would still spend their time taking splinters out of fingers, holding the hands of youngsters who have been poked on the playground, unlocking doors (which should not be locked) when the janitor cannot be found—largely because most schools cannot afford to hire anyone else to do these things. The important management tasks—personnel recruitment, teacher support and development, curriculum planning and so on—must often take a back seat to the day-to-day pinch-hitting for unbudgeted and unavailable staff.

The school administrator is also strapped by peculiar professional mores. Business generally does not tolerate incompetence, destructive attitudes or carelessness. But we professionals are special people. We protect each other in spite of failures and shortcomings that hurt the consumer. The most that many administrators can do about incompetent personnel is to promote them or move them out of the way without firing or demoting them. Until recently, schools traditionally transferred their incompetents into school districts where the parents were least likely to complain. This was usually a low-income, migrant and/or black school district. It was assignment to Siberia for the teacher but a fate even worse—death at an early age—for the students.

Too few teachers in the neglected and troubled areas are able to do a creditable teaching job. Others make some kind of adjustment—not because they want to compromise their principles, but because they want to survive. To fail is a threat to the teacher's sense of personal and professional adequacy and, like all human beings, he defends himself. For many, the obvious excuse is the child or his family—after all, everybody knows about culturally deprived or disadvantaged, hard-core children. What can one expect of the blacks, the poor, the lower class? "They don't care; they smell; they drink Cokes for breakfast; their parents are drunks." To survive, some run the classroom inflexibly. Others are too permissive, lower their expectations and let the children do whatever they want to do. Many are overwhelmed and leave. Some are driven out, battered and torn.

This constant, heavy turnover of teachers only increases the instability of the system. To look at a school and point with righteous indignation to teacher shortcomings alone is unjust. But such a school is the place where Walter Stoner, and other children with bad home experiences, get their second and maybe last chance. The Walter Stoners of America—without intent or malice—make it difficult for their classmates to get an education. When the school failed Walter, it was sabotaging more than one child's schooling. Like Walter, thousands of young people, a disproportionate number of them black, seek but do not find their chance in school.

It is into these deteriorating school systems that learned social scientists step—like clean, uniformed football substitutes onto a muddy field—with pencils, pads and test papers, to measure achievement levels. They compare the scores with those achieved by children with from two to five generations of good schools, good jobs and family stability behind them. They determine that the poor children (often black) cannot learn as well as the children from more privileged homes (often white).[5] They pretend that achievement scores have nothing to do with the relative amounts of money put into black education and white education over the years and over the generations and even today. They ignore the fact that the under-educated students of the 1940s are the parents of the youngsters in school today.

It is unjust and cruel to focus on the child and his family alone and ignore the many other variables that affect achievement and learning. Social scientists only confuse the issue when they close their eyes to under-financed, unstable school systems, and under–trained, under-supported staffs—while they focus only on the achievement of the child.

Child, teacher, and family-oriented research studies have contributed to a tendency to ignore a fourth party to the crime— those who appropriate funds, establish priorities and develop school policy. This group is probably as responsible for the crisis in education as the other three, if not more so. Only the naïve believe that the school board alone is to blame. Business, industry and government at the local, regional and national levels are all involved. These institutions should be held as accountable for the plight of Walter Stoner as is the teacher who could not help him, the father who deserted him and the school systems that under-educated his parents.

In addition, such studies produce simplistic solutions such as recommending that teachers care more, bussing black children to predominantly white schools, and the establishment of a variety of compensatory education and enrichment programs. Even if such treatment of symptoms were practical and possible, it ignores the fact that the underlying disease is rooted in the social injustices and inequities of the past and present—including the traditional denial by our society of money for black education and the instability it still forces upon so many black families. Until these conditions are corrected, youngsters like Walter Stoner will present themselves to the school and society in rapidly increasing numbers and in a condition that our teachers and helping workers cannot deal with.

Of course, it is still true that failure in school is not always a life sentence to poverty, under-development and unhappiness. Some people find well-paying jobs and self-satisfaction without much education. For some, a special talent—singing, athletics, sales ability—will pay off. But school failure in this complex age generally spells trouble and low-level adjustment at best.

Predictions for life and living in the year 2000—less than thirty years away—stagger the imagination.[6] Population growth demands that technology move full speed ahead, or people throughout the entire world, including the technologically advanced nations of today, will be underfed, diseased and in conflicts that could lead to world destruction. By the year 2000, the planet earth will hold more than six billion people. It is estimated that there will be only six inches of coastline for every American by that year. Barley bread, fish and the divine spirit will not feed this multitude! From one-half to two-thirds of the world's population live on the brink of starvation at this very moment. It will take skillful use of science and technology to feed, clothe and house the generations to come.

Technology has already reduced the man-hours necessary to plant, cultivate and harvest an acre of corn from forty-six in 1880 to two in 1965. In 1965, corn yields doubled those of 1950. Biological researchers are experimenting with insects or viruses that would feed on pests, and with the production of ocean algae as an important protein source. General Mills has perfected a process that can turn soybean protein into chunks of food that look like real meat. Over 15,000 farmers are already using computers to help them with bookkeeping, and in the future more farm planting and other operations will be computer aided.

In the relatively near future, scanning machines will be able to read any legible script. As soon as a typewriter now in development can distinguish between "bear" and "bare," it will operate in response to the sound of the human voice. Already on trial is a system of electronic credit in which a computer hooked up to homes, stores and employers will transfer credit from account to account—employer to worker to bank to merchant and round-robin again.

Scientific research has heart disease, cancer and arthritis on the run. Researchers think an artificial heart will be ready by 1980. But so rapid are the gains in the prevention and cure of heart disease that it may not be necessary. Geneticists believe that they will soon be able to control and alter genes, thereby controlling and altering the nature of people. These "advances" raise ethical, moral, developmental and policy questions with which nobody is yet prepared to deal. (Can you imagine the health officials in a small town in Mississippi deciding who should receive gene alterations that would increase intelligence? Can you imagine who would get them in New York, for that matter?)

The impact of science and technology is already greatly affecting the way the worker earns a dollar. The rate of growth in the employment of white-collar workers increased 43 per cent between 1950 and 1965, while the increase for blue-collar workers was only 13 per cent. There was a 98 per cent increase in the number of professional and technical workers in the same period. The number of school teachers increased more than 45 per cent, engineers more than 60 per cent, cashiers more than 100 per cent. At the same time, there were declines of 3 per cent in the number of machinists, 5 per cent in painters, construction and maintenance groups, and approximately 12 per cent for carpenters.

By 1975, one in every seven persons employed will be a professional or a technical worker; one in every six a clerical worker. In every employment sector, from mining to health, the percentage of white-collar workers will increase significantly over the 1960 levels, and the percentage of blue-collar workers will show a decline, beginning a trend that will become even more evident in the 1980s and 1990s. By 1975 the percentage of jobs available for laborers—unskilled and poorly educated—will have declined by more than 35 per cent since 1960. Training and employment discrimination as well as under-education have resulted in a disproportionate number of blacks being in the category of laborers, where the decline will be the greatest.[7]

An ad run in *Time* magazine by the Olin Company bears witness to the intellectual demands of the age as they relate to the problem of employment:

## American Industry Can No Longer Be an Asylum for Illiterates

Over eight million American workers have the reading, writing, and counting ability of a fourth grader or less.

In other words, 10% of our working force is functionally illiterate.

Until recently, there was a place for the illiterates in industry. But now technology is threatening to evict them, if possible. The problem is, they can't be retrained. Because they can't read the most elementary instructions.

And this is what we're dealing with at Olin.

Together with the Board of Fundamental Education, we instituted a literacy program—and then a high school program—in three of our plants, using company space and funds.

Despite initial obstacles (principally older men who didn't want to admit they were illiterate), we graduated our first classes several years ago.

And so far, the results have been so promising that we've broadened the program to include several of our other plants as well.

Nearly two hundred workers have completed the course. And in two of the programs nearly one hundred attained their high school diplomas, with a few going on to college.

In just about every case their work efficiency improved dramatically.

The more important was a complete shift in morale. These were men who had given up every hope of advancement who proved that they could *advance*.

These were men capable of growing with our company.

We're not the only corporation to start this program, of course, but we're still one of a small minority—too small to educate the millions who will soon have no place in our technological society.

It's time for every company to start realizing the problem. And solving it.

There's no growth potential in ignorance.

Adults unable to work are unable to meet the primary demand placed on them by the society—to care for themselves and their families. Thus, their self-esteem is damaged. The reaction to this condition by many of them adversely affects the development of their children. The problem is growing and will continue to do so unless our society faces up to its responsibility to enable families to meet the needs of children, and to take full responsibility itself for the needs of children without families.

Walter Stoner intuitively understood that society had let him down. In one therapy session he said, "You know, animals do better than humans. They take care of their children till they're able to take care of themselves. I know some of them animals are born that way, but humans call themselves so intelligent and lots of them don't do as well as the animals do. Them humans is somethin' else!"

Walter was too broad in his charge. Some humans do better than others. Humans in other industrialized, technologically advanced countries do better by their children than American humans. Sweden, West Germany, Russia, Israel and some of the Eastern European countries are much more supportive of child development than rich Uncle Sam.

In spite of the vast amount of money Israel must spend for military readiness, a great deal of its time, interest, and money go into concern for family stability, housing and youth development. Special projects for immigrant settlement to prevent family disorganization are numerous. Some of the Six Day War battlefields have been developed into handsome housing areas for immigrants. Soldiers—male and female—are utilized in a number of programs to assist children; thus the military is not associated in the minds of the people solely with violence. Sweden, without the burden of war, displays an even more remarkable concern for the development of its children.

Several government allowances assure every Swedish child a reasonably good childhood. The caretaker, usually the mother, of every child receives a special allowance of $240 per year in its behalf until the child is sixteen years of age. There is free health supervision in school for children between the ages of seven and fourteen. School lunch is free, for those who elect to have it. Mothers of handicapped children receive an allowance above that given to mothers of normal children. At sixteen, the handicapped child gets a pension just as the old-age pensioner does. Where one parent is dead, a child receives a pension of $340 a year, and an orphan receives $480 per year. For the low-income family there are clothing allowances, free holiday camps and holiday transportation allowances.

In 1970 there were 200 day nurseries for children between the ages of six months and seven years in Stockholm alone. Some 9,000 children were served, with children of unwed mothers, low-income and student parents receiving preference for admission. The cost depends on the ability to pay. There is a play-school program in Stockholm serving 10,000 children of mothers who do not work. In urban America, thousands of "latch-key kids" (the door key is kept on a string around the child's neck) play in the street after school, usually until their mothers come home from work. In Stockholm, there are 125 after-school centers serving 3,000 children beyond the day-care age, or between seven and fourteen years. Each of the 137 playgrounds in Stockholm employs two to three people to provide child-supervisory service. There are theater groups, clubs, youth organizations for 100,000 young people between the ages of fourteen and twenty. It is a kind of Swedish "substitute" for the youth gangs seen in American cities and the shopping-center loitering and shoplifting seen in the suburbs.

The physical plant and educational equipment I observed in what was called an average secondary school in Sweden compared favorably with America's best. On one occasion, I visited a vocational school for 120 mentally retarded youngsters (IQ 50 to 70) from Stockholm. It was one of the best-equipped and finest looking schools I have seen anywhere. American visitors in the vocational education field who were there at the time groaned with envy.

Every Swedish student receives a cash payment while in school. This amounts to $20 a month and may be increased to $55 a month after a test establishing financial need. Students over twenty are considered economically independent of their parents and receive $35 per month during the school year. All students in need of further economic assistance are entitled to annual loans of up to $1,300. Married students with families may receive more. Adult students may be partially exempt from repayment of these loans because of economic hardship or other reasons. All loans for higher education are interest-free and do not have to be repaid until the student is fifty years old. Study funds available to college undergraduates total about $1,600 per year per student, and some $350 of that is an outright grant. Students working on post-graduate research may receive special scholarships of $2,150 per year.[8]

The benefit of this approach is that no talented person is denied an education because of an accident of birth—the financial condition of the family into which he was born. There can be no excuse for not "making it." A source of anger and alienation is reduced, and a basis for a rational and responsible relationship with authority figures in the society is established. Young people have a real obligation to themselves and their country, and conflict–ridden dependency struggles with their parents and government authority figures are less likely. But the Swedes have not spent all of their energy coddling college or college-bound young people while ignoring everybody else, as a visit to the home of a young unwed mother demonstrated. The woman was employed as a secretary, and, like most of Sweden's unwed mothers, she was a productive citizen. Her apartment was clean and well furnished. The room of her six-year-old youngster looked like that of a youngster in a stable, middle-income family in America.

Our society permits and exacerbates conditions that handicap children like Walter Stoner and his family, and then turns them over to the social worker, the psychiatrist and other helping professionals and says, "fix them." Too often society has not provided enough people or facilities to do the "fixing." I have seen many desperate parents, children and school personnel looking for places where "salvageable children" can find help. I have often made phone calls and searched for days, only to disappoint the supplicants in the end. More important, we refuse to consider the possibility that the rehabilitation may be more than the helping professional can handle. The major disorder lies beyond Walter and his parents and teachers. Walter and others more severely disadvantaged are the primary victims of an inadequate social policy which cultivates racism and results in national priorities that put men on the moon before enabling other men to care for their families.

This may sound like an attempt at psychiatric justification for our societal ills. I grant that people are afraid to go out at night; that women are raped and men are mugged. Yet, the fact is that the marauders are also victims. (Walter possibly ended his failure cycle and probably his criminal potential by joining the military, but many others with experiences like his take anti-social directions.)

Many who commit anti-social acts are not simply "bad people." Numerous professionals who have worked in homes for delinquent children and in jails report that most inmates do not really want to be tough. Their behavior, for the most part, is the end product of a destructive developmental period. For example, I worked with one youngster from a troubled family background who would steal things from a nearby dormitory nearly every weekend. He knew that a youth home would offer more security than his own. He would be disappointed and angry when the judge repeatedly only shook a finger in his face and warned him not to appear in juvenile court again. Another youth pleaded to be sent to a residential treatment center because he had not been able to bring his destructive impulses and emotions under control in relationships with parents and adults. He was afraid he was going to hurt someone.

The neglected, abused and exploited in one generation are often the exploiters and abusers of the next generation. One neglected and abused child in one generation may account for four in the next and sixteen in the third. It is this problem, rather than too few police, too few street lights, lenient court officials, and urbanization which is at the root of our soaring crime rate. It is, in large part, this that accounts for the fact New York City has had more homicides in recent years than England, Scotland, Wales, Ireland, Northern Ireland, Switzerland, Spain, Sweden, the Netherlands, Norway, Denmark, and Luxembourg combined. (The overall population of these nations is approximately sixteen times that of New York City.)

There are thousands of damaged human beings who have not

and never will come to the attention of public or private authorities and will therefore lead lives of personal misery—psychological and social. They will exploit and abuse friend, foe and relative alike in search of a sense of personal adequacy, in a world where they cannot earn enough to provide for themselves and their families. My patient in the emergency room, disfigured for life over a bottle of wine, was one of the victims. Walter's girlfriend, hit in the head with an electric iron, was another. All these people were denied the kind of childhood that might have permitted them to relate to others in a more humane way. Instead, they live now with day-to-day abuse, frustration and anger which they displace on one another—killing, knifing and beating.

But wait. Many people who live under terrible conditions can cope admirably. Most black people have made it. "You made it," I am often told. ("Making it," by my definition, means being free to relate to others in a humane way and being able to cope with the demands of any society.)

Yes, many people make it over every obstacle their fellow human beings put in their pathway. But too many who could make it with ease do not. People should not have to overcome colossal obstacles to enjoy a decent way of life. And on the way to success in this society there is too much destructiveness among the seekers—pushing and shoving and cheating to get ahead, and stay ahead. As a result we have a conflict-ridden, exclusionary society rather than a cooperative, open society.

A situation I observed in one public school illustrates the point. In a midwestern kindergarten, a first-year teacher who was permissive had a classroom of total chaos. The most aggressive children destroyed property, harassed others, victimized the innocent and weak and attacked the teacher. With a different teacher in the second year, kindergarten children from the same neighborhood and background performed quite differently. When property was damaged, it was accidental. Extreme aggression was rare and brought under rapid control—by the children more than by the teacher. A handicapped and vulnerable child in the class, who would have been a victim the year before, was helped to perform by others who took pride in that effort. It was no miracle. The teacher was well organized, attuned to the needs of the students, protective of the rights of each child. She set necessary limits and just expectations, established tasks consistent with classroom goals, and promoted individual effort and interpersonal cooperation. These are the requirements for peace, order and achievement in any social system—be it the household, the classroom, the city or the nation. The powerful people beyond the home and classroom, the policy makers, must serve the same function as the teacher or parent to accomplish the same ends. This has not been the case in America.

But it is too easy simply to criticize Uncle Sam. In spite of its shortcomings, the United States has a record of concern for people that puts it high among the nations of the world. (True, it has had a blind spot for black people.) It is doing better. It can afford to do much better. Its size, its heterogeneity, its frontier, its mentality and peculiar history have created a confounding complexity of issues that have delayed its confronting the fact that human needs must be met if a society founded on the principles of justice and equality is to survive.

A close look at the black experience reveals that black problems are simply the most extreme examples of American problems; that blacks have been only the most victimized by a generally inappropriate social policy. It reveals that, while black and white conflict is very real and painful, the root problem is *beyond black and white*. The black experience can teach us all much about how America must change if it is to reach and survive the year 2000.

# Like
# It Is

My own experience, as a black man and as a psychiatrist, has continued to tell me that much of what white folks say about black folks is a white lie—and by no means a little one.

During a 1964 school-desegregation attempt, a group of low- and middle-income white parents in Queens, New York responded to the situation with traditional ignorance. Peggy Streit in the Sunday *New York Times Magazine* reported their remarks in response to bussing black and white students to achieve racial balance:

> Look at my father. Negroes can at least speak English, but when my father came here from Italy he had to learn the language, so he went to night school. Then he got a job as a wrapper in a bakery. He worked there 47 years and was a supervisor when he retired. The way I see it, if a Negro lives in Harlem, it's because he likes it there and because he doesn't want to work hard enough to get out of that environment.

> I worked with Negroes on a construction job for seven years. They don't work hard or help their children or care about their families or keep their homes clean.

> I don't think I have a moral obligation to anyone—to my family, my husband and child maybe, but no one else. If Negroes have been deprived of some rights, it is because

they haven't worked for them. They don't deserve them.
And the only way they're finally going to get them is through
hard work—not by having our children bussed into their
schools . . .

Color? It wasn't their color that was holding them back. It
was the kind of people they were and the things they did and
the things they didn't do . . . Substandard schools? But
why hadn't they done something about their schools before
now? White mothers would have. Why have they been so
apathetic all these years?

If I were God, what would I do to improve the lot of the
Negro? If I were God, I'd make everybody white.[1]

The longevity of prejudice is even more remarkable than that
of old soldiers. In 1969, *Newsweek* published a special report on
Middle America, those people who make up three-fifths of this
country's white population. They are the people who feel threatened, betrayed, scared and disgusted.

. . . feeling himself the spokesman of the oppressed majority, a hard-hatted San Francisco construction worker
gripes: "The niggers are all organized. So are the Mexicans,
even the Indians. But who the hell speaks for me? . . . We
spend millions and the Negroes get everything and we get
nothing."

A woman claims, "The Negroes want $200 a week after
six to eight months' training when my husband and father
had to work six or eight years to get that . . . Why can't
they work up to it like everybody else?"

According to an Ohio steel worker, the whites do all the
work. "The niggers have got it made . . . They keep closing in and closing in, working their way into everything. Last
three or four months you can't even turn on the damn TV
without seeing a nigger. They're even playing cowboys."

To soothe all these woes and more, a California repairman
offers a "solution to the black problem": "We should have a
Hitler here to get rid of the troublemakers the way they did
with the Jews in Germany." [2]

Middle America has gained much of its security through such government-assistance programs as the GI bill, Farmers Home Administration, Social Security, public education, the Small Business Administration, Medicare, and so forth. Their trade unions have guaranteed them additional security through medical and life insurance plans, tuition programs, cost-of-living increases, paid vacations and numerous other benefits.[3] Government and private assistance, not just "rugged individualism," has made opportunity available for large numbers of white Americans.

Nevertheless, white Americans keep asking why black Americans have had more difficulty than other ethnic groups. They seem to think that black experiences and black opportunities have been the same as their own.

Black people have been victims of economic, psychological and social exploitation, intimidation, violence and exclusion far beyond that of any white group. Adaptive mechanisms—economic opportunity first and foremost, a positive common bond (language, religion, nationality), family and community cohesion—have not been as readily available to blacks as to others. Like most simple answers and summary statements, this response to white America's naiveté tells us very little. To further investigate the question of why so few black Americans "succeed," we must ask another question: What are the criteria for success in America? Again, the answer is simple, but the implications are multiple and critical.

One of my high school teachers once made a remark that deals with this question very well: "You know, most of us are just average people. Only here and there do you find a Joe Louis, an Einstein, an Abe Lincoln, or a Rockefeller. The best most of us can hope to accomplish is to be man enough to take care of ourselves and our families." The implication here is that there are basic human needs and the driving force in an individual, group or society is the desire to satisfy these needs. One is presumed to have achieved moderate success when one has filled the most basic of these needs: food, clothing and shelter for oneself and one's family. This level of security permits the growth and development of young people that enable them to cope in any society. This level of security permits humane person-to-person relationships. Thus, the question of what happened to black people must be pursued in terms of the degree to which blacks were permitted or denied opportunity as compared with whites. The nature of black and white relations in America, from the very beginning, has resulted in the white masses denying the black masses the opportunities they sought for themselves, and that denial has had direct social and psychological consequences for both blacks and whites.

In pre-twentieth century America, the land provided a living for many. A job on the farm or in the mine or factory required little education or training. Apprentice training was the rule when any training at all was necessary. Until the turn of this century, a man could serve as an apprentice for a few years and become a surgeon, an occupation that now requires approximately twenty–seven years of preparatory education. The main requirement for meeting basic needs in the old days was a strong back.

While the rapid gains of twentieth-century technology have not eliminated all unskilled jobs, they have reduced the abundance of such jobs. Moreover, jobs requiring better education and training generally provide comfortable economic security as well as prestige and a sense of achievement. (A recent occupation-rating study shows that physicians rank second behind Supreme Court justices in prestige, and carpenters fifty-eighth. The sharecropper ranks eighty-seventh and the shoe-shine man ninetieth.) Thus, the major requirement for meeting basic and man-made human needs has moved, for most people, from a strong back to a "strong" or developed mind.

The first wealth of this country was made from the land and from trading. The English and Dutch granted charters to commercial companies—the London Company, Plymouth Company, Dutch West Indies Company, and others. English noblemen and gentlemen obtained vast tracts of land from these companies, and many immigrant poor worked the land as indentured servants, serfs and slaves. It has been estimated by Henry Pelling, an authority on labor history, that at the end of the colonial period, over one-half of the white population was made up of the last three groups.

Blacks were introduced into the colonies in 1619. To meet the

ever-present labor shortage, particularly acute for the Southern
planters, blacks were brought here in increasing numbers after
1650. The shipper profited both ways—by bringing black bodies
to till the soil and by carrying back valuable timber, furs, fish, rice,
tobacco and other riches. Enormous profits were also made by
the colonial planter, whose products were shipped back across the
Atlantic. The slave trade was a major source of the American
wealth that was later used to help finance industrialization.

Slaves had no influence on public policy, and the poor had only
scant influence. Land ownership, the requirement for participation in most policy-making, was generally not possible for the
underpaid free laborer to achieve. The landed aristocracy controlled most of the provincial assemblies, although in New England and New Netherlands, the assemblies had an appearance
of representative bodies. Large numbers of colonists, black and
white, freedmen, serfs and slaves, lived in abject poverty while
a few held great power and wealth. Gustavus Meyers, in *The History of the Great American Fortunes,* has shown that many of the
holders of huge estates lived in pomp and grandeur, in the style
of Old World monarchs. Only after the Revolutionary War was
the hold on the land by the aristocracy broken. Meyers wrote:

> No close research into pre-Revolutionary currents and
> movements is necessary to understand that the Revolution
> was brought about by the dissatisfied trading class as the only
> means of securing freedom of trade. Notwithstanding the
> view often presented that it was an altruistic movement for
> the freedom of man, it was essentially an economic struggle
> fathered by the trading class and by a part of the landed in-
> terest. Admixed was a sincere aim to establish free political
> conditions. This, however, was not an aim for the benefit of
> all classes, but merely one for the better interests of the prop-
> ertied class. The poverty-stricken soldiers who fought for
> their cause found after the war that the machinery of gov-
> ernment was devised to shut out manhood suffrage and keep
> the power intact in the hands of the rich. Had it not been for
> radicals such as Jefferson, Paine, and others, it is doubtful
> whether such concessions as were made to the people would
> have been made. The long struggle in various States for man-
> hood suffrage sufficiently attests the deliberate aims of the

propertied interests to concentrate in their own hands, and
in that of a following favorable to them, the voting power of
the Government of the States.[4]

After the Revolution, the trading class, long subordinate to the
great landholders and to British nobility, began to gain wealth and
power. The masses remained largely closed out of political power
by property requirements. Many Afro-Americans today express
anger toward the church for teaching the masses to accept their
reward in heaven and their "hell on earth." White poor heard the
same message from the same source in the days of feudal lords
and shipping fortunes.

Between 1781 and 1867, the federal government acquired large
quantities of land from the states and through the Louisiana Purchase. In this period, 1.8 billion acres came into the hands of the
federal government and were disposed of almost as fast as they
were acquired. After World War II, only 400 million acres remained. This acreage is now designated as public lands. Between
1871 and 1940, 1.1 billion acres were all but given away, distributed in the following ways:

1) 301.8 million acres sold at low cost through public auc-
   tions under various laws such as the mining laws
2) 287.3 million acres distributed via the Homestead laws
3) 330.5 million acres given to the states
4) 94.3 million acres were granted to the railroads to encourage railroad construction
5) 61 million acres were granted to veterans as military
   bounty
6) 68 million acres were granted for miscellaneous purposes.[5]

The aim of the 1862 Homestead Act was to foster the settlement and development of the land and to extend ownership opportunities to a broader segment of the population. If one was
white, it was easy to acquire land. Under this act, which was later
revised and extended in generosity, a settler could acquire 160
acres of free public land provided he reside on, cultivate and improve it for five years, and pay a nominal registry fee. The settler
then obtained full title and unrestricted ownership of that land.

In less fertile areas, 320 to 640 acres were made available to each settler. By the 1920s most of the land available under the Homestead Act had been disposed of.[6]

Land was also "sold" under the 1872 Mining Law, which allowed prospectors who discovered ore on public lands to stake a claim, mine and finally obtain a patent for the land and its resources. Filing a claim and paying from $2.50 to $5 per acre established uncontested ownership.[7] Although claims were to be filed only on the basis of definite evidence of a mineral deposit, in practice, flimsy proof was accepted. Once the claim was filed, the prospector had ownership rights to all surface and subsurface resources, including oil and gas, should they be discovered. Fantastic wealth was acquired from mineral land, frequently without hard work.

There is good evidence that "gift land" led to power. The white Comers, who eventually acquired great wealth and influence in business and politics, got their start from land granted for service in the Revolutionary War.

Between 1840 and 1870, the federal government also made large grants of land to encourage railroad construction. Approximately 130 million acres were granted (including 49 million acres provided by the states) to the railroad companies. The estimated value of the federally donated lands alone was $126 million to $190 million. The federal grants aided some seventy companies.[8] In addition to land grants, railroads received $853 million in assistance toward construction. This was provided through rights of eminent domain, government loans, and even by government purchase of stock in the railroad companies. The only thing Congress required of these "rugged individualists" in return was reduced rates for transportation of the mails and government personnel and property.

Federal aid to the railroads gradually diminished, but during the Depression, the federally backed Reconstruction Finance Corporation provided loans to aid railroads unable to obtain funds through normal commercial sources. These loans totalled over $1 billion. These facts indicate that the rugged individualists we read about in our history books were not as rugged as they were lucky to be in the right place, at the right time, with the right skin color.

The nation, in effect, was one big grab bag. Matthew Josephson, author of *The Robber Barons,* wrote: "The very fathers of the Republic: Washington, Franklin, Robert Morris, Robert Livingston, et al., were busy having land at one shilling or less the acre and selling it at $2.00, in parcels of ten thousand acres or more. The very occasion of choosing a site for the national capitol had been the outcome of collusion between the great land grabbers, securities speculators, and statesmen . . . The sequel of the Mexican War was an orgy of land grabbing and speculation in which the origin of the war is not hard to trace."

When the Illinois Central Railroad was awarded a 2.6 million–acre land grant between Chicago and Mobile, Alabama, the company heads sold chunks of land to their friends at $2.50 an acre along the line. Later the public bought it at ten to fifteen times the original price.[9]

Much of the land and potential wealth of America was given away while blacks were either in slavery or recovering from the effects of slavery. Almost all of it was dispensed before 1915, when 90 per cent of the black population lived in extreme poverty and oppression in the Deep South. White people acquired the primary wealth in America, and the powerful few who got it were able to determine who would procure the secondary wealth; who would receive education and training; who would be employed; in short, who would be able to take care of their families.

Just as land was used to attract settlers to the West and to promote the development of railroads, it was also used to promote education. This practice predominated in New England and was the predecessor of the federal land-grant system. From the early 1600s, land grants complemented the private endowment of schools. In 1785, Congress passed the Survey Ordinance for the disposal of lands in the western territory, reserving one section of every township for public school maintenance. The Ordinance of 1787, governing the Northwest Territory, provided that "not more than two complete townships be given perpetually for the purpose of the university."[10]

Before the middle of the nineteenth century, higher education was primarily classical and professional. Such education did not reflect the interests or needs of the agrarian and industrial segments of American society. Eventually the Morrill Land Grant Act of 1862 was adopted to insure the development of colleges answering such educational needs. The original act gave 30,000 acres of federal land, or the equivalent in money, to each state for the establishment of colleges specializing in agriculture and the mechanical arts. Alcorn College, founded during Reconstruction in Mississippi in 1871, was the first land-grant college for blacks. Only Mississippi, South Carolina and Virginia attempted to appropriate a share of the benefits of the 1862 Act for black education. The majority of the Southern states took no action until forced to by provisions of the second Morrill Act.[11]

The second act, passed in 1890, authorized annual grants to the states for operation of the land-grant colleges, and succeeding legislation expanded these financial grants. In addition, the 1890 Morrill Act contained a provision against discrimination by race: ". . . no money shall be paid out under this Act to any state or territory for the support and maintenance of a college where a distinction is made in the admission of students, but the establishment and maintenance of such colleges separately for white and colored students shall be held to be a compliance with the provision of this Act if the funds received in each state or territory be equitably divided as hereinafter set forth." [12]

The Southern states were slow to establish land-grant colleges for blacks, and even in later years the distribution of funds was far from equitable. In 1930, blacks were 23 per cent of the total population of the seventeen states maintaining racially separate institutions, but black colleges as late as 1936 received only 6 per cent of the funds given to each state for the support of land-grant colleges. In 1955, fifty-two land-grant colleges for white students received 25.7 per cent of their budget for education and general purposes from federal funds, while the seventeen black institutions received only 3.1 per cent.

In a 1964–65 survey of college and university endowments, only three black institutions—Hampton Institute, Tuskegee and Fisk—reported endowments above the average $9 million level of the 882 institutions reporting. Well-known institutions—Howard, Lincoln and Meharry Medical College—were among the twenty-eight black colleges in the study. Predominantly white Harvard showed an endowment of nearly $600 million. Its predominantly black counterpart, Howard, with only one-third fewer students, had an endowment of just over $5 million. In fact, the

1964–65 endowment of all 106 black colleges was about one-half that of the 1964–65 endowment of Harvard. The Harvard endowment is now over one billion dollars! [13]

In 1967, a building on the University of Oklahoma Medical School campus slated for demolition was in better condition than the main building of the predominantly black Meharry Medical School campus. Today, approximately 40 per cent of all black college graduates receive their training in black institutions. Prior to 1940, almost 90 per cent of black graduates went to black schools.[14] Graduates of under-financed black colleges teach a majority of the black children and serve the black community in professional roles. It must be emphasized that many of these graduates do an excellent job, but the preparation of many is below par. Many undertake expensive compensatory training to acquire what they were entitled to, but denied, in the first place.

Unfortunately, this is not an inequity that stems from economic circumstances alone. Many universities and colleges were formed simply to pacify blacks, with no intention of making them first-rate institutions. These institutions are located mainly in the South, where they are often controlled by racist school boards that often do not encourage creative and scholarly inquiry, particularly in areas that might affect the status quo. Progressive programming is often stymied by administrators, who must work with their staff keeping one eye on the program and the other on the white school board. Scholars, black or white, have difficulty working under these conditions. An African proverb says, "When the hawk hovers over the yard, the owner of the fowls feels uneasy." The frustration experienced by many young people attempting to buck the system frequently leads to their giving up or leaving. Thus there is a high turnover of personnel and a lack of continuity and growth.

Further indication of the lack of interest the white power structure had in black education is given by school-enrollment rates, median years of school completed, and the percentage of illiteracy in the population. In 1850, 1.8 per cent of the black population was enrolled in school as compared with 56.2 per cent of the white population; most blacks were still in slavery. In 1870, 9.9 per cent of the black population was enrolled in school as compared with 54.4 per cent of whites. It was not until 1950 that the black population came within five percentage points of the white in school enrollment.[15] But that figure is deceptive. It must be remembered that blacks were often in school for one or two months a year compared with eight or nine months for whites. The median number of school years completed by blacks in 1940 was 5.7 as compared with 8.7 for whites. As late as 1967, the median completed by blacks was 9.1 years compared with 12.1 for whites. In 1940, 1.1 per cent of native-born whites were illiterate, 9 per cent of foreign-born whites, and 11.5 per cent of blacks. In 1959, 7.5 per cent of the black population was illiterate compared with 1.6 per cent of the white.[16]

Could these findings mean, as is so often suggested, that blacks were not interested in education? John Hope Franklin wrote:

> It is difficult to exaggerate the eagerness of Negroes at the close of the War to secure an education. The several Negro conventions held in 1865 drew up resolutions requesting the states to provide educational facilities for Negroes. Most of the states turned a deaf ear. When Florida in 1866 made special provisions for the education of Negroes by imposing a tax of $1.00 on each Negro male between twenty-one and forty-five and 50 cents per month for each pupil, Negro parents seized the opportunity to send their children to school. Meanwhile scores of thousands of Negroes were availing themselves of their only educational opportunity in the schools set up by the Freedman's Bureau, religious societies, the philanthropic agencies. Booker T. Washington said that the desire and effort to learn were so great that anyone who did not witness it would have difficulty comprehending it. Washington further observed, "It was a whole race trying to go to school. Few were too young, and none too old, to make the attempt to learn. As fast as any kind of teachers could be secured, not only were day-schools filled, but night schools as well." [17]

The educational needs of black men were not adequately met. In fact, whites frequently burned down the few schools that were available for blacks in the post-Civil War period. While the poor white man was overtly antagonistic from time to time, it was the "responsible" white man who deliberately ignored and clearly failed to meet the nation's responsibility to black youth in the area of education.

As late as the 1930s, the nine states containing almost 80 per cent of the black population had an expenditure per pupil higher for whites than for blacks. During the 1931–32 school year these nine states spent an average of $49.30 for each white child and $15.41 for each black one. In 1931–32, Georgia spent $9.50 per pupil for black education compared with $41.02 per pupil for whites; Alabama, $10.72 for blacks, $40.90 for whites; Louisiana, $12.86 for blacks, $62.21 for whites; North Carolina, $18.08 for blacks, $41.12 for whites; Florida, $17.33 for blacks, $48.71 for whites; South Carolina spent $8.08 per black student, $53.81 per white student. This, in large part, explains why so many blacks from South Carolina I examined at the Welfare Clinic in Washington, D.C. had only a second or third grade education. Most of the whites seeking welfare whom I examined had a ninth or tenth grade education. Walter Stoner's father went to school in rural North Carolina in the 1930s. In Lowndes County, Alabama, original home of the Black Panther Party, the expenditure per pupil was twenty-five times as great for whites as blacks in 1930. The county was 90 per cent black.[18] Generally, the higher the percentage of blacks, the smaller their share per capita of education budgets.

The educational experience reported by Mrs. Annie Mae Passow, a black woman who grew up in Lowndes County in the early 1900s, is revealing. When she was in school, her mother, a leader of the black community, was called before the all-white school board and told that the crops had been bad the year before and that there "ain't goin' to be no nigger school this year." Rather than do without, the black share-croppers scraped together enough money to bring in a teacher from another state to run a school for their children that year. Sixty years later, white officers were still arbitrarily blocking the education of blacks. My uncle, who was the principal of a rural Barbour County, Alabama high school, told me that his assistant principal was whipped by a white county superintendent in the mid-1940s because he had insisted that black children not be removed from school "during cotton-picking season."

But come on now, is it not true that "those people" really do not have ability? Would it not be a waste of money to try to educate blacks in the manner and style of whites? Unfortunately, these are not yesterday's questions. In 1970, a leading American physicist suggested that the "urban crisis" is a matter of genetics and not environment or experience. (Urban crisis is, in part, a code word for "black folks.") Another scientist, a geneticist, has indicated that America, with its large black population, is less fortunate than other technologically advanced nations in that its "brain reserve" is not as good. I suspect that neither "scientist" knows anything about the black American experience. They operate from the erroneous assumption that equal opportunity has been a reality in America. The findings at a number of compensatory education programs indicate otherwise.

Over a three-year period, from 1964 to 1966, 159 black students, primarily from eight Deep South states, participated in a six-week Summer Study-Skills compensatory program. Fifty-three of them repeated the program. Most students were between the ages of fourteen and sixteen and the average Lorge-Thorndike Intelligence Score was 120. The students were usually in the top 10 per cent of their high school classes. One-third were from rural areas and towns of less than 10,000 population, one-third from cities of 10,000 to 50,000 and one-third from even larger communities. Family incomes ranged from $900 to $25,000 per year, and parental occupations ranged from physician, college president, air force pilot and school teacher to laborer, share-cropper, domestic worker and public-welfare recipient. Approximately 20 per cent of the students were in the poverty category, as defined by the Social Security Administration. Approximately 90 per cent were from two-parent families.

On an achievement test, standardized on a nationwide basis, the students made statistically significant improvement in mathematics, English and vocabulary. The performances of the fifty-three students who returned to the program for a second summer revealed not only that gains in mathematics were maintained through the intervening year but that significant additional gains were made the second summer. In English, on the other hand, they lost a little ground through the intervening year, but made even greater gains during the second summer.

The average percentile improvement in mathematics for the

212 subjects, or 159 students, over the three-year period was 10.72 percentile points. The average improvement in English was 11.25. There was a 5.49 improvement in vocabulary. Students who entered the program with the poorest educational preparation made the greatest advances. A group of sixteen such students made an average percentile gain of 34 points in mathematics in six weeks. The son of a sharecropper improved 34 percentile points in mathematics, 30 in English and 44 in vocabulary in one six-week period. He maintained and enlarged these gains during the following school year. To provide an education to match his ability, arrangements were made for him to finish high school in California. The daughter of a middle-income professional family improved 80 percentile points in mathematics in one six-week period and maintained this gain in the following school year.[19]

What do these remarkable changes indicate? The students often explained that this was really the first time they had had a mathematics course. In many rural areas and even some larger cities, advanced courses are listed to meet state requirements but the courses are not taught. A student from the Mississippi Delta described what had happened in one of his classes where test papers were passed out for a trigonometry final examination, and the students were required to put their heads on their desks and rest. His class had never been taught basic algebra, not to mention trigonometry! In one school, television equipment for TV teaching had been purchased, but was left in the storeroom for three years due to lack of trained staff. Students repeatedly pointed out that there was little competition and that their schools did not provide a learning environment. Teachers going through the motions of education in a social system that in essence says, "We don't want black people to learn," did not expect these black children to accomplish anything.

Some of the students had had first-hand experience with school integration and described various incidents. In one case, an attractive black girl was trailed through the school halls by white hoodlums who made obscene propositions and remarks, while white teachers ignored them. In one Mississippi town, a regulation was passed which would allow black students to return to the black school after a year if they were unhappy in the predominantly white school, which encouraged white students to provoke, antagonize and intimidate them. One youngster, with an IQ score of 132, wanted to become a pediatrician to help the poor children of Louisiana, but lamented, "I don't think I can make it because the subjects I need aren't given in my school and I don't think I could take all the trouble I'd have at the white school."

These were the best students from solid backgrounds and they obviously had the ability to achieve. They were prepared from an emotional and developmental standpoint, but were not receiving adequate training in their own schools. There are many students from more troubled backgrounds with equal potential but in need of special types of programs. If many of the Southern rural schools are not educating the best students, obviously they are not even touching the needs of the more troubled students. As we saw with Walter, conditions for blacks are not much better in the North. Certainly this situation exists for many whites, but generally, where society has failed whites it has more completely failed blacks.

In the final analysis, most Americans did not succeed as owners of large farms, as land speculators, as professionals or as big-businessmen. Most white Americans have been able to earn a decent income to support their families as a result of benefits derived from public education and membership in unions. Blacks were cheated in the area of education. North and South, blacks were largely closed out of the labor movement and barred from the better jobs and opportunities until the second half of the twentieth century.

After slavery, blacks—eager to get any kind of work—were used as strike breakers. This increased antagonism toward the black worker. On the other hand, it convinced the leaders of some craft and trade unions that blacks must be included in the labor movement. Intimidation of black and sympathetic white workers took place across the country—New Orleans, Canton, New York, Buffalo, and so on. Blacks were admitted to locals in some Northern cities, only to have their membership rejected in others. A white worker in Washington, D.C., who agreed to work with blacks was expelled from his union. In many places, when blacks came onto a job, whites walked off. Business and industry usually acquiesced to white demands. Such was the situation even in the nation's favorite pastime—baseball.

In 1884, the Toledo Mud Hens of the American Association took the field against the Chicago White Stockings. Cap Anson of the White Stockings took one look at the black Walker brothers and led his team off the field. When the Toledo manager promised to fire the black brothers the next morning, the game was played. By 1888, all black men were out of baseball. Because of this action, "Josh" Gibson, perhaps the greatest catcher in American history, never made the major leagues, and Satchel Paige, perhaps the greatest pitcher in history, made it when he was "over the hill." [20] From sports to science, America was denied the talents of blacks because of the fear and racist reaction of too many "little men" and the acquiescence of too many "big men."

A. C. Cameron, Samuel Gompers, William A. Sylvis and other white labor leaders pumped hard for the inclusion of blacks in the trade and craft unions, but in the end, they gave in to the forces of racism. Cameron said in a speech, "The systematic organization and consolidation of labor must henceforth become the watchword of the true reformer. To accomplish this the cooperation of the African race in America must be secured . . . What is wanted then, is for every union to inculcate the grand and ennobling idea that the interests of labor are one." [21] Cameron did not anticipate that a wanton disregard for law, order and justice would allow white men through fraud, violence and intimidation to disregard the rights and needs of the black population—in fact, to render that population powerless and dependent. Unions would not need black support to gain power.

For several years, Gompers refused admission to the American Federation of Labor to any union with explicit discrimination clauses in its constitution. However, by the 1890s, he relented somewhat because of the loss of at least one railroad brotherhood. He and other labor leaders chose to charter separate federations to represent black workers. The eventual loss of black political power, competition from white workers, and a lack of commitment by white employers eventually rendered most of the black unions ineffectual.

Sterling Spero and Abram Harris wrote in their book, *The Black Worker,* "Emancipation had its most immediate and profound effect upon mechanics and artisans . . . The rise of craft unionism with its apprentice system (exclusive of blacks) helped to consolidate the white artisan's position. Industrial changes and the introduction of machinery made much of the Negro's skill and training obsolete." [22] As a result, in 1890 there were more than 22,000 black carpenters in the United States, in 1940 there were less than 21,000; more than 9,000 black brick and stone masons in 1890, less than 8,000 in 1940; around 12,000 black iron and steel operatives in 1900 and around 12,000 in 1940, in spite of a large increase in the black population.[23] Blacks have consistently been closed out of these critical middle-step jobs which, meanwhile, have made the three-generation leap possible for white immigrants. These were and are the jobs of white Middle America.

While racism was a major factor, the exclusion of blacks from the labor movement was, in part, the result of the sheer magnitude of the influx of destitute Europeans.

Between 1820 and 1865, more than 7 million immigrants entered the country, settling largely in the North, Midwest and West. They came in large numbers just after the economic depression of 1812–1820 and during a period of industrial expansion. Agitation for free public schools grew in the 1830s and 1840s and educational opportunities were extended to greater numbers of the poor in the North. (The South did not provide much public education until the late 1860s.) The immigrants were arriving when the common man, through the sweat of his brow, could earn enough to participate in the land grabs made possible by the Homestead Act. Matthew Josephson wrote in *The Robber Barons:*

> The immigrant, in general, was the most aggressive, the coolest head, the least sentimental among his people, the least fettered by superstition or authority; he had no ties with any place or with the past, but lived only in the future. Having risked all and crossed the ocean in search of pecuniary gain, he was stayed by few scruples, he feared no loss from a bold stroke. A stranger, like the others all about him, whose past, whose credit was unknown, he often dealt with the others as strangers. Thus, in the rude, loosely controlled commonwealths of the frontier, the pioneer became, as Turner concludes, "strong in selfishness and individualism, intolerant of . . . experience and education, and pressing individual liberty beyond its proper bounds." [24]

Marcus Lee Hansen, author of *The Immigrant in American History,* has shown that the immigrant farmers pushed westward in great waves. They bought and took over the lands of earlier Americans in large numbers. In the 1820s and 1830s, they moved into Pennsylvania, Ohio and western New York. Missouri, Illinois and Wisconsin received them in large numbers in the 1840s; and in the 1850s and 1860s they moved into eastern Iowa and Minnesota. In the 1870s, even greater numbers, lured by the powerful appeal of free land available under the Homestead Act, rolled into the prairies.[25]

After the Civil War, the floodgates broke. Approximately 28 million immigrants entered the country from 1865 to 1914. Industrialization developed more rapidly than ever before, but again the growth was primarily in the North and West. The free public school was only beginning to get established in the Southern states during this period and it was primarily for whites. Many of the immigrant families, benefiting from the schools and employment opportunities of the industrial North, were able to make a three-generation leap—from unskilled and unlettered laborer in the first generation, to a lettered and better skilled worker in the second generation, to a highly trained business or professional person in the third.

Certainly the hardships of the immigrants should not be underplayed. Difficult crossing experiences, exploitation, abuse, the sign in the window reading "No Irish Need Apply"—these were all a part of their experience. But, the critical institutions of family and religion were not denied the immigrants. Indeed, many lived in "Little Irelands" and "Little Italys" with a minimal break in traditions or relationships, while they made adaptations to the new land. But there were no comparable opportunities for the blacks adapting to "emancipation" in those very same years.

For too long, far too many people (even the most liberal and most educated) have compared the black American with the immigrants who have come to America. The black experience was traumatic and unique. Benjamin Botkin's collection of narratives, *Lay My Burden Down,* reflects the great differences. Several ex—slaves interviewed in the early 1930s commented:

Joyful expectation:

   . . . A man named Captain Barkus . . . called for the three nearby plantations to meet at our place. Then he got up on a platform with another man beside him and declared peace and freedom. He pointed to a colored man and yelled, "You're free as I am." Old colored folks, old as I am now, that was on sticks, throwed them sticks away and shouted.

The reality I:

   . . . Then come the calm. It was sad then. So many folks done dead, things tore up, and nowheres to go and nothing to eat and nothing to do. It got squally. Folks got sick, so hungry. Some folks starved nearly to death. Times got hard. We went to the washtub—onliest way we all could live. Ma was a cripple woman. Pa couldn't find work for so long when he mustered out.

Reality II:

   . . . a few niggers was sticking sticks in the ground when the massa come up.

"What you niggers doing?" he asked.

"We is staking off the land, massa. The Yankees say that half of it is ourn."

The massa never got mad. He just looked calm-like.

"Listen, niggers," he says, "what's mine is mine, and what's yours is yours. You are just as free as I and the missus, but don't go fooling around my land. I've tried to be a good master to you. I have never been unfair. Now if you wants to stay, you are welcome to work for me. I'll pay you one-third the crops you raise. But if you wants to go, you sees the gate."

Rendered dependent:

When freedom, my mama said Old Master called all of 'em to his house, and he said: "You all free, we ain't got nothing to do with you no more, go on your own way." My mama said they go on off, then they come back and stand around just looking at him and Old Mistress. They give 'em something to eat and he say: "Go on away, you don't belong to us no more, you been freed."

They go away, and they kept coming back. They didn't have no place to go and nothing to eat. From what she said they had a terrible time. She said it was bad times . . .

Seemed like it was four or five years before they got to places they could live. They all got scattered.

True rugged individualists:

. . . When we gits to Texas, we gits married, but all they was to our wedding am we just 'grees to live together as man and wife. I settled on some land, and we cut some trees and split them open and stood them on end with the tops together for our house. Then we deadened some trees, and the land was ready to farm. There was some wild cattle and hogs, and that's the way we got our start, caught some of them and tamed them.

I don't know as I 'spected nothing from freedom, but they turned us out like a bunch of stray dogs, no homes, no clothing, no nothing, not 'nough food to last us one meal. After we settles on that place, I never seed man or woman, 'cept Govie for six years, 'cause it was a long ways to anywhere. All we had to farm with was sharp sticks. We'd stick holes and plant corn, and when it come up we'd punch up the dirt around it. We didn't plant cotton, 'cause we couldn't eat that. I made bows and arrows to kill the wild game with, and we never went to a store for nothing. We made our clothes out of animal skins.

Hardtimes I:

Several families had to live in one house. Lots of the colored folks went up North and froze to death. They couldn't stand the cold. They wrote back about them dying. No they never sent them back. I heard some sent for money to come back. I heard plenty 'bout the Ku Klux. They scared the folks to death. People left Augusta in droves . . .

Hardtimes II:

. . . That how us was. No money, no nothing. I git a job working for a white man on he farm, but he couldn't pay much. He didn't have nothing. He give me just 'nough to git a peck or two of meal and a little syrup.

Like It Is:

When you has work and some money in your pocket so you can go to the store and buy some meat and bread, then you has the best freedom there is.[26]

In a devastated, poverty-stricken, post–Civil War South, land was the primary source of power. The re–distribution of land was immediately recognized by blacks and whites alike as a prerequisite for meaningful emancipation. A wise Southern editor wrote in 1868, "Without confiscation [of land] the result of Negro suffrage will slip through their fingers." [27] Many black freedmen saw that their economic dependence on white landowners would force them to choose between voting and eating, and there was widespread demand for land from the black masses. Granting black freedmen land would not have been an unprecedented action, considering how much land the government had already given away to whites.

For a while, it did not seem far-fetched to believe, as many blacks did, that each freedman would receive forty acres of confiscated land as a reparation for slavery and to aid adjustment to freedom.

"Forty acres" was no figure of speech. The idea began with General Sherman. On his famous march to the sea, he authorized black refugees to settle on the Sea Islands, off the coast between Jacksonville, Florida and Charleston, South Carolina, and a strip of the mainland thirty miles inland along this same stretch. Each freedman was granted forty acres of land for the duration of the Civil War and was led to believe that Congress would eventually make ownership permanent. Approximately 40,000 blacks settled on this land and made remarkable improvements in a few months. Slave narratives indicate that blacks settled on land elsewhere in the South at the same time. When white Southern landowners were pardoned and attempted to reclaim land they had formerly owned, freedmen fought to retain possession of it, usually unsuccessfully. In the Sea Islands area, however, there was some success. Armed conflict forced the issue and Congress eventually made 38,000 acres of federal land in the area available to blacks at $1.50 per acre. Where blacks had been given leases under the order of General Sherman, they were allowed to retain their lands.

On March 3, 1865, the Bureau of Refugees, Freedmen and Abandoned Land was established by Congress. The agency, better known as the Freedmen's Bureau, was authorized to assign each freedman and each "loyal white refugee" not more than forty acres of land from the confiscated plantations. The freedmen were charged an annual rent of 6 per cent of the 1860 value of the land, considerably higher than the 1865 value. The Bureau held only

800,000 acres and it was expected to provide for the needs of 4 million freedmen located in the post-Civil War South. No provision for eventual ownership was contained in the bill that created the Bureau. In fact, the Bureau sold its best land to white speculators, and by 1868 held title to only 140,000 acres of poor land. On the other hand, the Bureau did provide emergency food, negotiated work contracts between the freedmen and their former masters and set up numerous schools. However, this work fell far short of meeting the needs of the black masses.

Congressman Thaddeus Stevens, a champion of black freedom and opportunity, pointed out that 394 million acres of land in the South were then owned by 70,000 people. The remaining 71 million acres were owned by persons having less than 200 acres. He proposed that those owning less than 200 acres be permitted to retain their land and that the estates of "leading Rebels" be divided into tracts of forty acres for each freedman. Stevens's bill was introduced in the House of Representatives in March, 1867, but it was not even supported by his own Republican party. The dream was over. The nightmare returned—more painful than before to men who were now told they were "free."

Men guilty of treason against the United States government were pardoned and their land returned. While blacks were being denied land, free land was being made available to encourage immigrants to settle the West. Blacks were unwanted. C. Vann Woodward in his book, *The Strange Career of Jim Crow*, wrote, "Generally speaking, the farther west the Negro went in the free states, the harsher he found the proscription and segregation. Indiana, Illinois and Oregon incorporated in their constitutions clauses restricting the admission of Negroes to their borders, and most states carved from the old Northwest Territory either barred Negroes in some degree or required that they post bond guaranteeing good behavior.[28] Only one black man was in Marinette, Wisconsin, in 1910 and seventeen had made it to Casper, Wyoming. It was less than a show of gratitude or responsibility to a people who had helped to finance the Industrial Revolution, worked the land for more than 200 years, and by 1865 had defended the country in numbers totaling over 250,000 fighting men.[29] For most of white America, "A peck or two of meal and a little syrup" was good enough for the niggers. Real freedom—the kind in which freedmen had some money in their pockets and could go to the store and buy some meat and bread—was not to be.

At the end of slavery, 4.3 million poverty-stricken blacks, who were without an independent economic base, were thrown into direct competition for jobs with 5.3 million poor white Southerners. In fact, the struggle between black and white workers began before the end of slavery and continues to the present. During slavery, blacks were often trained in various crafts to help maintain the plantations, and to earn money for the masters as hired-out hands.

It is a little-known paradox of American history that blacks had more freedom to compete with white workers during slavery than after emancipation. There is evidence of this in a rare law passed by the Georgia legislature in 1845, providing:

> That from and after the first day of February next each and every white person who shall hereafter contract or bargain with any slave, mechanic or mason, or free person of color, being a mechanic or mason, shall be liable to be indicted for a misdemeanor; and on conviction, to be fined at the discretion of the court, not exceeding $200.[30]

As Freud pointed out, laws are rarely passed unless whatever they prohibit is being done on a substantial scale and is a threat in the eyes of those who control society. So great was the economic competition from blacks in the North that, in 1860, the legislature of Pennsylvania was urged to reenact laws permitting Negro slavery. In New York City, unskilled German and Irish immigrants in the Democratic party were quite blunt about it. They opposed the freeing of slaves on the grounds that emancipation would bring increased competition for jobs and would reduce their wages. Like the freedmen, the immigrants understood that the best kind of freedom was the "meat and bread" kind.

The anti-black climate—North, South, East and West—was one of the reasons most blacks remained in the South. There was little to be gained by leaving. By 1910, of a total population of about 9.8 million blacks, only 50,662 lived in the West and just over 1 million lived in the North. The majority stayed in the South.[31] As late as 1910, almost 60 per cent of the black Southern population were employed as farm workers, and at least 75 per cent of these workers were tenants or sharecroppers—the lowest economic level and the least prestigious employment in America. Another 20 per cent worked as domestics and in personal service occupations. Thus, over 50 per cent of the black population of the United States were living as serfs, and about 90 per cent toiled at the most menial level of labor only six years before World War I. In 1910, less than 25 per cent of the white population lived in the South and the majority of this group held better jobs. In fact, whites earned from 30 per cent to 70 per cent more for the same job than did blacks, whether they were sharecroppers or school teachers.[32]

Serfdom was not the worst aspect of the early post-Civil War period for the freedman. From 1865 to 1867, white hoodlums and organized groups systematically terrorized blacks. A New York reporter wrote, "The public mind is not informed of a one-hundredth part of the wrongs endured by the patient freedman." [33] White teachers in the black schools were ostracized and schools for blacks were burned. Blacks seeking to vote were intimidated. John Hope Franklin wrote, "Already the pattern was emerging: bitter resentment of 'outside interference' that would contaminate the Negroes and yet no effort by white Southerners to improve the conditions." [34] In 1866, a series of bloody riots in Memphis, Charleston and New Orleans forced a reluctant Congress to take action. It responded with the Reconstruction Acts of 1867, which placed ten of the Rebel states (excluding the eleventh, Tennessee) under Federal military occupation and provided for the establishment of black suffrage and of state governments which included freedmen.

Reconstruction had a number of political, social and economic consequences, both good and evil. Few periods of history are more disputed than the years from 1865 to 1877. It is often argued that ignorance and mismanagement led to the Compromise of 1877, which ended Reconstruction, returned control of the South to the Democrats and ended black participation in government. Donald Comer, of the white Comer line, points to a passage from James Truslow Adams' *Epic of America,* to describe the white man's burden:

Scenes in the legislative halls of all the Northern states would have been laughable had they not been tragic. Crowds of Northern muckers and blacks who had been slaves a short time since swaggered about, smoking and drinking at the states' expense, ruling the South. There is no parallel in the history of modern civilized nations, and it is almost incredible that it occurred within our own country. No civilized victor was ever more ungenerous. The War had left the South prostrate. Reconstruction left it maddened.[35]

Donald Comer indicated that Barbour County, where my father was born—as, incidentally, was Alabama Governor George Wallace—had a particularly difficult experience with the carpetbagger Negro government imposed by federal occupation. (I suspect that he was talking about some of my relatives.) This was a widespread claim; however, John Hope Franklin has shown that it was a marked distortion. He wrote, "The national forces conducive to the decline of public morality were powerful and the South was not immune." Graft and corruption were widespread North and South. By comparison with the activities of Boss Tweed in New York City and other Northerners, corruption in the South was petty. On the other hand, says Franklin, "Alabama has provided some of the prime examples of big graft during Reconstruction. Numerous railroads fed at the public trough by bribing legislators and other officials and through the use and misuse of state funds placed at their disposal." Franklin concluded, "Corruption was bi-sectional, bi-partisan and bi-racial . . . During the Louisiana Convention of 1864, before any blacks were in the government, corruption and frivolity were rampant. It ran up a bill of $9,400 for liquor and cigars, $4,394 for carriage hire and $4,237 for newspapers for delegates. More than $156,000 was appropriated for printing the journal and debates of the Convention." [36] To this day, those debates are not available in print.

What, then, did happen when the black man had his day? Although black voters outnumbered whites in five states of the South, only South Carolina and Louisiana ever had black-controlled legislatures, and federal troops were out of all but three Southern states by 1870, having been withdrawn to facilitate the white takeover. At the time of Reconstruction, blacks were economically dependent and poorly educated and had had no experience in public affairs. In *Black Power U. S. A.,* Lerone Bennett, Jr., described the outcome:

> As soon as the first Republican governments [including blacks] were inaugurated, the counterrevolutionaries sprang into action, using internal subversion, civil disobedience, and Big Lie propaganda techniques in a concerted effort to deny the new governments the money they needed to operate . . .
>
> Artfully spreading confusion and dissension, the counterrevolutionaries abandoned the orthodox methods of presenting the case to the public, and relied almost entirely on corruption and secret influence—bribery . . .
>
> Subversion from within was facilitated also by the ambivalence of white Republican leaders, most of whom had no real interest in black people and little real faith in democracy. Like most men of their place and time, they looked down on poor men—black and white. Most of them, moreover, had a desperate desire for social acceptance by their enemies. The grand outcome, as Albert T. Morgan very astutely observed, was that most white Republicans "went forward with their work as though their first duty was to consult the enemies of the system." [37]

Blacks were interested in conciliation, and were therefore easy prey to the unscrupulous power seekers from North and South who sought to exploit and overthrow them. With all their effort at internal and external subversion, whites were unable to significantly decrease black participation in government. They then turned to systematic violence. Whites of all classes engaged in a war of terror against blacks. Thus, throughout the entire decade, black power was being eroded by distortions, manipulation of men and information—often by criminal means. One of the most severe criticisms of the black legislators by the Bourbon press was that they taxed the rich to provide for education for the poor.

It is ironic that the early Republican governments, formed by white Northerners and white and black Southerners—though vilified and condemned by the man in the street and some social scientists—laid the groundwork for Southern recovery. The Reconstruction legislatures ratified the Thirteenth, Fourteenth and

Fifteenth Amendments, passed legislation that fostered industrial development, revised tax laws, reformed judicial systems, finally established a public school system mandatory for blacks and whites, and provided for public charities for the needy—all against the opposition of the Southern landed class. Black leaders called for early return of the franchise to the Rebels. It is another irony that the return of the franchise led to blacks receiving only nominal benefits from the legislative action black leaders had made possible. This is one of the reasons that young black leaders today call for "black power" by any means necessary, rather than for love and forgiveness. Mindful of the record, many blacks do not believe that whites with power are capable of fair play.

The 1901 statement of Congressman George H. White of North Carolina, the last black congressman in the post-Reconstruction era, tells the story of the final outcome:

> I want to enter a plea for the colored man, the colored woman, the colored boy and the colored girl of this country . . . but for the constant and the persistent efforts of certain gentlemen upon this floor to mold and rivet public sentiment against us as a people and to lose no opportunity to hold up the unfortunate few who commit crimes and depredations and lead lives of infamy and shame, as other races do, as fair specimens of representatives of the entire colored race. And at no time, perhaps, during the Fifty-Sixth Congress, were these charges and counter-charges, containing, as they do, slanderous statements, more persistently magnified and pressed upon the attention of the nation than during the consideration of the recent re-apportionment bill, which is now a law . . . none have been more persistent in their determination to bring the black man into disrepute and, with a labored effort, to show that he was unworthy of the right of citizenship than my colleague from North Carolina, Mr. Kitchen. During the first session of this Congress, when the Constitutional amendment was pending in North Carolina, he labored long and hard to show that the white race was at all times and under all circumstances superior to the Negro by inheritance if not otherwise, and the excuse for his party supporting that amendment, which has since been adopted, was that an illiterate negro was unfit to participate in making the laws of a sovereign State and the administration and

execution of them; but an illiterate white man living by his side, with no more or perhaps not as much property, with no more exalted character, no higher thoughts of civilization, no more knowledge of the handicraft of government, had by birth, because he was white, inherited some peculiar qualification, clear, I presume, only in the mind of the gentleman who endeavored to impress it upon others, that entitled him to vote, though he knew nothing whatever of letters.[38]

Congressman White hardly sounds like the grinning, swaggering black legislators described in the *Epic of America* or in college texts read by students as recently as the mid-1960s. He skillfully pointed up the motive of Mr. Kitchen and the tactics of most Southern states in removing black representation:

He [Mr. Kitchen] insists and, I believe, has introduced a resolution in this House for the repeal of the Fifteenth Amendment to the Constitution . . . perhaps it would not be amiss to call the attention of the House to a few facts and figures surrounding his birth and rearing. To begin with, he was born in one of the counties in my district, Halifax, a rather significant name.

I might state as a further general fact that the Democrats of North Carolina got possession of the state and local government since my last election in 1898, and that I bid adieu to these historic walls on the 4th day of next March, and that the brother of Mr. Kitchen will succeed me. Comment is unnecessary. In the town where this young gentleman was born, at the general election last August for the adoption of a constitutional amendment, and the general election for State and county officers, Scotland Neck had a registered white vote of 395, most of whom of course were Democrats, and a registered colored vote of 534, virtually if not all of whom were Republicans, and so voted. When the count was announced, however, there were 831 Democrats to 75 Republicans; but in the town of Halifax, same county, the result was much more pronounced.

In that town the registered Republican vote was 345 and the total registered vote of the township was 539, but when the count was announced it stood 990 Democrats to 41 Republicans, or 492 more Democratic votes counted than were registered votes in the township. Comment here is unnecessary, nor do I think it necessary for anyone to wonder at the peculiar notion my colleague has with reference to the manner of voting and the method of counting those votes, nor is it to be a wonder that he is a member of this Congress, having been brought up and educated in such wonderful notions of dealing out fair-handed justice to his fellow man.[39]

Congressman White also pointed out that Alabama and other Southern states effectively eliminated black representation and participation in government through state constitutional amendments in some cases and fraud, intimidation, murder and violence in others. Nearing the close of his statement, Congressman White observed, "Mr. Chairman, in the trial of Lord Bacon, when the Court disturbed the Counsel of the defendant, Sir Walter Raleigh raised himself up to his full height and, addressing the court said: 'Sir, I am pleading for the life of a human being.' "

The black Congressman concluded, "The apology that I have to make for the earnestness with which I have spoken is that I am pleading for the life, the liberty, the future happiness and manhood suffrage for one eighth of the entire population of the United States." [40]

Loud applause from fellow Congressmen followed his speech, but little action. His plea for an effective lynch law, restoration of the Freedmen's Savings and Trust Company and other actions to improve the lot of black Americans fell on deaf ears.

Because of black powerlessness after the 1870s, the legislatures began to fill with racists. Violence, intimidation, unjust legislation and harassment kept blacks away from the polls. From 1900 to 1940, approximately 2,000 blacks were lynched, according to official United States Government records, as compared with fewer than 200 whites. This did not include the unofficial and official murders permitted by biased and irresponsible white judges and juries. Attempts to organize for group advancements were frequently met with violence. "Freedom" was a cruel joke. Langston Hughes gave a description of the Mississippi floods of 1927 which poignantly reveals the level of racism three generations after the Civil War:

White refugees were brought down the Mississippi to Baton Rouge in steamers with cabins and covered decks that protected them from the elements; the Negroes were loaded on flat-boats and freight barges that trailed behind the steamers and were open to wind and storm. At Baton Rouge the whites were housed in a group of tree-shaded buildings, the Armory or former barracks. The Negroes—men, women and children alike—were housed in small tents in an open field where the mud was ankle deep when it rained. The whites had three hot meals a day; the Negroes, two. The whites were given regular rations of tobacco, snuff and candy; the Negroes got what was left over, if there was anything.

Many Negro peons told horrifying tales of having to do forced labor at gunpoint on levees that finally gave way; of terrified whites fleeing in all the available boats, leaving their Negro sharecroppers to find their way to safety as best they could; of hair-raising nights on roofs or knolls or flood-surrounded portions of the levee, fighting off the snakes and small wild animals that sought refuge there too. Most of the refugees could not read or write; most of them had never seen a city before; some of them had never been off the plantation where they were born; some of the adults had never had ten dollars at one time in their whole life.[41]

Conditions were only slightly better for the black population in the North. Hughes wrote of the conditions in New York City at the turn of the twentieth century that led to the founding of the NAACP: "Racial violence, inadequate police protection, the blindness of political officials to vice and crime, underpaid workers, the mothers whose work as domestic servants left their children with no one to look after them all day, the young people with aspirations but little to which they might aspire."[42] Throughout the North, blacks were crowded into narrow residential strips. In the early 1900s, a sign was posted in Elmwood, Indiana which read: "No Negroes Admitted Here." By 1930, all but one-fourth of the residential property in Chicago was restricted to white occupancy.

Despite the animosity toward blacks in the North, forces developed that pulled large numbers northward. Around 1910, farm mechanization, floods and the boll weevil began to push large numbers of black farmers off the land and into destitution. Black leaders, with an eye on improving the group's economic and social lot, encouraged migration. Black newspapers circulated in the

South, particularly the *Chicago Defender*, urged blacks to move north. While the North was still no paradise, many black Southerners reasoned that they had nothing to lose. The great migration began.

From 1910 to 1930, the struggle for jobs and territory in the North led to increasing black and white conflict. Bloody riots resulted in more than 200 black and white deaths in Philadelphia, Washington, D.C., Chicago, Detroit and other cities. Until 1930, although the exclusion of blacks from the labor movement had kept them at low economic and occupational levels, the generally good economic conditions had made employment possible. When the stock market collapsed, blacks—who had been gradually moving back into semi-skilled areas as craftsmen, barbers, bakers and butchers—were pushed out almost totally. For blacks, conditions were bad in times of plenty and worse in times of scarcity. Hughes wrote of the black experience during the Great Depression:

> Thousands of complaints concerning the Federal Emergency Relief Administration poured into NAACP offices. Private charities—even a number of religious organizations —also found ways of favoring needy whites above needy Negroes. Some soup kitchens and bread lines shamelessly turned away Negro men and women. Angelo Herndon was sentenced to 20 years on the chain gang in Georgia for leading a hunger march that sought to petition the county Commissioner for relief that was legally due Negroes. Negro applicants were frequently locked up for what white relief administrators labelled "impudence" or "disturbing the peace." Hunger and discrimination kept official company from coast to coast.[43]

Blacks spent forty years in the wilderness between the parting address of the last black United States Congressman and Executive Order 8802. The Order decreed:

> There shall be no discrimination in the employment of workers in defense industries and in Government because of race, creed, color, or national origin . . . and it is the duty of employers and labor organizations . . . to provide for the full and equitable participation of all workers.[44]

This Order was given on June 25, 1941, one week before a planned March on Washington proposed by black labor leader A. Philip Randolph and supported by the National Urban League, the NAACP, church groups and other organizations. The Order paved the way for the eventual re-entry of the black man into areas of the labor market other than domestic and farm worker and into the mainstream of American life.

Those four decades between the dawn of the twentieth century and the onset of World War II were critical years for all Americans. Public education was made available across the country. Business and industry, except during the period of the Depression, were expanding. Technology was advancing. These should have been the years that prepared Americans for life in the complex second half of the century. The grandparents of today's young adults were born in the early 1900s and the parents in the mid-1920s. Many whites received a decent income as workers, permitting them to provide for their families; public education enabled their relatively secure children and grandchildren to get an average, if not good, education. Many ethnic groups in America finally "made it" during these forty years.

This was not the case for the black man. In the American system, power begets power and it trickles down within groups, families, and organizations. Group cohesion created through successful social action increases group unity, political and economic power. Through group power, opportunity is increased for individual members. Without power, the black man was not in a position to protect himself.

As late as 1960, the head of a black Chicago financial firm had to pretend that he was working for a New York white man in order to get attractive office space in Chicago. The black officers in banks, there to aid the black businessman, are still few in number. Indeed, few black businessmen have been successful in their poverty-stricken, powerless communities. Such conditions have made economic growth difficult, if not impossible. Without black big business, black small business cannot thrive. The contracts awarded by big government and big business do not go to the black filling station or stationery store.

When the Irish moved into a residential area, Irish power made Pat O'Malley the friendly cop on the beat. He did not have to take a Civil Service examination. He played on the corner with the children of his neighbors and friends. When blacks came in and the Irish left, Officer O'Malley remained, sometimes as the unfriendly cop on the corner. Blacks, under-educated and closed out of institutional life—courts, legislatures, businesses and so on —could not force an antagonistic majority to provide the opportunities they needed if they were to live decently.

It has often been argued, by blacks and whites who should know better, that the middle-class black does not care, does not help his less fortunate brothers. This ignores the work of the many black teachers, ministers and doctors who have given above and beyond the call of duty. My family doctor never charged us a cent because we were all trying to go to college. A black teacher from St. Louis went to rural Alabama to help out when the residents heard, "There ain't goin' to be no nigger school this year." Many black families already settled in the North cushioned the adjustment of rural Southern migrants. Why didn't they do more? Because they did not have the economic and political power and prestige to do more.

Blacks were not in the powerful unions. Blacks were either closed out of the education and political power structures or they were the captives of the more powerful whites. Most important, black folks did not have and could not control the amounts of money that white ethnics and old Americans had in their reach. When the whites were amassing fortunes which were used to shape social policy to benefit their various ethnic groups, there were no income taxes. Taxes were not a significant obstacle to accumulating wealth until the 1940s. Blacks were then just beginning to come out of the rural South and gain the kind of jobs that would support a minimally decent way of life.

To blame middle-income blacks for not doing more, economically and psychologically, to smooth the way of low-income blacks obscures the real obstacles.

Until the 1960s, our society kept almost all blacks equally powerless. "Middle-income" blacks had distinctly lower incomes than middle-income whites. They had more than poorer blacks chiefly in the sense that they had more to lose if they didn't "know their place."

Only in the past decade has it begun to be reasonably safe for a black who has theoretically "made it" to show that he is "still a brother" without expecting reprisals. There are now blacks who can help other blacks get good jobs, or decent breaks at the courthouse and in the schoolhouse. Such interest and power were badly needed in 1914.

In 1914, as war and the needs of war production began to spread across the world, American industrialists turned to the untapped black labor source in the South. After the war, restrictions were placed on immigration and the mass migration of blacks from South to North began to accelerate. Today, almost 50 per cent of the black population is in the North and West, mostly in urban areas. In the past fifty years, more than 5 million blacks have made the trek from the rural South to the urban North. From 1910 to 1920, almost 750,000 blacks moved north and in the subsequent decade about one and a quarter million newcomers swelled the black populations of a score of the largest Northern cities. Between 1910 and 1920 the black population of Detroit increased more than 600 per cent; in Cleveland, 300 per cent; in Chicago, 150 per cent. By comparison, the greatest increase in a Southern city—Norfolk—was 75 per cent. There were fewer than 400 Negroes in Gary, Indiana in 1910 and nearly 15,000 in 1930. Southern white farmers, for the most part, moved to Southern cities.

But, alas, opportunity for the black man was still limited. From 1900 to 1940 very few blacks were involved in industrial apprentice programs, so that when blacks got jobs in World War II industry, few were prepared for skilled labor. While the white population was employed first and in the best jobs, blacks did at least have work. This opportunity brought 1.5 million to the North in the 1940s and approximately the same number in the 1950s. During the mid-1950s, blacks were arriving in Chicago at the rate of 3,000 per month. In the late 1940s and early 1950s, blacks discovered California. The gold was gone but the chance for a decent job and improved life conditions prompted a "rush." Between 1940 and 1960, the black population of Los Angeles increased 600 per cent.

By far the largest proportion of the migrants poured out of the rural areas of the Deep South. Aside from the obvious adverse social conditions, one look at the impact of federal agricultural programs of the era explains the most important reason for "Operation Black Exodus." In the 1930s, the Agricultural Adjustment Administration gave preferential treatment to white applicants for development and mechanization loans. The result was not only an increase in the number of whites who owned farms but also a reduction in the number of blacks who either owned farms or worked on them as sharecroppers or cash tenants. The result of federal policy and local prejudice was that blacks were squeezed off the land. From 703,555 in 1920, cash and share tenants declined to 506,638 in 1940. Black owners and farm managers declined from some 220,000 in 1920 to less than 174,000 in 1940.[45]

A study of the impact of federal programs on black farmers in nine counties of South Carolina, conducted by the Southern Regional Council and published in 1962, tells it like it was and is.[46] Conditions in these nine counties are typical of those still existing throughout the several states of the Black Belt, where most black farmers are located. In fact, some 98 per cent of all black farmers are in the South.

Blacks constituted more than 50 per cent of the total population in eight of the nine counties. More than 50 per cent of the farmers were black in five of the counties and not less than 39 per cent in any county. Despite their numbers, blacks were closed out of all policy-making positions in all federal programs designed to help small farmers. In fact, blacks did not even hold clerical jobs in the program offices and official correspondence usually did not refer to a black farmer as "Mister."

Another program, the Farmers Home Administration of the United States Department of Agriculture, established in 1934, helps small farmers with poor credit ratings acquire and hold family-sized farms through easy credit and technical assistance. To ensure local control, three farmers from the community must pass on each application for a loan. As late as 1962, no blacks had ever served on this committee throughout the South. That probably explains why only nine loans enabling blacks to acquire their own farms were made from 1959 to 1962 in the nine counties studied by the S.R.C. Figures for the same nine counties show that loans for the purchase of farms totalled $1,222,630, of which only $55,550 went to blacks. Of the $1,328,915 loaned to build or improve farm housing, only $81,955 went to blacks, representing a total of only fourteen loans over the same three-year period. Based on the number of black farmers, blacks were expected to receive from 75 to 80 per cent of the funds for operating and emergency needs. They received about one-third of that. Obviously, the policy is, "We'll help you out just a little when you are in a pinch, but we sure won't give you anything to help you grow."

When my uncle received financing in Alabama and built a modern ranch-type house, a white farmer—who frequently spoke despairingly of blacks who let their property deteriorate—commented, "Damn, Bob, did you have to build the best-looking house in the county?" Keeping the black man down was a full-time task for many. If they couldn't keep him down by keeping him poor, they could maintain the myth that "they don't want to do any better" by looking at the victims of racism and poverty—and damning those who showed the myth to be a lie.

The Agricultural Stabilization and Conservation Service of the Department of Agriculture is involved in price and market stabilization through production adjustment and conservation assistance. The county ASCS office, with the assistance of a committee of local farmers, is responsible for ruling on a farmer's eligibility for price support and for determining crop allotments. As late as 1962, no black worked in any of the state or county offices in the South or belonged to the committees. In fact, of the 90,000 farmers in the nation who had served on county committees in 1962, only one was black. He lived in Vermont.

Public and private agencies extend credit to small farmers on the basis of the amount of allotted crops. By controlling the economic fate of the black farmers, white committee members can also intimidate blacks through threats of economic reprisal for political activity. This might explain why voter registration ranges from three to eleven times less than the black population eligible to vote in the counties covered in the Southern Regional Council Report, which concludes:

> The Negro farmer in these nine South Carolina counties seems not to receive anything like a fair share of funds appropriated for the aid of the small farmer, and receives shockingly little in the way of help for the acquisition of ad-

ditional farm land to make his farming more viable, or for
housing to give him and his family an incentive to stay on
the land . . .

No agencies of the Department of Agriculture nor of the
organizations over which it has general supervision have afforded South Carolina Negroes anything like equal job employment. The only jobs available, besides as janitors, have
been those within the segregated practices of some of the
agencies. There have been no clerical or administrative jobs
made available to Negroes in South Carolina . . .

Area redevelopment programs which do not from the onset provide for equal job opportunities for Negroes will only
strengthen and perpetuate the present system of inequalities.
It is ironic that Negro unemployment and under-employment
is counted to determine area eligibility for area redevelopment assistance, while the resulting projects exclude Negroes
from any direct job benefits.[47]

In 1965, the United States Commission on Civil Rights reported essentially the same findings. While the policy of the Department of Agriculture has been more equitable since 1968 than
at any time in the past, changes have been slower than is necessary
and just. Thus, the Department was a major target of the Poor
People's Campaign in Washington, D.C. in 1968.

By the late 1940s, blacks had begun to ease their way into the
economic mainstream, particularly through industrial jobs. In the
1950s, automation began to push them out. It abolished old
jobs and created new ones. But these often demand greater skills
—or else there are new educational qualifications that screen out
many who could otherwise do the work.

The black migrants have been the worst-educated and least-
trained people in America. (Belated efforts by many employers
demonstrate that many undereducated people are quite capable of
holding modern jobs. Indeed, research has indicated that even retarded people, black or white, may be better prepared for some of
the jobs of the automation age than are our "creative thinkers."
Nonetheless, there is a high correlation between better education
and better employment opportunities.) While many unions began
to drop racial barriers in the 1940s and 1950s, most of the craft
unions still maintain those barriers today. The old problems of

prejudice and denial, and the new problems of mechanization and training, have combined to keep the black masses from a "meat and bread freedom."

> While some social scientists in the 1950s were predicting the end of racial conflict in America in one more decade, the seeds of today's racial crisis were being sown. Indeed it is the children of the unemployed and marginally employed people of the 1950s, black and white, who constitute the most troublesome component of the "urban crisis" today. Yesterday's prejudice is, in large part, today's black poverty.

In the past several years, there has been a small but steady improvement in the economic picture of the black community, together with even brighter developments in education. The number of non-whites at the poverty level (as defined by the Social Security Administration) declined from 10.9 million in 1964 to 8.3 million in 1967. The unemployment rate for blacks declined from 12.4 per cent of the black labor force in 1961 to 6.8 per cent for the first six months of 1968. A 31 per cent drop in black under–employment was recorded between 1966 and 1967, compared with a 17 per cent decline for whites. During the present economic decline, however, the black worker was hurt first and most.

In 1960, there were 46 million whites, but only 3 million blacks, in the better job categories (craftsmen, operatives and white-collar workers).

Between 1960 and 1970, things got better. For example, there was a 47 per cent increase in the number of blacks in white-collar jobs, craftsmen and operatives (the better jobs), compared with a 16 per cent increase for whites. There was an 80 per cent increase in the number of black professionals and technical workers between 1960 and 1967, compared with a 30 per cent increase among whites. There was a 77 per cent increase in the number of black clerical workers as compared with a 23 per cent increase for whites; a 49 per cent increase in craftsmen and foremen in the non-white category compared with 13 per cent for whites. There has been a corresponding decline in private household workers, 17 per cent for non-whites compared with a 23 per cent decline among whites. A 7 per cent decline was registered among black non-farm laborers, compared with a 2 per cent decline among whites. These changes, though very significant, are not as dramatic as they appear. They reflect the fact that there were so few blacks in relatively good occupational positions prior to 1960.

In 1960, the median number of school years completed by non–whites was 10.8 compared with 12.3 for whites. In 1968, the median for non-whites was 12.2 and for whites 12.6. The percentage of whites completing four years of high school was 64 in 1960 and 75 in 1968. For blacks, it was 39 per cent in 1960, and 58 per cent in 1968.[48] Again the bright picture is misleading—because so many blacks who attend school do not receive the equivalent of a white, middle-class high school education.

Despite educational and job advancement, blacks are like the weary runner trailing the field in a long-distance race. Every step uses up more energy but often results in losing ground. Because blacks were kept so far behind prior to 1960, a disproportionately large number of them are still at the bottom of the labor force and have the least amount of training and education. The pace of scientific and technological change destroys the lower rungs of the economic ladder just as most blacks begin to reach them.

There are still far too many blacks who were left out of the statistical gains recorded in the 1960s. In Gary, Indiana, an investigator for the President's Commission on Civil Disorder asked Mrs. Mamie Barnes, an aging black woman, whether she was able to make ends meet. Mrs. Barnes provided major financial support and care for the four children of her deceased daughter. She was employed as a domestic worker six days a week and spent most of Sunday at the First Zion Baptist Church. In response to the question, she shook her head slowly and said, "Mister, I don't even try to make 'em meet anymo', I jes' try to make 'em touch every now and then."

A desperate young girl in Mississippi wrote to a near stranger:

> While sitting down thinking of you, I decide to write and ask you for a little help. I am in the ninth grade and my father is dead and we just need help. My mother have nine heads of children and six head are in school so you see we need help. We have to pay for wood for our heater and light bill, gas bill, meet bill on some of the thing that we have in

the house. Now please if you can help us a little bit we have
no daddy to help mama with us so please if you can I will be
looking to hear from you . . .

It was subsequently learned that, after the father's death, this
youngster's family had been asked to leave the plantation they
were living on. Refusing to give up, this spunky 14-year-old pulled
a likely name from a magazine article and appealed for help. But
their problem was more complicated than poverty alone. Her
mother was deeply involved in the work of the embattled Child
Development Group of Mississippi (CDGM), a Headstart
Program funded by the Office of Economic Opportunity.

Contrary to the claims of many whites, North and South, that
black parents do not care, the CDGM mothers in Mississippi
wanted to see their children get a good education. They involved
themselves in a self-help pre-kindergarten and kindergarten school
program in fourteen counties of Mississippi. The enormous influence of their Senator, John Stennis, one of the most powerful men
in America, was turned against them.

More than in any other place in the country, the Child Development Group of Mississippi carried out the mandate established by
the Office of Economic Opportunity guidelines—maximum feasible participation of the poor. More than in any other place in the
country, poor black people were attempting to help themselves.
Approximately 99 per cent of the more than 2,000-member staff
were non-professional, but enthusiastic and creative and determined to grow and improve themselves and their children. Some
faced threats, violence and economic reprisal, merely to participate in a Headstart program! (In some areas it has been almost
necessary to use such tactics just to get parents to bring their children to the Headstart programs.)

It might be expected that the United States Senator representing
such determined people would have their self-help program as a
model of individual initiative. This program should warm the heart
of the coldest conservative.

But in 1966, John Stennis, Chairman of the Senate Appropria-
tions Committee, led the attack against his own constituents.
There were charges by government investigators, instigated by the
Senator, that $500,000 was misspent by the Child Development

Group of Mississippi and forgiven by the Office of Economic Opportunity. As it turned out, everything was in order except one per cent of the budget that could not be accounted for by a staff short on professional training. The money is being returned by CDGM to the government through a special fund.

In a discussion with a youngster at the Summer Study-Skills Program, I was momentarily led to believe that Senator Stennis might have been correct. The youngster repeated a remark by his mother who worked for the program, "My mama said that it's not right for some of those workers to cheat the government like that." I hesitantly asked, "What do you mean?" He explained indignantly that a few workers overstayed their lunch period to cash their checks.

Fiscal conservatives, concerned about private and public work practices, must be delighted to know that such dedication to the notion that a full day's work should be required for a full day's pay still remains in the land. Nonetheless, the Mississippi congressional delegation managed to cut off the funds to a group with such dedicated and hard-working members.

During a six-month period while the funds were cut off, most of the staff continued to work and refused to go to a rival program supported by the white segregationist establishment. Only the efforts of numerous influential individuals, social scientists, civil rights, church and labor groups and finally the intervention of former Vice President Hubert Humphrey permitted the program to be funded again.

Attempts were made to link CDGM to SNCC, Stokely Carmichael and militant Black Power groups—a remarkable basis for concern in a state stained with black blood. It is even more remarkable that only a handful of program participants had associated with militants. Charges were made that the cost per child was $450 more than O.E.O.'s estimated national cost figure, when indeed it was considerably lower than that figure.

Ironically, this complaint was made in a state where one county has spent nineteen times more on the education of white children than on black children. In the end, all of the sixteen charges leveled against the CDGM were proven to be major distortions of fact.

Why were the accusations made? Harold K. Schulz, of the National Council of Churches, writing in *Christianity and Crisis*, gave the likely but shameful answer:

> CDGM has troubled the politicians and segregationist whites of Mississippi by successfully involving persons in such a way that their lives are being changed. The demonic cycle of poverty is being broken as the poor begin making decisions about their own affairs. CDGM influence did not end with kindergarten education, but included policy making, planning, hiring and firing, and other decisions that affected the entire life of the community . . . Such an organization is a threat to the entrenched political power within the state.[49]

While Senator Stennis was attacking these black folks displaying "the spirit of our forefathers," his colleague, the senior Senator from Mississippi, James Eastland, was being paid more than $100,000 a year by the government for not planting crops on his farm—and thereby keeping black folks out of work. People who are aware of the guaranteed annual income this senator receives find it hard to accept opposition to a guaranteed annual income for all Americans.

The incongruity between the attitude toward CDGM and the farm payments to Senator Eastland highlights a long-standing paradox. Black folks, maligned as lazy and without initiative, have worked longer and harder for less money than any other people in America. Blacks worked as slaves, then as tenant farmers from sunup to sundown, and as domestics and laborers in greater proportion than any other group, often not making enough to meet the basic needs of their families. In 1968, about 750,000 black heads of families worked all year around and still landed in the poverty category. The proportion of blacks in the "working poor" category is five times as great as that of whites. It is not true that blacks will not work. The truth is that most blacks have always worked for nothing.

The black experience "like it is" explains why there are so many families like Walter Stoner's. It is unfair and misleading to focus on Walter and his family without looking at the social system that made them what they are.

While so many black people are in such misery, millions of other Americans enjoy the good life. In 1967, Americans spent over $1 billion for radio and television repairs. In the same year, Americans spent over $1 billion on flowers, seeds, and potted plants; over $4.7 billion on foreign travel. From the end of World War II to the present, we spent over $100 billion on foreign aid. In 1966, the total expenditure for elementary and secondary public school education in the fifty states was approximately $26 billion—about the same amount of money Americans spent for personal recreation in that year. All the federal funds available for the higher-education student-loan programs in 1967 amounted to $238 million. The school-lunch program did much better; it received $448 million in 1967. But in 1968 alone, the federal space program cost $6.5 billion. The result of our inappropriate priorities is that we have failed to meet the needs of Americans at home, and made unnecessary enemies abroad.[50]

But poverty is not the only cause of black and white conflict. Much of white America does not see, feel or think that a wrong has been done and is still being done. It does not understand that compensation, justice and change are necessary. This is the other major cause of black and white conflict. In Homestead, Florida, after a black student protest, the South Dade High School voted 1,010 to 47 to keep the symbols of injustice that angered blacks: the nickname "Rebels," "Dixie" as the school song, the Confederate flag as the school emblem, Confederate uniforms for the band, blue and gray as the school colors, and the name "Rebel Review" for the student newspaper. Given American history like it is, few things could be more insulting to black students.

A white girl asked the leader of the black student group why he was angry. The black student told of his feeling as a band member, "There I was, wearing the uniform of the man who fought to the death to keep my ancestors in slavery. That I looked ridiculous is not important. It actually hurt. It really does mean a lot to me."

After John Carlos and Tommie Smith, two black members of the 1968 U.S. Olympic Team, raised their fists and dropped their heads in a Black Power salute during the victory ceremony, a section of the statement made by the U.S. Olympic Committee read:

The untypical exhibitions of these two athletes also violates the basic standards of sportsmanship and good manners so highly regarded in the United States.

A black student laughed and said, "He dares to speak of sportsmanship and good manners when we have been cheated coming and going . . . you know, the white man is ridiculous!"

# The Making
# of
# the White
# Mind

From the standpoint of the "Black Mind," it is inconceivable that an intelligent white high school student would not understand why a black student would not want to wear a Confederate band uniform and play "Dixie" under the flag of the Confederate States of America. From the standpoint of the "White Mind," it is an exhibition of poor manners and unsportsmanlike conduct when two black Olympic athletes make a symbolic gesture of dissatisfaction with life conditions for black Americans. Both the Black Power salute and the Confederate flag are symbols of defiance, anger and pride; yet one is viewed as legitimate and understandable, the other is viewed as negative, impudent and undesirable. It would appear that if one is in poor taste, so is the other. There are numerous similar situations in American life in which the "Black Mind" sees it one way and the "White Mind" sees it another or does not see it at all.

A white colleague in the District of Columbia Health Clinic viewed most blacks who came to the clinic as taking a free ride on public welfare. I watched an elderly black clinic aide continuing to work as she slowly died from cancer. I observed that most of the black patients had worked all their lives for less than a living wage and with illness and old age were forced to go on public welfare.

An irate white woman argued to a *New York Times* reporter, "If Negroes have been deprived of some rights, it is because they

115

haven't worked for them." The fact is that blacks have been powerless to overcome the intimidation, violence, fraud, economic reprisals and illegal restrictions that whites have continued to impose on them. It is also a fact that hard work by blacks alone cannot bring them the economic, social and psychological advantages that whites have guaranteed for themselves by keeping blacks down.

When the late Congressman Adam Clayton Powell was denied his seat in Congress and stripped of his seniority, many liberal whites considered the action of Congress justified. Many of the most thoughtful blacks considered it a move to destroy legitimate black power. The reaction was the same when Muhammad Ali was stripped of his heavyweight boxing crown.

After the civil disorders following the assassination of Dr. Martin Luther King, Jr., the pastor of the Trinity Episcopal Church in the wealthy Fauquire County of Virginia, remarked, "We are asked to consider the Negro as our brethren, so they say, but I think really if we want to understand the situation that is going on in this country we should not look at them as our brothers but look at them as our children." The minister spoke of blacks as "really children in their capacity for understanding their position in life." He declared, "They do not have the mind, the intellect, the ability, or the position which we have. And so they behave as children, and we will have to look after them." [1] A black surgeon, holder of a Phi Beta Kappa key from a predominantly white college, quipped, "If the whites are the parents and we are the children, it is the most obvious case of the neglected and battered child syndrome I have ever encountered." (In this syndrome, immature and unstable parents view the legitimate wants and needs of their children as an assault upon themselves and often retaliate with assaultive behavior.)

Blacks live and experience and know it "like it is" in spite of the pressure from many whites to keep them thinking otherwise. That is why, in spite of my need as a youngster to be an accepted member of my school class, I had a funny feeling inside when I recited the Pledge of Allegiance and came to the last line . . . "with liberty and justice for all." My experience said, "that's not like it is." My white classmates did not have a quiver of discomfort. They were protected by the magic of the white mind.

Observers who have not grown up in America are often perplexed by the ability of the white mind to remain impervious to racial realities. A student recently asked me whether this did not indicate that all white people were mentally ill. Her reasoning is based on the fact that a prime indicator of good mental health is an individual's ability to perceive the external world as it really is and not as instinctual wishes or psychological needs would have it be.

When I first began to ponder the meaning of the many bizarre racial incidents I had experienced, I asked myself this same question. I now understand the phenomenon not as mental illness, but as a kind of collective defect in the national ego and superego; a blind spot that permits otherwise intelligent people to see, think and act in a racist way without the expected level of guilt and pain. The syndrome is what I call the "white mind."

To many observers, this failure to see, acknowledge or understand the peculiar experience and special problems of blacks is white racism, pure and simple. White racism it is, but simple it is not. The white mind is a quite complex aberration. It was formed in response to the circumstances of our African, European and American pasts. It is maintained by conditions of our American present and future. For some, it is a low-level adaptive mechanism, a way to feel adequate in the face of psychological, social and economic insecurities. For others, the white mind is the unwanted product of growing up in a society where racist viewpoints are transmitted from generation to generation by people and by their institutions. The white mind operates consciously and unconsciously to deny that white racism gives whites an unbeatable social, psychological and economic advantage over blacks.

American identity is rooted in the events surrounding its founding and the principles and doctrines that establish its purpose and direction. If Uncle Sam could talk, he would say, "I stand for the principles of the Judeo-Christian religion; I am democracy; I am justice; I am opportunity for the strong and willing; I am compassion and assistance for the weak and needy." When Americans violate these principles they are failing to live up to their commitments; this violation normally results in varying degrees of individual and public guilt and anxiety. In *Soul on Ice,* Eldridge Cleaver said to Uncle Sam, in effect, "Man, you are a damn liar."

Blacks and whites have had a kind of secret pact over the years which has helped whites minimize their guilt and anxiety. Whites have said, "Don't show me my white mind. Don't break down my defenses. Don't challenge the structure on which I base my identity. If you don't, I shall approve of you, I shall even open up a few token opportunities for you." The black protest movement has stopped keeping the black side of the bargain, and this has been getting white people upset. Because of their visible success, black athletes have been able to jolt the white mind most. Recently, they have been saying, "Don't do me any favors. Remember that I earned my way." The Black Power salute of two black athletes at the Olympics drew the ire of sportswriters because it symbolized the finishing blow to the already weakening pact.

To avoid anxiety and guilt, it has been necessary over the years for many whites to deny that the human and constitutional rights of blacks have been violated. But the violation has been so flagrant that denial alone is not enough. So the white mind adds rationalization and justification.

Through these psychological mechanisms, the white mind has managed to establish the notion that no consequential violation has ever taken place; that, in fact, blacks and whites have had essentially the same experience in America, particularly since slavery. Whites can then comfortably assume that blacks have special problems in America only because they are either inferior or lazy. Thus we can understand the irate white East Coast woman who told a reporter, "If Negroes have been deprived of some rights, it is because they haven't worked for them."

It is this notion—that blacks and whites have had the same experience—which leads to faulty analysis, planning and action in efforts to deal with problems confronting blacks. This is one reason why some social scientists compare black and white school achievement scores and draw erroneous conclusions and inferences. Because of the same-experience notion, many think that the black ghetto of 1972 is the same as the white ghetto of 1932. Thus, if white capitalism brought education, opportunity and well-being to poor whites, black capitalism should do the same for poor blacks. This is why a Maryland newspaper editor argued that Dr. Martin Luther King, Jr.'s civil-disobedience approach was unjustifiable because the same due process of law that is available to whites is available to blacks. Volumes of Justice Department reports show just the *opposite*. In spite of glaring differences, the white mind says, "We have all had the same chance—we started even."

The pervasiveness of the white-mind defect is remarkable. If some of the examples were not so tragic, they would be amusing: Mrs. Ellen Craft escaped from slavery riding in a train carriage disguised as an ailing white gentleman. An occupant of the train carriage, a Southern white lady, provided conversation for part of the journey with stories about slaves and slavery. The lady accepted slavery as her responsibility, but considered the slaves who ran off as ungrateful and wasteful. "If my son and myself had the money for those valuable [runaway] niggers, just see what a great deal of good we could do for the poor, and in sending missionaries abroad to the poor heathen, who have never heard the name of our blessed Redeemer." [2]

The men who framed the American constitution counted the black man as two-thirds a man with no rights and privileges, without a pang of conscience. Even when the nation began to develop a conscience, it was not completely shared. On one occasion, when troops were sent to integrate the public schools in Tennessee, a white bystander remarked disgustedly, "A million-dollar army to get a twenty-five cent nigger into school."

The white mind has an identical twin in some black people. Blacks have gone to white-controlled schools, listened to and read the white-controlled media and have been influenced by their relationships to powerful white personalities—teachers, politicians, employers and others. White information and rationalizations about blacks transmitted by powerful whites have often been accepted by blacks. Black people and, in turn, black institutions—churches, schools, and so on—have often transmitted the white message about blacks. That is why some blacks are as anti-black as some whites. That is why so many blacks, prior to the black–pride movement, wanted to be white.

The white mind has cost white people, black people and the nation dearly. It is impossible to calculate the price in dollars and cents. In 1960 and 1961 it cost the people of Louisiana almost $1 million for five special sessions of the state legislature to develop laws designed to maintain segregation. It has meant the loss of an enormous amount of human talent. The number of black lives snuffed out by white violence is beyond counting. The number of black lives crippled and maimed is even greater.[3] The psychological and social development of America's children—white as well as black—has been stunted. As a result, the nation is not prepared for an advanced scientific and technological age.

The nation has managed to see the problems of blacks as blacks' problems. Blacks are seen largely as those people over there—separate and distinct. The reality is that blacks are to the United States what an arm, a leg, or one-tenth of a heart muscle is to the body. When blacks are in trouble, the nation is in trouble. The black condition should have been an indicator, a warning trumpet, that told us our society was malfunctioning and not preparing for the demands of the times. Problems of blacks, caused by powerlessness, hopelessness and despair—welfare dependency, apathy, excessive drug addiction, self-destruction and so on—were viewed as results of racial inferiority. Now they are affecting greater numbers of whites and threatening national stability and we have had little experience in dealing with such problems because we have rationalized them away. In fact, many Americans still deny that these problems are related to adverse social conditions.

Excessive denial and rationalization gradually interfere with an individual's capacity to cope with situations that threaten his well-being. Like an individual, a society that engages in excessive denial and rationalization cannot deal with its internal social problems, and eventually begins to deny the realities of the outside world as well. In America that kind of denial has been going on for a long time. The roots of America's white mind are older than white America itself.

The documented information about Africa began drifting back to Europe in the fifteenth century. Basil Davidson, the English historian, wrote, ". . . if European attitudes toward Africans in these early times displayed a wide range of contrast, they were generally uniform in one important respect. They supposed no natural inferiority in Africans; no inherent failure to develop or mature." [4] Prior to the latter half of the sixteenth century, Europeans and Africans often looked upon each other as equals and partners in commerce. European traders had a healthy respect for the power of African armies and—long after the myth of African inferiority was established in Europe and the New World—African armies controlled most of West Africa. Europeans brought slaves, gold and goods out of this area through trade with powerful black African rulers rather than through conquest.

In *The Lost Cities of Africa,* Davidson presented evidence of stable and enlightened black Sudanese kingdoms as early as 1,500 years before the arrival of Europeans. Ghana was a centralized state at the time the Arabs first wrote about it in A.D. 800. Mali peaked in development during the thirteenth and fourteenth centuries and Songhay persisted as a power through the fifteenth and sixteenth centuries.

Timbuktu of the Mali empire was a center of commerce, learning and religion. Travelers in the fourteenth century described it as a place of great wealth. There were many judges, doctors and clerics. Manuscripts were imported and exchanged with outside scholars. Ibn Battuta, a traveler in Africa from 1325 to 1354, wrote of Mali, "The Negroes of this country are seldom unjust, and have a greater abhorrence of injustice than any other people. Their sultan shows no mercy to anyone who is guilty of the least act of it. There is complete security in the country. Neither traveler nor inhabitant in it has anything to fear from robbers or men of violence." [5]

Present-day Afro-Americans are descendants of people immediately south of these Sudanese kingdoms. A completely reliable description of the life and times of the pre-slavery period in this area is not possible. The motives of European writers affected their vision. Winthrop Jordan, an American historian, wrote of the problem, "Englishmen were fully aware that Negroes living in different parts of the Coast were not all alike; it was not merely different reactions in the observers which led one to describe a town as 'marveilous (sic) artificially builded with mudde walles . . . and kept very cleane as well in their streetes as in their houses' and another to relate how 'they doe eate each other alive in some places but dead in others as we wolde befe or mutton.' " [6]

Nowadays we have the facts a little straighter. The old black Africa was tribal but not primitive. Maurice Davie, a Yale sociologist, wrote, "In this general area we find native culture so complex that it can be called primitive only in the technical sense of

the word, that is, of a folk who never developed a written language . . . The basic self-maintenance is agriculture supple-
mented by fishing and hunting. There are domestic animals such
as sheep, goats and fowl. . . ." ⁷ Highly complex governmental,
economic and social systems characterized the area. Art and craft
work were highly developed and weaving and the manufacture of
pottery and iron implements were common. In short, it was far
from the Africa of savages running naked through the jungle that
eventually came to be the image held in some of America's best
minds.

While West Africa was forging its own unique culture before
the coming of the slaver in the fifteenth and sixteenth century,
Europe was undergoing social change that would forever affect
the face of Africa and set the stage for present-day black and
white conflict in America. Europe had moved from the slave-based
civilizations of antiquity through the tribal era and feudalism. Now
it was developing a system of cities and workers, merchants and
capitalists which would foster both human exploitation and a
greater recognition of individual human rights. At the center of
this new development was the Protestant Reformation, which began in 1517.

The Reformation was a mixed blessing. It spawned the belief
of man's direct accountability to God and his responsibility to his
fellow man. Man, as the direct communicator with God, implied
the greater dignity of the individual and his right to shape his own
destiny. The belief is easily recognizable as the foundation of principles, however badly neglected or abused, that guide and under-
gird Western civilizations, particularly the United States.

At the same time, Calvinists and Puritans held values that supported the rise of capitalism and the expansion of the bourgeoisie.
John Calvin adhered to St. Augustine's theory of predestination
as to who would be saved and who would be damned. Conve-
niently, prosperity was a mark of God's favor, hence salvation.
Idleness and poverty were scorned. The Puritans believed in the
right of each individual to achieve success or wealth. Indeed, these
were signs of virtue if they were achieved by honest hard work.
Puritans considered poverty a punishment for sin, and today's
opposition to a guaranteed annual income carries familiar echoes
of the old Puritan creed.

The conflicting principles of the Protestant Reformation eventually collided head on, like two inexperienced halfbacks, and helped create the contradictions that still characterize America's white mind. Prior to the Reformation, the exploitation of one group by another for economic, social and psychological purposes did not need justification. Every race of man has been subject to slavery, and the enslavement of women for sexual exploitation remains as old as the institution of slavery itself. William Graham Sumner, a political and social scientist, wrote of Roman slavery: "The free men (Romans) who discussed contemporary civilization groaned over the effects of slavery on the family and private interests, but they did not see any chance of otherwise getting the work done." [8] But, with the development of a concept of "dignity and individual rights," it became necessary to justify exploitation. Even Queen Elizabeth was burdened with the awesome choice between religious values and personal greed. When she heard of the activities of the capricious slaver, Captain John Hawkins, she said, "It was detestable and would call down the vengeance of heaven upon the undertakers." [9] English historian Daniel P. Mannix notes that when Hawkins showed her majesty his profit sheets, she not only forgave him but also became a shareholder in his second slaving voyage. Suddenly black Africa looked different. Thus the birth of the white mind. In the seventeenth century, America, the new and rich land across the sea, incessantly demanded hands and bodies to exploit it. There was great wealth to be made. Because slavery violated new concepts about the dignity of man, it could not be business-as-usual; it was necessary to devalue the man who would work the new land.

Europe had experienced its last attack from the outside in the tenth century; by the eighteenth century it was in a stage of rapid industrial and economic expansion. During the last decade of the sixteenth century, the last of the impressive black African kingdoms, Songhay, fell to the firearms of the Moroccans. Decline set in and permitted the European traveler to doubt that an impressive black civilization had ever existed.

Little had changed south of the Sudanese empires. But Europeans did not care to notice the stable and complex social systems; the Iron-Age art and tool-making; the dignity of the African as a fighter, a farmer, a father. The European preferred to see heathens, savages and lustful beasts. What he needed to justify slavery, he managed to find.

But the notion that Africans were an innately inferior race was a distinctly American touch—probably more marked in the United States than anywhere else in the New World. Several conditions facilitated the complete debasement of blacks in America.

Africans kidnapped for transport to North America entered a vast, rich, undeveloped territory. Because of the limitless frontier, neither government nor religion exercised any real deterrence upon the abuse and exploitation of people who could not protect themselves. Yet the rhetoric of religion and enlightenment was everywhere. The rhetoric of a rigid and restricting religion forced wrongdoers to deny wrongdoing. The rhetoric of a revolution for a noble cause increased the need to deny social evils. This boded ill for blacks.

An expanding society needed labor and did not care how it got it. Whatever arrangement was most workable—slavery, indentured servants or free laborers—would suit those in a hurry to exploit the riches of the new land. The sky was the limit on opportunity—if not in Boston, surely on the ever-widening frontier. Yet hard times and bad luck reduced many to poverty as wretched as in the slums of Europe. The early Americans were many people—different races, religions, classes, with different styles and goals. This was not conducive to trust and concern for each other. It produced suspicion and fear of the outsider or newcomer, and exclusion and exploitation of anyone who was vulnerable. The notions that poverty was a sign of sin, and that any decent man could pull himself up by his bootstraps, thrived in this atmosphere. Every man was an island.

It is likely that most early Americans took the attitude of the early Romans and were not deeply troubled by the moral contradictions that slavery posed. Some, however, needed a justification.

In an atmosphere where freedom, justice and individual worth were being promoted, it was necessary to show that the black man was a different kind of man, neither fit nor eligible for the privileges due white men. Carter Woodson, a historian, wrote:

In the eighteenth and nineteenth centuries, when the Europeans were engaged in the exploitation of the New World, slaves were no longer merely taken over as a sequel of war but became also an object of commerce to supply the colonies with cheap labor. This change of attitudes was justified by the Christian world on the ground that, although it was contrary to an unwritten law to enslave a Christian, this principle was not applied to the unconverted Negroes. Driven later from this position when numerous Negroes accepted Christianity, they salved their consciences by a peculiar philosophy of the officials of the church. These ecclesiastics held that conversion did not work manumission in the case of the Negro who differed so widely from the white man. The substance of this was soon incorporated into the laws of the colonies and the decrees of the Bishop of London, the spiritual head of the colonial Church.[10]

From the notion that the black man was "different" and therefore inferior, it was only a small step to the sanctifying of slavery as a kind of "white man's burden," carried unselfishly as a social duty. Many slave owners argued in effect that they were assistants to God, *civilizing* and *improving* the lot of the blacks. Far from being a crime against humanity, slavery was for the black's own good.

In 1837, John C. Calhoun of South Carolina said on the floor of the United States Senate:

Never before has the black race of Central Africa, from the dawn of history to the present day, attained a condition so civilized and so improved, not only physically, but morally and intellectually. It came among us at a low, degraded and savage condition, and in the course of a few generations it has grown up under the fostering care of our institutions, reviled as they have been, to its present comparatively civilized condition. This, with the rapid increase of numbers, is conclusive proof of the general happiness of the race, in spite of all the exaggerated tales to the contrary.[11]

William J. Grayson, South Carolina planter, scholar and politician, made essentially the same argument as Calhoun in—of all possible ways—a poem:

In this new home, whate'er the Negro's fate—
More bless'd his life than in his native state! . . .

Instructed . . . in the only school
Barbarians ever know—a master's rule,
The Negro learns each civilizing art
That softens and subdues the savage heart,
Assumes the tone of those with whom he lives,
Acquires the habit that refinement gives,
And slowly learns, but surely, while a slave,
The lesson that his country never gave.[12]

Grayson and Calhoun were men of power and influence. They both served in the United States Congress, from which platform they were in a position to affect the thoughts and actions of all classes of whites. They also received support from the leading "scientists" of the day.

The work of anthropologist Dr. George Morton helped establish the notion of black inferiority and defect. Prior to his "scientific research," the scriptural declaration of a single Creator and the Jeffersonian doctrine of equality had complicated the work of justifying slavery. Morton, using techniques that would make today's scientists nervous, determined that the mean internal capacity of the Caucasian skull was significantly larger than that of the Ethiopian blacks. He did not go to Africa, but by observing the skulls of dead men was able to draw a remarkable number of conclusions. He decided that Caucasians had the "highest intellectual endowments." He found that the Ethiopian was "joyous, flexible and indolent" in general, but diverse—with some tribes constituting the "lowest grade of humanity."[13]

His followers assumed: the bigger the skull, the better the brain. The evidence of modern science suggests that human capability is determined by the complexity of brain structure and central nervous system, and not by skull size. To our best knowledge, all populations have the same mental complexity. It is of interest that women have brains that are smaller, on the average, than those of the men they often out-think and out-perform.

With data on Egyptian crania provided by George Robins Gliddon, a former U.S. vice-consul at Cairo, Morton laid to rest the conjecture that the Egyptians of antiquity were black. He wrote a book which established the "fact" that the great Egyptian cultures were developed by white men. William Stanton, author of *The Leopard's Spots: Scientific Attitudes Toward Race in America 1815–59,* reports that when Gliddon returned to the States, he made Morton's book available to Southern politicians. They welcomed it and used it well in defense of slavery.[14] A high-ranking government official told me in 1970 that some leaders of government are using research as shaky as Morton's to avoid providing equal educational opportunities for black children today.

The "defective-black" thesis was a comfort to the white mind at every level of society and paralyzed the intelligence of even the best white thinkers. Dr. Benjamin Rush, for example, was strongly opposed to slavery, and had even aided some blacks to escape. He determined that black skin color was a symptom of endemic leprosy. His prescription was to get rid of the disease. Stanton wrote, "Dr. Rush prescribed pressure from 'cloathing,' which tended to absorb 'the coloring matter,' friction, depletion through 'bleeding, purging, or abstinence,' fear, 'oxygenated muriatic acid,' and 'the juice of unripe peaches' as well tested remedies for the Negro's color." [15]

Even the work and literature of the abolitionists give us pause today because white opponents of slavery did not as a rule deny the doctrine of black inferiority. The major concern was that slavery was a blot on the religious and political record of America. There are clear indications that some men prominent in the movement did not view blacks as equals. Anti-slavery literature is replete with expressions of concern for blacks as victims of political and economic exploitation and physical abuse. The violation of black women and children was denounced. But the Reverend Gilbert Haven was one of the few who sensed how the white mind operated in America, even among abolitionists. In 1863, he said, "It was with us, at the worst, equality of white people, and the slavery of all other complexions; at the best, equality of the whites, and the liberty, but not fraternity, of the blacks. Not the oneness of man as man, never, never." [16]

The making of the white mind did not cease with the end of slavery. The job of debasing the black man was of course more difficult once he was free. Was not a free black man just like a free white man in the land of the free? C. Vann Woodward, in

*The Strange Career of Jim Crow,* demonstrated that post-slavery social policy and resultant attitudes toward blacks fluctuated on this point before solidifying into strict discrimination and repression by 1900. Whites used black barbers, carpenters, and doctors for a while until it was established that this was unnatural. Blacks sat where they pleased on public transportation for a while until it was determined that this was immoral. I. A. Newby in *Jim Crow's Defense: Anti-Negro Thought in America, 1900–1930,* illustrates the many ways in which scientists, religious leaders, historians and politicians cooperated to re–establish the idea that there was something wrong with blacks—and that blacks should be kept separate because of it.[17]

In every sphere of American life, leaders transmitted a negative attitude toward black people. It is understandable that the man in the street, hearing the words of doctor, lawyer and government chief, developed racist attitudes. Everywhere he went— to church, to an election rally, to a labor meeting—the message was driven home: "blacks are inferior and not entitled to the privileges of white men."

The white working man had been carefully tutored by his leaders in the doctrine of black inferiority. But he scarcely needed to be taught. He knew his own interest. The man in the street was the refugee from the ghettos of Poland, the famine in Ireland, the politics of Germany, and the crowded conditions and uncertain economics of Italy. Who needed competition from free black men? Poor whites had of course felt threatened by black competition even while the blacks were still enslaved.

Frederick Law Olmsted, the architect and city planner who traveled in the antebellum South, wrote of a conversation between two white men he heard while boarding a train loaded with black slaves in North Carolina:

One said to the other:
   "That's a good lot of niggers."
   "Damned good; I only wish they belonged to me."
I entered the car and took a seat and presently they followed and sat near me. Continuing their conversation thus commenced, they spoke of their bad luck in life. One appeared to have been a bar-keeper; the other an overseer. One said

the highest wages he had ever been paid were two hundred dollars a year, and that year he hadn't laid up a cent. Soon after, the other, speaking with much energy and bitterness, said:

"I wish to God old Virginia was free of all the niggers."

"It would be a good thing if she was."

"Yes sir; and I tell you, it would be a damn'd good thing for us poor fellows."

"I reckon it would myself." [18]

Many other poor whites had felt that slavery, with its plentiful supply of unpaid black labor, was helping to keep them poor. The plight of the poor white could have endangered the slave system. People with a vested interest in the system recognized that a coalition of slaves, free blacks and poor whites might overthrow it. Thus, they were ever ready to drive home the social advantage of the system to the poor whites. J. D. B. De Bow, editor of the most influential pre-Civil War periodical in the South, *De Bow's Review,* made the point quite explicit. He wrote:

The non-slave holder of the South preserves the status of the white man, and is not regarded as an inferior or a dependent. He is not told that the Declaration of Independence, when it says that all men are born free and equal, refers to the negro equally with himself. It is not proposed to him that the free negro's vote shall weigh equally with his own at the ballot box, and that the little children of both colors shall be mixed in the classes and benches of the school house, and embrace each other filially in its outside sports. It never occurs to him, that a white man could be degraded enough to boast in a public assembly, as was recently done in New York, of having actually slept with a negro . . . No white man at the South serves another as a body servant, to clean his boots, wait on his table, and perform the menial services of his household. His blood revolts against this, and his necessities never drive him to it. He is a companion and an equal. When in the employ of the slaveholder, or in intercourse with him, he enters his hall, and has a seat at his table. If a distinction exists, it is only that which education and refinement may give, and this is so courteously exhibited as scarcely to strike attention. The poor white laborer at the North is at the bottom on the social ladder, whilst his brother here has ascended several steps and can look down upon those who are beneath him, at an infinite remove.[19]

Those white workers in Georgia who managed to get the legislature to pass a bill in 1845 forbidding whites to hire blacks as mechanics or masons had got the message. Rich whites will help poor whites maintain their advantage over blacks—if poor whites will help rich whites maintain the slavery system. The German and Irish immigrants in New York City, and white workers in Pennsylvania who in 1860 urged the reenactment of laws permitting slavery, had got a similar message: the repression of black competition is necessary for the security of whites.

The abolition of slavery made it more important than ever to promulgate the myth that blacks were inferior. The most potent fuel firing this myth was the damage done by slavery itself.

Slavery had broken the patterns of family and cultural life. It established a forced dependency. All these have a harmful effect on behavior. As early as the Greeks, we find written evidence of the effect of slavery—Homer wrote:

> . . . whatever day
> Makes a man a slave, takes half his worth away.[20]

Some of America's Founding Fathers had a certain insight into what enslavement can do to people. Thomas Jefferson wrote:

> No person living wishes more sincerely than I do, to see a complete refutation of the doubts I have myself entertained and expressed on the grade of understanding allotted to them [Negroes] by nature, and to find that in this respect they are on a par with ourselves. My doubts were the result of personal observation in the limited sphere of my own State, where the opportunities for the development of their genius were not favorable, and those of exercising it still less so . . . But whatever be their degree of talent it is no measure of their rights.[21]

Jefferson was right, as far as he went. The trouble is that he went no farther. The republic that he had helped to found continued to protect the institution of slavery.

This kind of rationalization would not have gone on for so

long unless it had been doing a lot of white people a lot of good. The role that economic, social and psychological advantages played in the production of the white mind is obvious. However, there is a subtle, seldom recognized but very powerful psychological force involved in forming and maintaining the white mind —the projection of evil. We all have a conflict between the "good" things we are supposed to do and the "bad" things we want to do. We are guilty and anxious about our "bad" impulses, most of them sexual and aggressive. We unconsciously deny them by attributing them to somebody else—preferably somebody different. The physical and cultural differences of a group that does not have the power to protect themselves make them a safe receptacle for the projection of our guilt. People who are "different" can be blamed not only for our sins but for our failures. Thus, all the troubles of an inadequate or anxiety-ridden man are due to his wife; all the problems of Nazi Germany were reduced to the Jews; and all the problems of some frightened, insecure white Americans are due to the niggers.

The religious climate of the colonies was sin-conscious and inflexible. It created a pressing need for potential sinners to deny their evil wishes and impulses. Jonathan Edwards, Cotton Mather and other colonial ministers preached the hell out of their flocks. Sex and sin were synonymous and sexual expression forbidden except within the confines of marriage. But, man and woman being what they are, forbidden thoughts, wishes and impulses did intrude. It was easy to see the black man—the outsider—as the personification of danger, sexuality, aggression and evil. The white man denied his own aggressivity, but, knowing such impulses existed, he had to attribute them to somebody. And somebody was available—the naked, lustful African.

Not only were Africans naked and lustful, they were also black. Psychoanalysts have repeatedly found among their patients a psychic association of blackness with night, fear, evil, danger, sexuality and aggression. Louis Jolyon West wrote, "For man, daytime is a good time, the safe time, the healthy time, when he can see what is going on and make his way in the world. The day dream is aspiration; but the nightmare is consummate terror . . . Night is the time of secret, mystery, magic, danger, evil; and the man of the night is black." [22]

Night is the time when father sleeps with mother and the child tries not to hear what is going on, but is tempted by a guilt-provoking wish and the ultimate sin—incest. The outcome is the association of sex with sin and evil. Psychiatrists have observed that some men who associate sexuality with badness or evil are able to enjoy intercourse only with promiscuous women. To some white men, this means black women. The strong antipathy of some black women for white men reflects an understanding of this motivation.

Malcolm X reported that during his days as a hustler, the sexual exhibition that whites most frequently asked to see was black men having intercourse with white women. I suspect that the observers gained pleasure by watching their own forbidden, repressed sexual desires acted out by the evil black who seduced the good, beautiful, white, mother. (The fact that the white women involved were prostitutes is not incongruous. Some of the unconscious thoughts of males about mother are not flattering, and the reaction formation to these "unsavory" thoughts is a part of what Philip Wylie called "Momism.")

Watching others act out our forbidden desires often gives us pleasure, and despite ourselves we are attracted to the people who are doing it. But watching them may weaken our ability to control such desires in ourselves. The "other" who does what we don't dare will then be hated with a special passion. But, at the same time, there is a deep-seated awareness that the "badness" is in us and not merely in him. We fear that he understands that, feels wronged by our reactions and will seek retribution. This can lead to a masochistic tolerance of abuse from him. This love-hate-love cycle is often at play at an unconscious level in black-white relationships.

Not everybody associates blackness with evil, aggression and sexuality. Some people associate blackness with beauty and strength. The difference between white attitudes toward the dark-skinned Indian and the dark-skinned African could not be explained were it not for the fact that whites were *taught* to associate Africans with evil, aggression and sexuality. Again, West's observations are helpful. He wrote, "In spite of the historical fact that for more than 250 years in North America whites were often raped, enslaved, and slain by Indians while the Negro was the white man's helper, it is still the Negro who appears in the white Oklahoma maiden's dream as the ominous rapist, and the sight of a Negro boy dancing with a white girl still moves Oklahomans to feelings and acts of violence." [23]

Charles Pinderhughes, a psychoanalyst, states that if a group is different in appearance, culture and behavior—particularly when a low value is given the specific differences—the group can be associated with "low" things—such as the buttocks, genitals and sexuality.[24] Couple these deep-seated psychic associations with a need to debase blacks to justify their exploitation, and a very potent anti-black force emerges as a highly charged component of the white mind. The Indian was considered an enemy not a helper; to be destroyed not to be exploited—the noble savage. He was never considered a potential competitor within the white man's system. Thus, denial, rationalization and debasement were not carried as far in the Negro's case.

Recently, an army officer stationed in Virginia received psychiatric treatment after sexually attacking his attractive eighteen-year-old daughter. For the previous three years he had forbidden his two daughters to go into the nearby District of Columbia unless he accompanied them. He had warned them that they were in danger of being raped by some of the black men who lived in the District. What occurred instead was an acting out of his own "sin-filled" desires. The usually unconscious association of blackness with dirt, evil, sin and sexuality is very close to consciousness in many American whites. That is why the white coed ran off in panic when she saw my "Ichabod Crane" roommate innocently coming down the hill at dusk; and also why the other white coed flinched at the sight of blacks dancing.

It is not sinful to express thoughts, wishes and actions when they are directed toward something evil, bad, dirty or threatening. This permits a feeling of having done good. It is helpful of course if there is an individual or a group serving as a target who is prevented by law or circumstances from fighting back. When the attack can also serve to preserve economic, social and psychological advantages for the attacker, it is like killing two birds with one stone—or two blacks with one rope. The long and bloody chapter of the lynching of blacks in America had social gain and psychic need as powerful moving forces behind it.

The conduct of the whites who participated in murdering and lynching blacks suggests that these grisly events served as a catharsis by purging the evil the whites feared in themselves and "projected" onto the blacks. Black victims were castrated, tortured, burned and mutilated by white men, women and children in drunken, orgy-like atmospheres. The throwing of the Christians to the lions might well have been more humane.

The Southern Commission on the Study of Lynching reported in 1931 that in at least half of the twenty-one cases that year, there was doubt that the lynched victims were guilty of the crimes they were "punished" for. The *Knoxville East Tennessee News* reported in 1920 that a black man was spared his fate when a white woman regained consciousness and stopped a search party looking for a "big, black brute" when she identified her attacker as "James Harvey, a prominent white man." In *The Algiers Motel Incident,* John Hersey's investigation of the shooting of black males found in the motel with white females indicates that the old demons are still near the surface of the white mind.[25]

The role of the black as a convenient target for the discharge of white aggression is deeply embedded in American folkways. When I was a boy, the Riverview Amusement Park in Chicago offered a "game" called the "African Dip." A grinning, taunting Negro man was in a cage above a target. A direct hit of the target with a ball thrown from a distance would open the cage and dump the Negro into the water. The Negro intuitively understood what excited the white men lined up to play "dump the darkey." He yelled barbs to those who missed, like, "You ain't nuthin'. You ain't got it. Man, is you a man?" Or, if they were with women, "I don't see what she sees in you!" The "Dip" had one of the longest lines of eager participants of all the sideshow events. I was ten years old; I could not watch and I could not leave. And every time there was a direct hit and a splash, I went down as well.

It must be stressed that many, if not most, black-white relationships are not pathological. But society has permitted the white mind to take out its problems on whatever blacks happen to be around. Extreme, rabid, irrational response to blacks is often caused by more than a fear of losing an economic or a social advantage. It is often related to unconscious motivations, normal and abnormal.

Young whites develop a white mind quite early. Recently, the wife of a black physician in Mississippi called his office, half laughing and half crying. She had just been trailed down the street by a white toddler dressed only in a diaper with a bottle in one hand, pointing at her and yelling, "Nigger, nigger!" He was about two years old.

During the acts of civil disobedience that followed the assassination of Dr. Martin Luther King, Jr., I was working with a 16-year-old white boy in an inner-city clinic. It became necessary to discuss his feelings toward blacks in general and me in particular. He acknowledged that violence made him angry. (One of his problems was his own inability to control his violent potential.) He explained that he knew he should not be mad with blacks or they would not want to work for him when he grew up. This was a youngster of low average intelligence and poor school performance, yet he had got the message about who stood where in this society. He was white. He was the top man—*with* or *without* ability.

The white family and the white institution transmit the white mind from generation to generation. Sometimes the racist message is emotionally charged. Mostly it is matter-of-fact, like teaching a child his name.

During the early days of the school integration struggle, a white youngster watching the news on television asked his mother why the whites were screaming. She calmly replied, "The Negroes want to come to our school and they are not ready yet." It was a racist message, accepted as truth by the child, and yet the mother was not a rabid racist but an average white American.

Her cleaning woman, who told me the story, was sending three youngsters through college on a day-worker's salary. She indignantly recounted the incident saying, "Can you imagine that? I can beat her doing anything she will ever try. And we're not ready yet!"

The message can also be passed along in a much more emotional way—with unexpected emotional results. A white adolescent girl was sharply scolded by her father when she put a coin in her mouth. He yelled, "Get that money out of your mouth— it might have been in a nigger's hand!" His message: blacks are untouchables, contaminating and not to be taken in or inserted.

In psychoanalysis, she discovered that his "simple" admonition had been one way her father had helped himself to deal with her provocative and sexually stimulating overtures. While he had helped himself control his own impulses, he had also associated blackness with sexuality and badness. Human nature being what it is, he had helped establish a sexual attraction to black males in his daughter. The forbidden incestual wish was transferred to blacks—symbolic of unrestrained pleasure and evil—the living id.

Attitudes, values and information transmitted while a child is dependent become part of the psychic baggage of his adult years. Even when people "learn better" at a later date, it is an intellectual understanding, and the internalized effects of emotionally charged communications from the past are difficult to eradicate. The early input which says that blacks are untouchable often lurks in the background awaiting moments of intellectual confusion when it says, "See, I was right in the first place." That is why so many "reformed" whites, reared in a racist environment, seek out the blacks and the black culture that prove racism is unjustifiable. The gut-level conviction can come only when a new white generation grows up getting fewer racist messages as it matures.

Parents simply transmit the mores, beliefs and values of the larger culture. Until very recently, our society and all its institutions transmitted as gospel the belief that whites are superior, and therefore entitled to rights and privileges that blacks are not worthy of in every aspect of life. The institution of slavery said it clearly, as Thomas Jefferson noted:

> The whole commerce between master and slave is a perpetual exercise of the most boisterous passions, the most unremitting despotism on the one part, and degrading submission on the other. Our children see this and learn to imitate it; for man is an imitative animal. This quality is the germ of all education in him. From his cradle to his grave he is learning to do what he sees others do. If a parent could find no motive either in his philanthropy or his self-love, for restraining the intemperance of passion towards his slave, it should always be a sufficient one that the child is present. But generally it is not sufficient. The parent storms, the child looks on, catches the lineaments of wrath, puts on the same

airs in the circle of smaller slaves, gives loose to the worst of passions, and thus nursed, educated, and daily exercised in tyranny, cannot but be stamped by it. . . .[26]

The stamping of minds continued after slavery. The water fountain marked "colored" sent a message. The "white school" sent a message. The cafeteria line with all black servers and a white cashier and manager sent a message. The Alabama statute that read, "No person or corporation shall require any female nurse in wards or rooms in hospitals, either public or private, in which Negro men are placed for treatment . . ." sent a message.[27] The "black bus" going toward the suburbs in the morning and the executive offices downtown devoid of black faces sent a message. The disparity in wages and privileges for whites vis-à-vis blacks working on the same jobs sent a message. The "black latrine" sent a message.

Schools and textbooks transmitted the myth with special efficiency. While my fifth-grade classmates were reading aloud about General Washington crossing the Delaware, I turned to the middle of the book and found a picture of "happy darkies" singing and dancing on a wharf stacked with bales of cotton. I slammed the book shut and everybody turned around and looked at me. The teacher asked me what was wrong. "Nothing," I replied. That was the only reference to blacks in that history book. My white classmates protected me when we got to that section. They all looked away. But I had a funny feeling they were all looking at me anyway. I knew they had got the message.

School children are led to believe that there is no black achievement comparable to Washington's crossing the Delaware. From the perspective of the white mind that may be true. But then, they have not been taught about the efforts of blacks to escape and overthrow slavery, to preserve the rights they gained under Reconstruction, and to eliminate segregation and discrimination. Is there really any difference between the courage shown by Dr. Martin Luther King, Jr., marching in Selma, Alabama, and by General Washington crossing the Delaware? In fact, the Delaware might have been less hazardous.

The National Archives display important documents that record the making of our nation. The decision to display one document and not another transmits a message about what and who is important.

Recall that when the last black representative, George H. White of North Carolina, left the United States Congress in 1901, he said, "This, Mr. Chairman, is perhaps the Negroes' temporary farewell to the American Congress; but let me say, phoenix like, he will rise up some day and come again. These parting words are in behalf of an outraged, heart-broken, bruised and bleeding, but God-fearing people, faithful, industrious, loyal people—rising people, full of potential force." [28] The departure of White from the Congress marked the complete loss of Reconstruction-gained power for black Americans. It was a critical and historic turning point in black and white relations. But this brilliant, prophetic statement is not in our National Archives or any other place of national prominence. How could it be? It is not seen or heard because it challenges, confuses and distresses the white mind. But is it less significant than, "Give me liberty or give me death"?

The white mind is changing. Old rationalizations and justifications no longer work. Denial is possible only for a few. Television and modern transportation have undermined the old defenses. The emergence of black African nations has destroyed the image of blacks as slaves, servants, an inferior and dominated people. To the "manhood" games of baseball, football and basketball came superstars Jackie Robinson, Jim Brown, Willie Mays, Bill Russell and Wilt Chamberlain. Brave and unarmed black people and white people "crossed the Delaware" at Selma, Birmingham and Jackson. Tear gas and bullets from the hands and guns of unjust and frightened white men destroyed the great white lie: "We all have had the same chance in America." Black frustration has exploded in the streets and in the ballot boxes. Black emergence continues in every phase of American life.

A new generation of whites grew to young adulthood in the decade of black emergence, the 1960s. Among their heroes were Jim Brown, the football player; James Brown, the singer; and Muhammad Ali, the boxer. In fact the heroes of some young whites are anti-establishment groups and personalities like the Black Panthers, Rap Brown, Malcolm X, Angela Davis, Eldridge Cleaver and Stokely Carmichael. These young whites can see that "liberty and justice for all" is not a reality. Many were raised a long way from the insecurity of the frontier, or the white ethnic ghettos. They had less need for the rigid, racist indoctrination of the past. But even if they had the need, gratifying it was less easy. The pulsating beat of black awakening cannot be shut out. Television—the newscast, the ballgame, the variety show—weakens racist stereotypes. Everywhere the myth of black inferiority is under siege.

While white racism is still a fundamental flaw in American life, there has been a basic change in the white mind. White men no longer slap black strangers on the back and say, "Hi, boy." Many frankly racist whites will acknowledge that blacks have a right to earn a living and exercise basic human and constitutional rights. But, because of the legacy of the past, it will be a long time before there is a single American mind instead of a black mind and a white mind. In fact, the black mind, like the new white mind, is still being found.

# The Black Mind: Lost and Found

*Slim nose, narrow lips, straight*
*hair and a fair complexion are*
*all beauty to me;*
*I am black with a broad nose and nappy hair.*
*What else can I be but ugly?*

> From a poem entitled *Beauty,* written
> by a seventeen-year-old black girl.

The conditions of life in America have had a devastating impact on the minds of black people. At the 1967 Black Power Conference, an angry speaker charged that "white America's greatest wrong was not the violation of our women and the lynching of our men." Rather, he said, it was "the processing of our minds . . . The black man has been taught to believe that white is good, that black is bad; that white is strong, that black is weak; that white is intelligent, that black is stupid; that white is moral, that black is immoral; that white is beautiful, that black is ugly . . . Before we can do anything, we've got to get ourselves together and undo all of this brainwashing!"

There is ample evidence that the black mind was indeed washed, processed or lost. Until it is restored, our society will not be a healthy place for either blacks or whites.

There are some verses by the poet Waring Cuney that might

almost have been composed in direct response to the seventeen-year-old girl quoted above. In his poem, "No Images," he gave the reason she does not know her beauty.[1]

The black woman who *does* "know her beauty" has problems too. Recently the five black finalists in an Indiana University Homecoming Queen Contest charged officials with racial discrimination. The charges were upheld and the contest was declared void by university officials who ruled that "no beauty contest can fairly consider entries of different races or ethnic groups whose physical and behavioral characteristics differ materially from the standard of the dominant segment of society, which in this case means an American Caucasian standard."

The handicap that white racism inflicts on a black girl in a beauty contest may seem like a small and superficial thing, but it is the visible tip of a giant iceberg.

The teenager who equates blackness with ugliness will also equate it with personal inadequacy. Waring Cuney spoke of palm trees and rivers, streets and dishwater, but he was also talking about the destruction of meaningful black culture in America. The white yardstick challenged by black contestants in a beauty contest is the same one that is used to brainwash blacks into feeling inadequate wherever they turn.

The brainwashing or "processing" begins at an early age. A black youngster in the 1940s jumped on a bus in front of a white woman. Several white men pulled him off and beat him. His father did not try to protect him or to seek justice, but just scolded him, "You ought to know better than to get on the bus before the white folks." The youngster got two messages at once. First, that white folks said blacks were no good. Second, that black folks seemed to think so too, or if not, could do nothing about the attitude of white folks.

A ten-year-old patient said to me, "My mamma said my daddy is a good-for-nuthin' nigger and I'm gonna be just like him."

A white child psychiatrist once told me that he was alarmed to find that what many of his young black patients really wanted was to be white. Indeed, a number of studies have shown that black children prefer light colors in people and in things. On a children's television show, a very dark four-year-old girl was asked what kind of animal she would like to be; her pathetic response was, "A white rabbit." I asked a black ten-year-old in a therapy group that I was conducting how he felt about the disruptive behavior of another member of the group, and he angrily snapped, "He's a black nigger, that's what's wrong with him!"

Studies of black adults show that even some who achieve at a level our society considers high have a problem accepting their own blackness.

A black lawyer in the Midwest donates valuable property to a state university, but forecloses the mortgage on a black fraternity. In Kansas, a wealthy black widow gives property to the city but nothing to black charities. Both the work and the life of the poet Paul Laurence Dunbar show that he found his blackness a burden. My own positive response to the Black Muslim minister demonstrated that, for myself, achievement by total society standards was not enough to lighten the burden of being black in America. Given the message about blackness and whiteness, responses in blacks reflecting a rejection of blackness should be expected. They can range from the bizarre to the tragic.

A black public official purchased a house in Maryland from a white lawyer. The key was left with the black live-in maid, who was to turn the house over to the new owner. When the black man arrived, the maid was stunned. "Mister," she said, "you don't want to buy this house . . . it's . . . it's dirty!" She forgot that if it was dirty it was her fault. What she really meant was that the new black owner was dirty and not wanted in that kind of neighborhood. As things turned out, the new black owner found that his white neighbors had less trouble with his color than the black maid had.

During my medical internship, I treated an intoxicated black man with multiple facial lacerations. He kept muttering, "I'll kill you . . . I'll kill you, you dirty black nigger . . . I'll kill you!" Finally, I could contain my curiosity no longer and asked him who he was after. (I wanted to be sure he wasn't talking about his doctor.) "My friend—the guy that did this," he said, pointing to his face. A friend had disfigured him for life over his refusal to share a bottle of wine. Of course, it may be argued that many things contribute to making life and limb so cheap to such men, but it is clear that the major one is the damage done to the black mind by white racism.

A huge black football lineman from Mississippi was being pushed around the field at a western college by his white teammates in an early scrimmage session. He was unable to "be physical" because in the part of America he came from, black males are taught from early childhood that black aggression will not be tolerated. His insightful coach was eventually able to convince him that aggression toward whites—at least on the football field—would not bring retribution, and the black lineman went on to become an outstanding player. His fears, of course, had been solidly grounded in the racial realities of the South. An "aggressive" action by fourteen-year-old Emmett Till—whistling at a white woman—cost him his life in Mississippi in 1955.

The ways in which America's racist culture can warp the black mind are not always immediately visible, and the results are not always dramatic; sometimes they just make ordinary human problems a little too hard.


A twenty-year-old black college student, Bob Young, was referred to me for psychiatric evaluation and treatment. He had an IQ of 136 but had been a consistent under-achiever since he was fifteen. He had shown flashes of academic excellence which were spoiled by poor follow-up performance. His high potential always won him attention and opportunity, but he generally blew it. Teachers and supporters ended up accusing him of laziness and of a lack of the desire to succeed.

Bob's mother was a well-meaning but aggressive woman who was the archetype of the strong, black matriarch. Her own father, who had been a postal worker, although he had a college degree, had deserted his family. Her mother was left with the burden of sending three children to college. Bob's mother had a low regard for black people in general, and for black men in particular. In many ways she taught Bob to be as white as possible: to purse his lips "so they won't be so thick and ugly"; to walk quickly "so you don't look like you're walking in a cotton patch"; to speak distinctly "so you don't sound like you just crossed the Mason–Dixon Line"; to do well in school "so you won't be stupid like the rest of them." Her own marriage, like her mother's, was unhappy, and she over-invested in Bob, giving him too little room for psychological growth. She wanted to know what he was doing, when he was doing it and with whom he was doing it, even after he entered college. Thus, she was often unconsciously destructive of his healthy self-assertive and aggressive tendencies.

Bob's father, unlike Bob's grandfather, did not desert his family. He just abdicated and let his wife raise their son. He was not a failure in the usual sense; in fact, he was a successful professional man. But he always seemed to be in search of his own manhood. His search took the form of a strong drive for trophies—professional advancement, expensive cars, and women—particularly white women. These pursuits kept him and his family on the brink of disaster. One extra-marital affair almost ended both his marriage and his career.

The worst time for Bob came when he was fourteen and his parents were on the brink of separating. He felt trapped between his mother and father, afraid he would be hurt if he took sides with either one. His response was to do nothing. He began to have a recurrent dream that he was walking on ice with two white polar bears watching him. The bigger bear wore ice skates and would chase him, getting closer and closer until—just in time—Bob woke up in terror.

The student of the subconscious will suspect that there was probably a reawakening of the Oedipal conflict, and that Bob's uneasy role in the family triangle made him fear an attack by his father who was represented by the larger bear. Bob demonstrated an excessive need to be dependent, which gave rise to disquieting homosexual impulses and feelings of sexual and social inadequacy. He defended himself against dangerous wishes and impulses with a paralyzing inhibition of action. His response to most conflict situations was to do nothing. If his natural drives or talents led him to act assertively, or aggressively—or even capably—he would compulsively undo them, as though he might be punished for letting his achievements stand. As a result his academic performance declined to an average level, far below his natural capacity.

On the face of it, Bob's psychological problems were like those of many other potentially successful middle-class students for whom the term "under–achiever" was coined. Nor was his family's problem unlike those of many other middle-income families. This is understandable in that black people struggle with the same problems as whites except that the American race issue complicates things for blacks. Some of Bob's experiences illustrate how the race issue exaggerates normal developmental problems.

Bob was reared in a racially integrated community where acceptance in school came easily, but the outside social situation was more ambivalent. When he was fourteen, he should have been building adolescent relationships that could turn his interest away from harmful involvement with his parents and improve his chances for healthier psychological development. As a result of his anti-black training he ignored black girls. Dating white girls led to trouble.

He recalled that during that time a white girl who had a crush on him suddenly cooled their relationship. Her mother had seen him walking her home. He also remembered studying with a white girl in the library and pretending that he had to drive in the opposite direction so that he could avoid risking trouble with her parents if he took her home. At other times, mainly through his attentions to white girls, he put himself in a position to be hurt as he had been hurt when he was trapped between his parents. The anguish, excitement and morbid pleasure that he felt in the family situation were reproduced in the social situations that he compulsively repeated.

If we now consider his dream again, we see that the large polar bear menacing him was perhaps not only his father but also the white world, angered by his interest in the other polar bear, who was undoubtedly female, and perhaps represented not only his mother but also symbolized white girls and all the other opportunities and objects that are forbidden to blacks. Such a double meaning for the dream would also explain why the bears representing his parents were polar bears, which are white.

The outside world, into which Bob tried to escape, became only a reflection of the family trap. The family situation and the racial situation interlocked to keep him from achieving his potential as a student or as a man.

For Bob, as well as for his parents, the question of adequacy was tied up with race. Despite all their ability, neither Bob nor his father believed he could be a man without being a white man.

Mrs. Young despised them for their weakness, which she blamed on their blackness. They, in turn, retaliated by continuing to fail her and cooperated by proving that she was right.

Given the struggle of black Americans for a sense of adequacy in a society that has bombarded them with messages about how bad it is to be black, it should not have been surprising that an attempt to dignify blackness would catch on. But hardly anyone was prepared for what began to happen on the day in June, 1966, when Stokely Carmichael called for "Black Power."

The slogan ripped through America like a shock wave because it touched deep-seated needs in many blacks and deep-seated fears in many whites. The words *black* and *power* are psychologically loaded in this country. Using them together was unthinkable. The linking of these two common English words somehow violated a taboo as fierce as the one against joining a black man with a white woman. In fact, the violence of the white reaction to the slogan indicated that what it was "loaded" with—in the white mind—was the threat of black sexuality. But to blacks it meant something different. The lost, processed, brainwashed black mind was about to be found.

Certainly there have always been blacks who were proud of themselves and of their race, as there have always been efforts to establish black political and economic power and pride. But the Black Power slogan became a catch phrase because it articulated an urgent and pervasive need at a critical time in the development of a positive black identity. It was the same need the Muslim minister stirred in me in 1962. For a group to establish a positive identity, it must be able to protect its members from exploitation and abuse. It must be able to enhance its members' capacity to cope in the larger society. It must provide its members with a sense of adequacy and security. To achieve these aims in America, a group needs unity and political and economic power. The first step toward these goals is self-esteem. The quest understandably turned toward the search for pride-evoking cultural roots.

Within a short time, blacks were sporting dashikis and learning Swahili. Black art and black cultural institutes sprang up across the country; so did schools indoctrinating young black students with positive feelings about blackness. Students began to call for programs of Afro-American studies.

Women who had formerly spent hours straightening their hair and despairing of its texture were proudly displaying Afro hair styles. Once-conservative black students became militant. A black student from Harvard turned down a high-paying job and went to Mississippi to register voters and to work with the black poor. The reserved widow of one black professional man and the mother of three others stood up in a public meeting and angrily accused the local school board of being "a bunch of white racists!" Blacks began to reject some of the American values they had never questioned before. Self-help and black community development began to replace racial integration as a goal. On campuses where students once protested segregation policies, blacks have formed their own student groups, some of which advocate separation. Across the country, black students at predominantly white colleges have called for all-black dormitories. Black anger is expressed openly. Black children in the first and second grade have begun to manifest a consciousness of race and of freedom, and have begun to discuss it as never before. Unlike the black maid in Maryland a few years before, a black day-worker for a black family recently said with pride, "Getting so nowadays some colored people have homes just as nice as the whites."

Certainly there are many individuals who have hardly been affected by the spirit of positive blackness. No doubt some of the most exhibitionistic advocates of black beauty and adequacy do not completely believe in positive blackness. Thus the occasional black militant by day with the pretty blonde at night. But few black people have been left untouched at some level by the psychic revolution that rejects the notion of black inferiority.


What happened? From pursed lips to Black Power salutes in three years. Why now, when social and economic conditions are getting better for many blacks? Why is the need for a sense of positive blackness so intense, even among blacks regarded as successful by total society standards? Where is the psychic revolution going?

It would be presumptuous to claim to know all the answers, but what has been happening makes sense in light of where black America has been.

Economic factors have been cited as the sole or primary explanation for black unrest, but they cannot explain the depth, breadth and variety of feeling and action in the black community today. Even where there are enough jobs and every black man who works is earning a decent living, there is ferment. The Black Power Conference speaker who complained about processed minds was closer to the mark than those who claim that the unrest is totally a matter of economics. The poet Cuney, concerned about the absence of palm trees and the presence of dishwater, was on the right track.

The black mind is being born out of a prideful struggle for human dignity against formidable resistance. Social and psychological forces that have been building up for 350 years are at work today. They make the intensity, timing and nature of the quest for a positive black identity appear logical and even predictable. They must be understood if the just demands of blacks are to be granted and black-white conflict reduced.

According to the planter, William Grayson, blacks are lucky that they were seized from Africa and enslaved.

> In this new home, whate'er the Negro's fate—
> More bless'd his life than in his native state! [2]

Had he said the same about the Irish peasants fleeing the potato famine, the Italians choosing immigration over starvation, and the destitute and psychologically traumatized English leaving slums and prisons, he would have been nearer the truth. Anyone who had an opportunity to share in America's abundance was lucky. But blacks did not share in it, although they helped produce it. More important, the move from Africa to the conditions of slavery, segregation and exclusion destroyed or damaged all the cultural heritage that gives a people stability, pride and a sense of group and individual competence.

In current attempts to establish a basis for black pride, the historian and poet hark back to Africa's Golden Age. Study of the ancient black empires of Ghana, Mali and Songhay and of the great tribal nations of the Ashanti, Yoruba and Fanti assumes a new importance. Knowledge that black men had intellectual centers, smelted iron, developed great cities and had an appreciation of art came to me as a welcome relief from my lurking suspicion, based on cartoons depicting Africans with nose rings boiling "civilized" white men, that black men had achieved nothing . . . that in fact Grayson was correct:

> The Negroes schooled by slavery embrace
> The highest portion of the Negro race . . .[3]

But more relevant to the present struggle of black Americans than the Golden Age is a study of the social organization and function of the peoples from which Afro-Americans are descended. The fact of African empires tells little about the majority of the people of that age. Only through some understanding of the social organization of the period during which most slaves were brought to America does the cataclysm of the American experience become clear.

Most Afro-Americans are descendants of the people of the West African Gold and Ivory Coasts, around the Niger Delta and Dahomey. Life in West Africa was different from life in Europe and early America in significant ways. While conditions varied between groups, certain structural and functional elements were common or similar. A close-knit family or kinship structure was at the core of all political, economic and social organization. Weaving, blacksmithing, wood-carving and other traditional crafts were usually hereditary within a lineage (a group of people numbering from twelve to five hundred who can trace their descent to a known ancestor or lineage founder). Each lineage had its own ancestral shrine, history, taboos and rituals. Art, music and literature (story-telling or folklore) were not reserved for professionals. They were an integral part of life, present and utilized in every aspect of life, from birth to death. Every African was literally his own musician, bard and artist, although some were better than others and there was some degree of specialization.

Lineage members generally lived together in one section of town and had a special responsibility to each other. Each lineage was usually composed of a number of extended families. The relationship of adults to children and of children to adults was well-defined and was transmitted from generation to generation. In general, there was a reverence for age in African societies that was more marked and institutionalized than in European societies. For example, government decision-making was often in the hands of the older men; and deference was given to age even in the expression of an opinion.

While children were to show respect toward adults, adults in return were expected to be supportive of and helpful to the children. Thus, a child in need could call upon any adult within his lineage and tribe and expect concerned attention. Parents expected others to be concerned about the conduct of their children. They welcomed the help of others in setting limits for their children and even in punishing them for misbehavior. Generally, kinship arrangements were formally established for the counselling, care and disposition of wives, children and property during the life of a man and after his death. For example, in the Afikpo Ibo tribe, the oldest brother in a family was the counsellor and adviser to the sons of his sisters, even while their father lived.

Among the Yoruba, a group significantly represented among present-day Afro-Americans, each lineage had its own farm land. The land belonged to all members of a lineage; no man had to work for hire. The Yoruba women did not work in the fields; instead, they cared for the livestock and the home. In the Yoruba town of Ado—which was raided for slaves in the nineteenth century—there was a royal lineage from which came the Ewi, or king. The Ewi and three grades of chiefs constituted the government and there were chiefs representing each lineage. The opinions of people within a lineage were expressed through the junior chiefs to the senior chiefs, who made the decisions. When possible, a dispute between two members of a lineage was settled within the lineage. Where this was not possible, disputes were settled by the elders at the village and town level. In cases of irreconcilable disputes between the lineages, the king's decision was final. Thus, government was not only by the people, for the people and of the people, but government by the kinspeople, for the kinspeople and of the kinspeople.

An important element of social organization was the age-set and age-grade system. Specific structure and operation varied from place to place, but the system was widespread in West Africa. Among the Afikpo Ibo an age-set comprised all the people of the town or village born within approximately three years of one another. Membership was automatic and crossed lineage lines. Several age-sets combined to form a larger body, an age-grade, with a specific village function or service to perform. Among the Afikpo, the young adult age-group was responsible for maintaining law and order in the village. The next older grade formed the executive arm of government. The middle age-grade, or older men, made up the legislative and judicial bodies and the younger men learned their future roles while acting as apprentices. Parallel age-grades existed for women, and the male and female grades supported each other in social and ceremonial activities. However, the women's age-grades generally were not as well developed. Age-set members were extremely supportive of each other and had strong feelings of loyalty. They often participated in village and tribal ceremonies as a group and they usually attended the personal ritual and ceremonial events of fellow members.

Child-rearing among the West African societies from which many black Americans are descended ranged from the informal and non-coercive to the strict and authoritarian. Among the Dogon tribe, children at birth do not officially exist until ritual and ceremony infuse the ancestral spirit into the child to make him a part of the physical and spiritual world. Circumcision is performed to accentuate masculinity because the foreskin is culturally symbolic of femininity. After circumcision came the naming ceremony, which was very important to the African. This is particularly significant in view of the fact that in America the male slave was often referred to by the name of his master or his woman, "Mister Carter's boy" or "Sophie's man."

West African societies were particularly history-conscious. Important lineage functions—religion, government, justice—were based on history, yet there was no written language. For this reason, according to African anthropologist P. K. Onwauchi, the child was made a part of the adult world. Extensive contact with adults running the society prepared the young to take over adult functions when they met the proper requirements. Specific attention was given to the narration of folklore and of important events in the history of a tribe. Through such stories, the youngsters learned what was expected of them in the present and in the future.

In some West African societies the age-sets were only for adults; in others, children were in an age-set from the moment of birth. They moved from one age-group to another, usually in groups rather than as individuals, and this was again a time of ceremony and festivity. In many tribes, boys were initiated into adult society in their late teens. Initiation usually required some test of strength, courage and responsibility. Among the Polanee tribe, maturity was not defined by chronological age but according to one's awareness of responsibility to himself and his people. Indeed, to court a woman, a Polanee had to demonstrate strength and courage in a ritual test of pain-tolerance. Those who could not pass never achieved decision-making status, and spent their time among the youngsters.

The young age-sets and age-grades carried out their own responsibilities and maintained their own organization, thus giving the young a chance to practice community participation away from the total society, while having real status in it. These age-groups permitted youngsters to have some social and psychological distance from adults but usually upheld and reinforced the norms of the adult world. Criticism by an age-set member—particularly when the sets functioned as tight-knit associations—was more effective in maintaining adherence to the values and rules of society than criticism by parents or courts.

Most West African societies, during the age of the slave trade, had agrarian economies. The historian, Stanley Elkins, points out that West African land was "no Garden of Eden" and that "traditions of toil and self-discipline" were necessary to maintain a stable, agrarian society.[4] His observations undermine the myth of undisciplined, lazy blacks. And the strong male dominance of many African societies counters the argument that the strong female leadership of many black families in America is of African origin.

The African described by serious students of these societies is a far cry from the wretched savage dreamed up by Grayson, Calhoun, De Bow and a host of other apologists for slavery. West Africa had a social system that maximized participation by each individual in every aspect of life. Meaningful representation of each member took place at the decision-making level. Life's demands, limits and opportunities were clearly defined. Meaningful mechanisms, from kinship ties to courts, encouraged acceptable behavior; meaningful ritual and ceremony shared with members of one special age-set gave the African an intense sense of belonging and being a part of things. These elements guaranteed a sense of security that is in marked contrast to the anomie and alienation of modern "advanced" societies.

It is not strange that the pre-colonial Africans, as poverty-stricken as some were, did not have the identification problem that plagues many of their black American cousins today. When the pre-colonial African said, "Who am I?" his social experience said, "If you have adhered to the dictates of your society, you are somebody of worth and value, wanted by your people and important to them." The Yoruba child received an answer from his social experience which explained that he was a descendant of Oduduwa—the creator of all men and the direct ancestor of the Yoruba! (The Yoruba creation story is no less dubious than the Judeo-Christian.) Small wonder that the black African mind was generally a proud one, viewing the self as capable and adequate.

Nothing has been said which suggests that West Africa was Utopia. Clearly, some of the West African societies functioned better than others, much as New York State outclasses South Carolina. Certainly some were more humane than others, much as Colorado outstrips Mississippi. There is no reason to believe that the African who was enslaved was "the lower sort." Daniel Mannix and Malcolm Cowley have shown that the ancestors of present-day blacks belonged to the "relatively advanced and highly industrious people of Upper Guinea." [5] Onwauchi points out that most slaves were captured in raids and wars and were not formerly domestic slaves as the popular American myth holds. Thus, warriors and other young and healthy individuals from all ranks were among the captives forced into slavery.

Given full participation within American society, blacks could have made generally the same adaptation as everyone else. Indeed, blacks in America who did not experience severe and traumatic living conditions did just that. In fact, most blacks, even after 350 years of slavery and discrimination, have made an adaptation—with certain subcultural variations and differences—which is comparable to that of most other Americans. In their old African culture, blacks had a sense of belonging, adequacy, value, worth, power and control that would have been immensely valuable in America had it not been systematically destroyed.

The 250 years of slavery not only destroyed the African immigrant's sense of his own worth and value but bred a sense of personal and group inadequacy. The impact of slavery was even more traumatic than the Jewish experience under the Nazis was to those who survived. Adult Jews and even Jewish children took a positive self-image and meaningful heritage into concentration camps and many were able to hold on to it, even use it, to protect themselves from psychological damage. Most traumatic for blacks was the fact that children were born into the degrading slave system, and were socialized and developed in ways that defined them as inferior and incapable. After the first few generations, the most important and supportive elements of the African past were lost. The African became what slavery made him.

The ferment in black America today is of a people in search of a place in society, or against society if need be, which will protect them from the forces that say, "Black is bad, black is weak, black is stupid, black is immoral, black is ugly." The effort is sometimes individual and sometimes collective; sometimes planned and sometimes spontaneous; sometimes beneficial and sometimes destructive—to blacks and whites alike; sometimes rational and understandable and sometimes irrational and perplexing. A white school official who had supported integration for years, responded to a black student's request for separate housing with, "What do I do now?" The debate over the use of the words "Negro" and "black" reflects a deeper issue. "Negro," to many, symbolizes all that blacks became under slavery. "Black," to many, symbolizes a man of dignity, worth and competence on his own terms.

Nothing can explain the nature of the trauma that the black mind is now trying to overcome half so clearly as the accounts of ex-slaves, slave owners and intimate observers of the slave system. The following by a woman who had been a slave in North Carolina illustrates how slavery—even under a "good" master—destroyed the old African feeling of adequacy and worth, replacing it with a state of mind that can only be called infantilism:

We had the best mistress and master in the world, and they was Christian folks, and they taught us to be Christian-like too. Every Sunday morning Old Master would have all us niggers to the house while he would sing and pray and read the Bible to us all. Old Master taught us not to be bad; he taught us to be good; he taught us to never steal nor to tell false tales and not to do anything that was bad. He said: "You will reap what you sow, that you sow it single and reap double." I learnt that when I was a little child, and I ain't forgot it yet . . . God called my Pa to preach and Old Master let him preach in the kitchen and in the back yard under the trees. On preaching day Old Master took his whole family and all the slaves to church with him.

We had log school houses in them days, and folks learnt more than they does in the bricks today.

Down in the quarters every black family had a one- or two-room log cabin. We didn't have no floors in them cabins. Nice dirt floors was the style then, and we used sage brooms. Took a string and tied the sage together and had a nice broom outen that . . . We kept our dirt floor swept clean and white. And our bed was big and tall and had little beds to push under there . . . Our beds was stuffed with hay and straw and shucks, and believe me, child, they sure slept good.

We used to play at night by moonlight, and I can recollect singing with the fiddle. Oh, Lord, that fiddle could almost talk and I can hear it ringing now. Sometime we would dance in the moonlight too.

Old Master raised lots of cotton and the womenfolks carded and spun and wove cloth, then they dyed it and made clothes.

We wore drawers made out of domestic that come down longer than our dresses, and we wore seven petticoats with sleeves in them petticoats in the winter, and the boys wore big old long shirts. They didn't know nothing 'bout no britches till they was great big, just went round in they shirt-tails. And we all wore shoes 'cause my pa made shoes.

Master taught Pa to make shoes, and the way he done, they killed a cow and took the hide and tanned it . . .

All Old Master's niggers was married by the white preacher, but he had a neighbor who would marry his niggers hisself. He would say to the man: "Do you want this woman?" And to the girl, "Do you want this boy?" Then he would call the Old Mistress to fetch the broom, and Old Master would hold one end and Old Mistress the other and tell the boy and girl to jump this broom, and he would say: "That's your wife." They called marrying like that jumping the broom.

Now, child, I can't 'member everything I done in them days, but we didn't have to worry 'bout nothing. Old Mistress was the one to worry. 'Twasn't then like it is now, no 'twasn't. We had such a good time and everybody cried when the Yankees cried out: "Free." T'other niggers say they had a hard time 'fore they was free, but 'twas then like 'tis now. If you had a hard time, we done it ourselves.[6]

For other slaves, conditions were less comfortable. An ex-slave from Georgia gave the following account of some of his experiences.

I mighty nigh wore out from all these hard years of work and serving the Lord.

. . . But I just keep on living and trusting in the Lord, 'cause the Good Book say, "Wherefore the evil days come and the darkness of the night draw nigh, your strength, it shall not perish. I will lift you up 'mongst them what 'bides with me." That is the Gospel, boss.

You can see boss that I is a little bright and got some white blood in me. That is 'counted for on my mammy's side of the family. Her pappy, he was a white man. He wasn't no Kendrick though. He was an overseer. That's what my Mammy she say, and then I know that wasn't no Kendrick mixed up in nothing like that. They didn't believe in that kind of business. My old marse, Arch Kendricks, I will say this, he certainly was a good fair man. Old Miss and Young marse, Sam, they was strictly tough and, boss, I is telling you the truth, they was cruel. The Young marse, Sam, he never taken at all after he pa. He got all the meanness from Old Miss, and he sure got plenty of it, too. Old Miss, she cuss and

rare worse'n a man. 'Way 'fore day she be up hollering loud
enough for to be heard two miles, 'rousing the niggers out
for to git in the fields ever 'fore light. Marse Sam, he stand
by the pot handing out the grub and giving out the bread,
and he cuss loud and say: "Take a sop of that grease on your
hoecake and move along fast 'fore I lashes you.". . . All the
cooking in them days was done in pots hanging on the pot
racks . . . At times they would give us enough to eat. At
times they wouldn't—just 'cording to how they feeling when
they dishing out the grub. The biggest what they would give
the field hands to eat would be the truck what us had on the
place, like greens, turnips, peas, side meat, and they sure
would cut the side meat awful thin too, boss. Us always had
a heap of corn meal dumplings and hoecakes. Old Miss, her
and Marse Sam, they real stingy. You better not leave no
grub on your plate for to throw away. You sure better eat it
all iffen you like it or no . . .

Just to show you, boss, how 'twas with Marse Sam and
how contrary and fractious and wicked that young white man
was, I wants to tell you 'bout the time that Aunt Hannah's
little boy Mose died. Mose, he sick 'bout a week. Aunt Hannah, she try to doctor on him and git him well, and she tell
Old Miss that she think Mose bad off and ought to have the
doctor. Old Miss she wouldn't git the doctor. She say Mose
ain't sick much, and, bless my soul, Aunt Hannah she right.
In a few days from then Mose is dead . . . Us toted the
coffin over to where the grave was dug and gwine bury little
Mose there, and Uncle Billy Jordan, he was there and begun
to sing and pray and have a kind of funeral at the burying.
Everyone was moaning and singing and praying, and Marse
Sam heard 'em and come sailing over there on he hoss and
lit right in to cussing and raring and say that if they don't
hurry up and bury that nigger and shut up that singing and
carrying on, he gwine lash everyone of them, and then he
went to cussing worser and 'busing Uncle Billy Jordan. He
say iffen he ever hear of him doing any more preaching or
praying round 'mongst the niggers at the graveyard or anywhere else, he gwine lash him to death. No sir, boss, Marse
Sam wouldn't even 'low no preaching or singing or nothing
like that . . . Old Miss, she mighty stingy, and she never
want to lose no nigger by them dying. Howsomever, it was
hard sometimes to get her to believe you sick . . .[7]

Many slaves were denied the meaningful ceremony and ritual that had been central to African social organization, and which could have reinforced a sense of worth and value. Some slaves were completely powerless under the total power of white sadists and hoodlums who treated them like animals. The experience of another ex-slave from Georgia demonstrates this situation:

Massa Earl Stielszen captures them in Africa and brung them to Georgia. He got kilt, and my sister and me went to his son. His son was a killer. He got in trouble there in Georgia and took him two good stepping hosses and the covered wagon. Then he chained all he slaves round the necks and fastens the chains to the hosses and makes them walk all the way to Texas . . .

Massa had a great, long whip platted out of rawhide, and when the niggers fall behind or give out, he hit them with the whip. It take the hide every time he hit a nigger. Mother, she give out on the way, 'bout the line of Texas. Her feet got raw and bleeding, and her legs swoll plum out of shape. Then Marsa, he just take out he gun and shot her, and whilst she lay dying he kicks her two or three times and say, "Damn a nigger what can't stand nothing." Boss, you know that man, he wouldn't bury mother, just leave her lying where he shot her at. You know, then there wasn't no law 'gainst killing nigger slaves . . .

He come plumb to Austin through the snow . . . He cut logs and built he home on the side of them mountains. We never had no quarters. When nighttime come, he locks the chain round our necks and then locks it round a tree. Boss, our bed were the ground. All he feed us was raw meat and green corn. Boss, I et many a green weed. I was hungry. He never let us eat at noon, he worked us all day without stopping. We went naked, that the way he worked us. We never had any clothes.

He brands us. He brand my mother before us left Georgia. Boss, that nearly kilt her. He brand her in the breast, then between the shoulders. He brand all us.

My sister, Emma, was the only woman he have 'til he marries. Emma was wife of all seven Negro slaves. He sold her when she's 'bout fifteen, just before her baby was born. I never seen her since.

Boss, Massa was an outlaw. He come to Texas and deal in

stolen hosses. Just before he's hung for stealing hosses, he marries a young Spanish gal . . . whips her 'cause she want him to leave he slaves alone and live right . . . She cry and cry every time Massa go off. She let us a-loose, and she feed us good one time while he's gone. Missy Selena, she turn us a-loose, and we wash in the creek clost by. She just fasten the chain on us and give us great big pot cooked meat and corn, and up he rides. Never says a word but comes to see what us eating. He pick up the whip and whip her till she falls . . . I swore if I ever got a-loose I'd kill him. But before long after he fails to come home, and some people find him hanging to a tree . . .

You know there was some few free niggers in that time even 'fore the slaves taken outen boundage. It was really worse on them than it was with them that wasn't free. The slaveowners, they just despised them free niggers and made it just as hard on them as they can. They couldn't get no work from nobody. Wouldn't any man hire 'em or give 'em any work at all. So because they was up against it and never had any money or nothing, the white folks made these free niggers 'sess the taxes. And 'cause they never had no money for to pay the tax with, they was put up on the block by the court man or the sheriff and sold out to somebody for enough to pay the tax with what they say they owe. So they keep those free niggers hired out all the time 'most, working for to pay the taxes.[8]

Frederick Law Olmsted, who traveled through the South in the 1850s, left a valuable record of slave life. He described the cruelty, slave resistance, paternalism, forced dependency and infantilization of slaves with an objectivity rare among the fiercely pro- or anti-slavery writers of the period. Of cruelty and resistance, Olmsted quoted a white overseer of black slaves, "Why, Sir, I wouldn't mind killing a nigger more than I would a dog." The overseer pointed out that some slaves were determined never to let a white man whip them and often resisted and in some cases had to be killed. Of cruelty and submission, Olmsted wrote of the brutal beating of a teenage girl by a white overseer because she apparently lied to escape work. The girl received forty lashes without resistance, only writhing, groveling in the dirt and screaming, "Oh please don't, Master! Oh please don't, Sir!" The overseer, unperturbed, considered it all in a day's work. Of paternalism, dependency and infantilization, Olmstead quoted a Virginia slave owner, "Oh, they [black slaves] are interesting creatures, sir . . . and, with all of their faults, have beautiful traits. I can't help being attached to them, and I am sure they love us." Olmsted described the slaves of this master as childlike. Given a task, they had to come back seeking more instructions or approval for their work. How unlike the proud African youth who withstood ritual pain to gain adult status! [9]

Even if a man had made an accommodation to slavery or had been reared to accept it, the system occasionally produced acute psychological trauma. The Reverend Josiah Henson was born a slave in Maryland, escaped to Canada and told of what he and his parents had experienced. On one occasion, a white overseer brutally attacked Henson's mother. His father rushed to her defense, a violation of slave code. Henson wrote, "A nigger has struck a white man; that was enough to set a whole country on fire; no question was asked about provocation." [10] Slaves were summoned from surrounding plantations to witness the penalty of fifty lashes administered by a powerful blacksmith. From that day on, the senior Henson, who had been good-humored and light-hearted, became sullen and morose. Finally, no longer of value, he was sold away from his family.

The traumas did not stop with the sale of his father. Soon afterward, the white master died and young Henson was sold away from his mother. On her knees, clutching the legs of her new master, his mother begged not to be separated from her child. The new master violently and repeatedly kicked her to disengage himself. Young Henson observed the beating and abuse of his father and mother, and their total powerlessness, when he was between five and six years of age. This is the age when children identify strongly with parents of the same sex who are seen as powerful and protective. This could not have been young Henson's assessment.

Separated from his mother and placed in slave quarters with forty others who cared little about him and who showed little affection or concern for him, Henson almost died. (What strange conduct in people in whose cultural past the responsibility of an adult to a child in need was sacred. However, mutual support and concern of people for people can be reduced or destroyed in a situation of extreme powerlessness, purposelessness, and insecurity.) No one provided him with emotional support and he was only occasionally given food or drink. By chance he was returned to his mother, recovered rapidly and grew to a vigorous adulthood.

Reports about the Hensons and other slaves upset Susan Dabney Smedes, who became the mistress of a Mississippi plantation after her father's death. She felt that history would be unfair to kindly slave-holders like her father, and she described plantation life under him to balance the ledger. So kindly was he that when he moved from Virginia to Mississippi, the slaves—given a choice —chose to leave their friends and kinspeople rather than separate from their "beloved Master and mistress." So respectful were the white children that they called the adult slaves "aunt" and "uncle," except on very formal occasions when they were called "Mr." and "Mrs." (That was indeed odd for Mississippi in the 1840s and 1850s. In 1962, a Southern-born white medical officer was transferred from a clinical assignment in Mississippi by federal officials at the insistence of the Mississippi governor, because the doctor constantly referred to black patients as "Mr." and "Mrs." and dared to disagree with the governor's stand on public school integration.)

When Mrs. Smedes traveled through Ohio, her "mammy," Mammy Maria, was afraid that she would be forced to go free. When questioned by a white stranger, "She got down on the floor of the coach and squeezed herself under the seat on which her master and mistress sat, and could not be persuaded for some hours to leave her hiding-place." [11] Mrs. Smedes felt that these circumstances demonstrated that the tie between master and servant was sacred and close to the tie of blood. While it is true that strong ties developed between blacks and whites under the conditions of slavery, they became the basis for "bad blood" and racial conflict, rather than for the mutual respect and positive feeling associated with healthy relationships.

The slave experience stripped the African of the social organization he had developed to serve his needs, and replaced it with a new one that served the needs of the white man. The needs of the slave were met only when they did not interfere with those of the master. Thus, singing and praying for the dead child, Mose, would have helped the slaves deal with loss and sorrow. It would have enhanced their appreciation of themselves as individuals, but it embarrassed and threatened the master. It was vigorously quelled. Even humane treatment was motivated by a master's self-interest. An ex-slave said, "Marse always say being mean to the young-uns make them mean when they grows up and nobody gwine to buy a mean nigger."

Many slaves resisted. Some escaped to the Indians, some fled to the North and Canada. There were those who hid in the wooded areas surrounding plantations and occasionally raided the planter, while others sabotaged tools and equipment. Some plotted and planned rebellions. Three major insurrections and numerous small ones took place. Others stole from the master, fought with overseers, even when it meant death or severe punishment, and some worked as slowly as they could without getting punished. But, for the most part, the African had to accept his lot as a slave. This is a painful reality to some black Americans. I recall a classmate in a college bull session passionately asking, "Why? Why didn't they fight back like men?"

It has been argued that there was less resistance in North America than in South America and the Caribbean because the black slave brought here was inherently passive and child-like. A more likely explanation is that blacks were initially a small minority. In addition, the slave holdings were small, an average of two to five slaves per master. Tight social and psychological control was easier here than in places with large holdings and a slave majority. By the time they were in large numbers in the Deep South, a sufficient number had been thoroughly conditioned —infantilized or rendered dependent and passive—and were not able to resist.

Conditioning to the point of infantilization is obvious in the case of Mrs. Smedes' mammy, Maria. Like many other slaves, she had been rendered totally dependent—an adult child. The literature of slavery abounds with examples of slaves who had become infantile, passive, dependent and depressive. Indeed, Josiah Henson's father apparently experienced an acute depressive reaction after the beating he got exposed his humiliating powerlessness. I suspect that it was because of the dependency relationship, and not pure affection, that the slaves of Mrs. Smedes' father could leave their friends and kinspeople to follow their "beloved Master and mistress." This was far from a healthy relationship.

The aggressive militancy in the black community today shows us that the passivity of the slaves was not biological but was produced by the experience of slavery. How was it possible to destroy the pride of African warriors to such a point that it was replaced by dependence upon a white master?

The answer is in the total power of the master and the total powerlessness of the slave. The African was far from home, easily identifiable, surrounded by hostile whites. The organizational elements of his culture—the kinship systems, courts, chiefs, age-grades—were wiped out. In addition, recall the words of the ex-slave who said, "You know, then there wasn't no law 'gainst killing nigger slaves." Unlimited force was used until a slave submitted.

If a slave was killed, there was no lineage group to stand in judgment on the killer. If he was killed by his master, the killing was automatically justified. If a stranger killed a slave, he compensated the master, not the family of the slave. The situation sent a message to the slave that clearly told him he had no value except as somebody's property.

In Africa, the importance of the individual was ceremonially acknowledged at every stage of his life—from the rites of birth to the tests of manhood and the rituals of death. In slavery every function of life was subject to the will of the master: Marriage . . . "That's your wife." Sex . . . "My sister Emma was the only woman he have 'till he marries." Work . . . "rousing the niggers to git in the fields ever 'fore light"; and Worship . . . "Old Master let him preach in the kitchen . . ."

The master provided basic necessities: Food . . . "At times they would give us enough to eat. At times they wouldn't." Clothing . . . "They didn't know nothing 'bout no britches 'til they was great big." Shelter . . . "Down in the quarters every black family had a one or two-room log cabin," or, "Boss, our bed was the ground."

The male slave did not provide for his family. He did not go to battle in the name of his lineage, tribe or nation. He did not return from battle as a conquering hero to be feted and honored by his people; nor could sacrifices be offered in his honor if he failed to return. He was neither farmer, herder, nor chief. He was a slave who derived his only identity and value in a degrading relationship with his owner no matter how kind the master or how humane the treatment.

The functions served by the master were obviously parental in nature. The master's relations with the slave were like those of an adult with a very young child. The white master—not the head of the black household—provided protection, defined the social role, and represented the only security a slave had. It is understandable then, that many slaves looked to the master for almost everything and not to their kin and to other slaves. The slave child observed the helplessness and powerlessness of his parents and recognized the master as the highest authority. When the child did look to the parents, he was taught through scolding and beating to submit to the system for his own safety. While the African parent had often been a strict disciplinarian, child-rearing practices in Africa were preparation for taking an honored role in adult society. Child rearing in slavery prepared the young to be "good" slaves but inferior human beings. In Africa, the parent asked the child to give up excessive assertion, aggression and self-indulgence for a mature and honored adult role that would bring self-fulfillment. In slavery, the parent was simply the agent of the master and conditioned the child to fulfill himself by doing the master's bidding.

Hard work did not lead to wealth or success or pride. There was no chance to define oneself as adequate through personal effort. Josiah Henson wrote, "One word of commendation from that petty despot [overseer] who ruled over us would set me up for a month." [12] The only way a slave could define himself was in terms of the white man who owned him. The current Bureau of the Census designation of blacks as non-whites is a significant reminder of this unequal relationship; no wonder it is offensive to so many blacks.

This situation explains a great deal. This is the reason that Josiah Henson, as a helpless child, could be placed with forty adult slaves and be ignored by them. Slave literature often makes the point that some blacks appeared to care more about the master's white children than about their own. This is understandable. The black child, in the final analysis, did not belong to the black parent. He belonged to the master and was thus degraded. The white child also belonged to the master but was highly valued. It was inevitable that many blacks would value what the master valued and reject what the master considered inferior. This would be particularly true where the slaves lived under harsh and uncertain conditions.

Slavery inexorably led to the association of whiteness with power, blackness with powerlessness; whiteness with goodness, blackness with badness; whiteness with intelligence, blackness with stupidity; whiteness with morality, blackness with immorality; whiteness with beauty, blackness with ugliness. It established the psychic association of blackness with child-like behavior and whiteness with adult behavior; blackness with inadequacy, whiteness with competence.

This was the black experience in America that prompted the seventeen-year-old black girl to write, "What else can I be but ugly?"

Her tragic lament is to be expected. Snatch a free man from his own culture, enslave, exclude, degrade and abuse him; and his sense of worth, value and adequacy will be destroyed, reduced or under constant and severe challenge.

That is why the signs carried by black garbagemen who were on strike in Memphis, Tennessee, when Dr. Martin Luther King, Jr., was assassinated did not read, "We Want More Money" but "I am a Man."

Slavery has been over for more than 100 years. How, I am often asked, can you claim that it is relevant to present-day events? This is an odd question since the practices and policies of the Greek and Roman civilizations that flourished 2,000 to 2,500 years ago affect our own lives daily. The impact of slavery is still being felt by Americans, both black and white. The conditions that destroyed the black psyche anew in each generation were little changed until very recently.

When slavery was finally abolished, blacks who had been controlled by their owners found themselves controlled by a government and an economy run by openly racist whites. Recall that, until 1915, more than 90 per cent of the black population lived in the most restrictive and oppressive section of the country, and over 50 per cent of all blacks lived as serfs. Until one generation ago, nine out of ten blacks toiled at the lowest, most humiliating jobs in America—if they were permitted to work at all. Only in the decade of the 1960s did employment opportunities at the better job levels begin to open up. But whites still wonder why blacks have not accomplished more in a hundred years of "freedom." And even whites who are well educated still find it possible to ignore the evidence of how blacks have been controlled, contained and brutalized. Only recently have blacks in "democratic" America been better off than people living under dictators. The white mind has been able to look without seeing.

Fraud, theft, economic reprisal and open violence against blacks existed until the 1940s, when they began to give way to measures more covert but equally effective. United States Census Bureau statistics show that over 3,000 blacks were lynched between 1882 and 1935. The records of Tuskegee Institute show that more than 4,700 blacks died from mob action between 1882 and 1955. From 1882 to 1901, there were more than 150 lynchings in an average year.

The motives for violence were mixed, but all were in the interest of maintaining white privilege. When black brakemen on the Yazoo and Mississippi River Valley Railroad did not quit their jobs as ordered by whites in 1921, one was lynched and others were beaten. Six blacks were lynched in Georgia, in 1916, after one killed an overseer who had whipped one of them. *The Savannah Tribune* reported that, in 1912, a black recruiter for a Back-to-Africa movement was so successful that the white farmers began to fear they would have no one to harvest their crops. The recruiter was lynched. In 1944, a black Mississippi minister was lynched on his 220-acre farm after he hired a lawyer to protect it from whites who suspected there was oil on his land. Such events moved an ex-slave to remark, "It's hard for colored folks to keep anything. Somebody gets it from 'em if they don't mind." [13]

In 1916, a young black man running for a train in Cedar Bluff, Mississippi, accidentally brushed a young white girl; he was beaten and hanged. In 1914, according to the *New York Age,* a seventeen-year-old black girl was criminally attacked by two white men. Her brother shot one of them and fled. When the local authorities were unable to find him, they hanged his sister, the seventeen-year-old victim! [14]

In 1911, the Governor of South Carolina, Coleman L. Blease, expressed public approval of the lynching of a black man. Twenty years later, when he was a United States Senator and running for re-election, he said, "Whenever the Constitution comes between me and the virtue of white women in South Carolina, I say to hell with the Constitution." [15] Because of such leadership, it is easy to understand how in Tylertown, Mississippi, in 1920, a black man was dragged from the courtroom where he was being tried, and lynched. In 1921, a black Texas strikebreaker was seized from a hospital and hanged. (To get jobs at all, blacks often had to work as strikebreakers.) A wounded black man was taken out of an ambulance in Florida and lynched by a mob in 1941.[16]

So intimidated and helpless were blacks that in Munroe, Georgia, in 1946, the relatives of a lynch victim were afraid to attend his funeral. Concerned about law, but not order and justice, a Harvard professor, A. Bushnel Hart, suggested, "If the people of certain states are determined to burn colored men at the stake, those states would better legalize the practice." [17] Essentially, lynching *was* legal, because the federal and state authorities who now claim to be so deeply concerned about law and order were content to look away from Dixieland and let whites lynch blacks at will.

Whites who tried to defend blacks against lynch mobs fared little better than the blacks themselves. Is 1916, a Lima, Ohio, sheriff was nearly lynched while protecting an intended black victim. In 1925, the mayor of Omaha, Nebraska, was less fortunate. He died of injuries sustained while he was attempting to prevent a mob from lynching a black man. In 1927, Clarence Darrow fled Alabama after publicly condemning lynching. He was denounced from the pulpit and in the press and menaced by a mob. Darrow's speech, as reported by *The Chicago Defender,* was perhaps ahead of the times. He said to a black audience:

> I can't help you; you will have to help yourselves; but I
> advise an attitude of defiance toward the white man who

calls himself your "friend." How has he manifested his friendship?

By hanging and burning you, by making you do his work and use his back door, refusing to let you enter the best hotels and use the best coach in the train, and making you sit in the rear of the street car.

The only front place the white man has ever given you is in the battle line. There you can stop the bullets; but when you return home you can't use the sidewalks. You have to use the road. What can the colored man do to help himself?

I see you pray, but I don't see why. Your God must be a "white" man, considering the way He treats you. No doubt there will be a "Jim Crow" law in your heaven when you get there.

You can sing. I hear you sing "Sweet Land of Liberty," but I don't see how you can. I don't sing it because I know it's not true.[18]


Perhaps it was because I also knew that I flinched when, as a youngster, I stood tall in the classroom with my hand across my chest saying, "One nation, indivisible, with liberty and justice for all." Indeed, it is for the same reason that my legs would not move and my mouth would not open when the national anthem was played before a ball game while I was at Indiana University. It was five years before it was clear to me that the nation was going to change and I could stand up again.

These oppressive conditions did not permit the emergence of many defiant black men. The absence of protection under the post-slavery laws forced black men into subservient, dependent, degrading relationships with whites, that were only slightly changed from those of slavery. Most blacks remained laborers and domestics. The white Comers who had owned my relatives during slavery, employed them in the kitchen and the fields after slavery. One of the stories I recall hearing my father tell often was the warning of "Boss" Comer, "If you get into trouble in town, get back to the place [plantation] and I can protect you. I can't help you in town." I am sure that arrangement saved some of my relatives' necks, but it did not help their minds—their sense of their own personal adequacy, worth and value.

It is obvious that after slavery the black man in America was still in a spot psychologically as well as socially—stripped of his African lineage ties, and largely deprived of the strong family ties around which American life is structured. "Jumping over the broomstick" at the master's command and being separated for the master's benefit had not contributed to enhancing the sanctity and strength of a family. U.S. Senators who prided themselves on putting racist violence ahead of the Constitution could not give the black family a sense of belonging and security in the society.

In addition, freedmen were isolated in large numbers in some of the most remote and socially backward areas of America. The effects of industrialization, public education and other social forces that changed the face and style of the rest of America passed them by as they passed the whites of Appalachia by. The significant point here is that there was a greater percentage of blacks than whites in isolated areas of the rural South without opportunity to participate in the social system. For a hundred years, many isolated blacks necessarily maintained life styles very close to those formed in slavery.

Nonetheless, most freedmen attempted to do the only thing then possible—become a part of the American mainstream. Establishing and maintaining a family was the first move. Even before the end of slavery, some freedmen purchased their wives and children from white masters. After slavery, some who had been separated from their families made great efforts to find them. A college classmate of mine, now a prominent Virginia lawyer, told me of his great-grandfather who walked from Washington, D.C., to southern Virginia to be reunited with his family. Most freedmen settled down to a two-parent family arrangement, but some maintained the weak sexual liaisons that slavery had established. Some wandered from place to place, unable to adjust to a new life style.

But, for even the most determined family man, working at the lowest level of the job market made it hard to support a family. Getting ahead was hardly in the realm of possibility. For the black man who was interested in getting an education, the obstacles were great. Participation in business or government after Reconstruction was out of the question. Under these circumstances, it was difficult for blacks to live a normal life. Those who were overwhelmed, or who acted out of their frustrations, became the basis for the stereotype—the hopeless, the violent, the irresponsible, with conflict-ridden family and community relationships. They were the originals of the "Sambo" stereotype. My patient who had had his face disfigured for life in a fight over a bottle of wine was among this number. So was the mother of Walter Stoner's girlfriend, who hit her child in the head with a flat-iron.

The white mind, needing justification for the violation of its religious and political principles, looked on and said, "That's the way niggers are!" The white mind was not interested in knowing why some blacks acted anti-socially. Neither was it interested in knowing that most blacks did not act that way at all. The tribulations of a small segment of the black community, disproportionately large when compared with groups who had a less traumatic history, was not seen as a cause for national action but as a source of thigh-slapping amusement. The laughter continued late into the first half of this century. The "comedy" of *Amos and Andy* and the stupidity of the lawyer, Calhoun, tickled millions of Americans. Youngsters laughed heartily at the antics of Little Eight Ball, the white mind's notion of a black child. Cartoons in *The New Yorker, The New York Times,* and some of the most liberal periodicals poked fun at the antics of black folks. The white mind could not understand why blacks objected to the clowning of white minstrels in black-face.

When my mother worked as a maid for a prominent judge in my hometown, she heard the judge, a prosecutor, and a defense attorney laughing heartily over the antics of their black clients. One finally asked the others, "How much should we get out of these crazy coons?" Needless to say, my confidence in the American judicial system was shaken by my mother's account. The white doctor who, during my internship, laughed about the black woman who was kicked in the stomach by her husband reflects the same mood of amusement at the tragedy of black life in America. Would he have laughed at a man trying to free himself from quicksand?

Blacks growing up when I did had no defense against this contemptuous white laughter. My textbooks told me nothing about the black man's past or present achievements, or about the dramatic struggle for survival, adequacy and freedom. Watching Little Eight Ball at the theater sent shivers up my spine. That was me . . . us. Indeed, there were black youngsters who had come from isolated areas of the South in my community who were close to this stereotype. I had no way of knowing that the life conditions of their parents and grandparents had made them what they were. There was a lawyer in my hometown who could have been the prototype for Calhoun. We joked about what the judge had once said to him in court when he had erred on procedural matters, "Don't you know anything? You're out of order, sit down!" Had I known how much less was spent to educate blacks than to educate whites, I would have understood.

When the white mind was not overtly antagonistic toward blacks or amused by their struggle for survival, it often reflected an air of insulting paternalism. Any white man could walk up to a black stranger and slap him on the back in a gesture of "friendship," or refer to him as "George" or "Sam" or "boy." At a racially integrated off-campus restaurant in Indiana, a white drunk told a waiter in a loud voice, "Serve those colored boys." Then, putting his arms around our shoulders he said, in a fatherly manner, "I'm looking out for colored people. I like colored people." We were outraged, but had we done more than quietly ignore him, we would have been in trouble.

Blacks had to hold on somehow. I, in self-defense, did such things as read *Thirteen Against the Odds,* the story of thirteen successful blacks, symbolic of 13 million blacks struggling to gain a foothold in America. And I found myself delighted when a black lawyer who could hold his own in any courtroom finally came to town. I was even more delighted when the open display of black anger in the 1960s caused most white strangers to think twice before they laid their hands on me in a gesture of friendship. But there is no doubt that society's messages about my powerlessness, my inferior status, and my stupidity that bombarded me during the formative years of my youth put my sense of worth and adequacy under a constant and severe strain.

Blacks did not take the overt and covert battering lying down. Human beings with any degree of aggressive spark will fight back when oppressed or abused; but without economic independence, the fight could not often be in the open. A visiting Southern relative once described an incident that reflected a common pattern utilized to "get back" at the white man. The incident challenged Mrs. Smedes' notion of the sacredness of the slave/master tie.

When Governor Comer died, my great-aunt, a family servant, was overcome with sorrow. My great-uncle finally said, "Sitting up here crying like you're a member of that family, you better get some of this here silver and stuff while everybody is upset." That story amused even my father, who came pretty close to being a black Puritan. I now understand that incident as a case of getting the white man when one can, retaliating for the white man's daily exploitation of the black man. Indeed, this is one of the motivations of the looting that sometimes accompanies violent racial disturbances.

This exploitation-retaliation cycle became so common that many white employers underpaid their black employees and purposely left money around to be stolen, evidence of a truly sick relationship. The practice even followed the black man north. On one job where my mother worked as a maid, her employer deliberately left money around for her to snitch. When nothing happened after a few days, the employer explained the stratagem, and my mother promptly quit. Her employer asked her to return. "But that's the way I thought I was supposed to do it," she said. Elliot Liebow, in *Tally's Corner,* has shown that the exploitation-retaliation cycle is still with us today.[19]

The entire system, from white violence and white laughter to the endless cycle of exploitation and retaliation, worked to deny the black man a positive self-image. It is easy to imagine what must have happened in family after family. Just as the slave mother taught her son to be a slave, the black mother after slavery had to teach her son to be less than a man, and in turn despised him for it. She had to teach him to listen to and obey white folks, right or wrong, lest he pay the supreme price exacted for black self-assertion. She had to teach him not to aim too high because there was nothing up there for him. She protected him from the taunts and the slights, but found herself warning her daughter to be strong because her future husband was probably going to be like brother and daddy; they were not going to make it as men. The product? My ten-year-old patient saying, "My mamma said my daddy is a good-for-nuthin' nigger and I'm gonna be just like him."

While there is hard truth in that description of life for black people, some of it is the social scientist's distortion and the propagandist's tool. A young black social worker, distressed after a psychiatrist's discussion of the problems of black folks, said, "They make us sound sick. Look around you. You can see that we are not sick. We took everything they could throw at us and we hung on and now we are fighting back. We are a vibrant, determined people!" Well-meaning social scientists, this writer concluded, attempting to explain the circumstances in the black community, have sometimes reinforced the stereotypes instead of demolishing them.

The "black matriarchy" theory is an example. In a true matriarchal system, there is female control of property and economics, government and culture, and there is a defined and acceptable role for men. Certainly that is not the black American situation, or has it ever been. E. Franklin Frazier, the foremost student of the black family, pointed out more than twenty years ago that when black men were able to provide for their families, they jealously guarded their leadership position. Social scientists miss the fact that the black female often was the "public leader," while behind the scenes the male was in charge. Since the black female was considered less of a threat to the status quo than the black male, she was less subject to violent reprisal for self-assertion in public.

My Alabama-born father said very little in public, but when my parents were making the payday decisions about how to spend the money, I heard the leader . . . my father. The mere absence of a father in a relatively small percentage of families does not make a society a matriarchy. About 78 per cent of all black families are two-parent families as compared to 89 per cent of all white families.[20] The difference between the black and white percentage has more to do with economics than with family organization. In *Tally's Corner,* a study of black street-corner men, Elliot Liebow pointed out that these men wanted clearly to be husbands, fathers and breadwinners—not their wives' dependents. Young Walter Stoner thought men were "s'pozed to take care of women." So did some of the men who stood on the corner in front of the Frat in my hometown. That society has produced and perpetuated a disproportionate number of fatherless black families is a fact. Deliberately or inadvertently suggesting that the situation reflects an acceptable cultural pattern confuses the issue.

Black people held on while a culture was destroyed, through a period of exclusion and oppression in America, and came out looking pretty good by all the indices of social function. There is so much attention given to the problems of black folks that we often forget that the majority never go to jail and are never on public welfare, but maintain two-parent families and work whenever whites permit them to.

There is no contradiction here. Slavery, discrimination and abuse were traumatic. However, there are traumas and traumas. It is not sheer speculation that the slaves who lived under sadistic conditions fared worse from a post-slavery adaptive standpoint than those who lived under well-ordered conditions. Recent studies of data on school performance, crime and welfare confirm the obvious: that people who come from disorganized and chaotic home and community environments fare worse than those surrounded by order and stability. An ordered life without opportunity is likely to be disabling, but less so than a disordered life. Whatever the circumstances during and after slavery, most blacks made adaptations that permitted them to achieve a stability very close to that of the more fortunate white majority. How did this miracle happen?

There is a fundamental difference between black adaptation and white adaptation. Many more whites than blacks were able to make largely instrumental, or economic and environmental adaptations with less need for affectual or emotional relationships and supportive cultural forces. The record shows that whites established and controlled the levers of American social organizations —government, business, industry, education, unions, and so on. They established and modified social policy in a way that enabled the vast majority of white people to obtain a reasonable level of economic, social and psychological security. Black hands reaching for those levers were crushed. Blacks held on and, largely through interpersonal, creative and affectual mechanisms, helped force the powers to change. An allegorical oversimplification of the outcome would be to say that whites got the body and blacks got the soul.

In some blacks, this debilitating relationship to the white power structure interfered with adequate personality development. Frustration led to apathy and withdrawal that destroyed potential and ruined lives. But major adaptive pathways were available that did not include a close relationship with oppressive and abusive whites. There were physical and creative outlets that the white world could not obstruct. And there was the mechanism of religion. These provided blacks with the sense of well-being that more whites achieved by controlling the world around them.

The slave system had demanded the destruction of all things that might lead to black social control or to rebellion. But certain elements of African culture that were not threatening to the whites helped sustain the slaves psychologically. The smart master—faced with slave depression and unhappiness, hence possible violent rebellion or suicide—fostered these sustaining elements. Music, dance, story-telling, humor and banter were the most important of these non-organizational remnants of our African heritage. Slave literature reveals the frequent presence of the fiddle and the dance in the slave quarters. Music was heard in the fields, in the church, and in every aspect of slave life.

Thus black music was more than entertainment. It was sustenance. And from every period of black existence in America came a new and appropriate form; the resignation of the work-song and the spiritual of slavery; the hopelessness and sorrow of blues; the joyful note of swing, hot jazz, cool jazz, rock 'n' roll. My mother hummed spirituals as she washed greens for the evening meal or went about her work. She once described her experiences as a day-worker, doing a week's work every day for one dollar. When I asked her how she had managed, she replied, "I just sang and prayed that the Lord would bring a better day."

Like the spiritual, the tale, humor and banter survived slavery and served very specific functions. Long before the black comedian made it in the big time of television and posh supper clubs, he held forth with earthy, cryptic and caustic humor in black night spots across the country. But, more important, the black man in the street and the barber shop was pretty good at telling the tale also. I can see now that it was the tall tale and the sharp banter, "downing" or kidding each other, that kept the black locker room in the steel mill more warm and alive than the white one. Joe Johnson at the Frat kept the place cracking with his long rendition of "The Signifying Monkey." It was fun but it was not just fun. Let us examine this bit of foolery as Oscar Brown, Jr., the entertainer whose material often contains a soulful slice of the black subculture, presents it.

In Brown's version of "The Signifying Monkey," the mischievous monkey goads the allegedly tough lion by telling him that the elephant is talking in a scandalous way about the lion's mother, his grandmother, and indeed the lion himself. (Those in the know will recognize the "dozens"—that is, talking in a derogatory way about an adversary's relatives—the supreme put-down, or expression of anger and hostility.) A real man has no alternative but to fight when challenged in this way. The lion, enraged, challenged the elephant. Surprised and probably innocent but equal to the task, the elephant took up the gauntlet. The lion got his head whipped to a fare-thee-well.

The monkey was most amused and began to "signify"—that is, to question the lion's title of supremacy; threatening, from a safe distance, to whip the lion himself. In his glee, the monkey's foot slipped and he fell to the ground. The lion instantly sprang upon him. The monkey began to plead for mercy, claiming that he had some information the lion needed to know. When the lion paused to listen, the monkey leaped back into the tree and began to signify once again. The lion could only warn the monkey that his survival depended upon his staying in his place, up in the trees.

In "The Signifying Monkey," the less powerful animal, with a pretense of friendship and concern, pits the more powerful against the most powerful one and enjoys the outcome, sharing in the triumph of the latter. The powerful King of the Jungle was degraded, abused and ridiculed. With humans, the least powerful person would experience a feeling of triumph, power, control and a release of pent-up aggressive impulses in this situation. When he almost has to pay the price for his moment of pleasure, the monkey resorts to cunning to survive. The chilling reality of the situation—the fact of the lion's superior power—is tacked on at the very end. It is too close to human struggles to be a meaningless bit of "foolery."

The student of human behavior will recognize this amusing and innocent tale as a wish-fulfillment fantasy, which is a psychological mechanism for satisfying impulses or desires in an almost-but-not-quite manner when the consequences of overt action are too great. Black people have often utilized such mechanisms to deal with excessive anger and frustration generated by the oppressive social system. Otherwise these emotions might have manifested themselves as direct violence toward whites with severe repressive consequences for blacks. The fact that humor and banter were an inadequate way of handling the repressed emotions is reflected in the fact that the highest percentage of black assaults is on other blacks. The low percentage of black assaults on whites speaks to the degree of intimidation and control of blacks in America.

Black humor, frequently heard in private, is filled with tension–relieving tales of black success through devious and cunning methods, sometimes even direct black aggression toward whites. I recall college bull sessions that had the same central theme—outwitting and beating the white man in spite of all his power and control. What was verbalized in jest only reflected what was frequently being acted out in the black and white relationship . . . slaves breaking the master's plow, my great-uncle and the silverware, the welfare recipient holding a job while drawing public assistance. Beat the system, beat the man; beat the white man who is the system. The spirit of the interaction is captured in James David Corrother's poem, *An Indignation Dinner*.

> *Dey was hard times just fo' Christmas round our neighbor-hood one year;*
> *So we held a secret meetin', whah de white folks couldn't hear,*
> *To 'scuss de situation, an' to see what could be done*
> *Towa'd a fust-class Christmas dinneh an' a little Christmas fun.*
> *Rufus Green, who called de meetin', ris an' said: "In dis here town,*
> *An' throughout de land, de white folks is a'tryin' to keep us down."*

*S' 'e: "Dey bought us, sold us, beat us; now dey 'buse us*
*'ca'se we's free;*
*But when dey tetch my stomach, dey's done gone too fur foh*
*me!*
*Is I right?" "You sho is, Rufus!" roared a dozen hungry*
*throats.*
*"Ef you'd keep a mule a'wo'kin', don't you tamper wid his*
*oats.*
*Dat's sense," continued Rufus. "But dese white folks nowa-*
*days*
*Has done got so close and stingy you can't live on what dey*
*pays.*
*Here 'tis Christmas time, an', folkses, I's indignant 'nough to*
*choke.*
*Whah's our Christmas dinneh comin' when we'se mos' com-*
*pletely broke?*
*I can't hahdly 'fo'd a toothpick an' a glass o' water. Mad?*
*Sa, I'm desp'ret! Day jes better treat me nice, dese white*
*folks had!"*
*Well, dey 'bused de white folks scan'lous, til Old Pappy Sim-*
*mons ris,*
*Leanin' on his cane to s'pote him, on account his rheumatis'*
*An' s' 'e: "Chillun, whut's dat wintry wind a-singin' th'ough*
*de street*
*'Bout yo' wasted summeh wages? But, no matter, we mus'*
*eat.*
*Now, I seed a beau'ful tuhkey on a certain gemmun's fahm.*
*He's a-growin' fat an' sassy, an' a-struttin' to a chahm.*
*Chickens, sheeps, hogs, sweet pertaters—all de craps is fine*
*dis year;*
*All we needs is a committee foh to tote de goodies here."*
*Well, we lit right in an' voted that it was a gran' idee,*
*An' de dinneh we had Christmas was worth trabblin' miles*
*to see;*
*An' we eat a full an' plenty, big an' little, great an' small,*
*Not beca'se we was dishonest, but indignant, sah. Dat's all.*[21]

Alienated, rejected and suppressed people everywhere develop
passive-aggressive and anti-social relationships with those in
power and control. Such relationships are anti-social only to people who feel they are a part of or have a stake in the established
social system. To the excluded or rejected, violation of the op-

pressor is legitimate. Indeed, the multi-million-dollar-a-year shop-lifting problem, largely involving middle-income white youngsters, is in large part a product of faulty relationships between powerful but neglectful parents and young people without purpose, power or a meaningful place in society.

Important though music, dance, story-telling, humor and banter were in helping blacks deal with oppression, the major adaptive mechanism was religion. To some young black brothers, this is a disturbing fact. A militant young man told me that the only good things he could say about religion relative to blacks are that God is dead, the church is dying, and some ministers are less Uncle Tom-ish than others. It is well known that the church provided black men with a creed and value system that permitted them to adjust to slavery, as well as a place of catharsis that enabled them to react to the violence and oppression of the whites on Sunday and face it again on Monday. Indeed, it is true that too many black brothers of the cloth drove Cadillacs while their flock picked cotton in the fields or labored at the lowest level of the job market in the steel mills, without attempting to change the situation at all.

A former chaplain at Howard University pointed out that the black church largely failed to recognize its position as more than a religious institution. The black church was a substitute society. As such, it should have been a power base that produced political, economic, educational and social change. Such development at a much earlier period might have given blacks the kind of power necessary to crack the oppressive social system. Nonetheless, the church fulfilled important social and psychological needs which, unmet, would have resulted in more severe psychological and social trauma for greater numbers of blacks.

The truth of the matter is that the vast majority of black slaves had no choice but to lean heavily on religion for psychological and social survival. Man always strives to create a social system that gives him a sense of worth and security—not that he ever succeeds. Most slaves could meet these vital needs only through a relationship with the master. But in this relationship, the black slave or black man was defined as inadequate. He had to look elsewhere for a more positive definition of himself and to release feelings that might have cost him his life had they been directed at the white oppressor. He found a better master—the Lord.

Religion was the only part of life where the needs of the slave system and the needs of the slaves coincided. The master, who wanted the slave to learn "Obey thy master as thy God," and the slaves, who wanted to hear that submission and suffering were for a better life in Heaven, had no conflict around religion. Thus, whites often permitted blacks to participate on a second-class basis in white religious services or permitted them to have their own—under supervision or under a white minister. The most talented leaders among the slaves often became the ministers. They buried the dead, prayed for the sick, bolstered the spirits of the sick-at-heart and promised the oppressed that there would be a better day in Heaven. The minister's role was second only to that of the master. When slavery ended and the freedman was without social organization of any kind, most slaves turned to the organizational potential of the minister, the church and religion.

E. Franklin Frazier has pointed out that the church played a critical role in the development of a new kind of community life among the freedmen, including the stabilization of the black family. After slavery, the more stable freedmen began to work as farmers and artisans and eventually bought land. Many of the leaders, as would be expected, were ministers who built a church almost before they built their homes. The church of the new freedmen merged, after considerable conflict, with the church of the small body of blacks freed before the Civil War, and became the center of organized black community life.

Consider here a fundamental principle of human behavior. Once basic behavioral patterns are established, they are not easily changed because they are acquired in childhood through a "charged," or meaningful relationship with parents and other important adults. This is a significant point in regard to blacks. Frazier wrote, "Under slavery the Negro family was essentially an amorphous group gathered around the mother or some female on the plantation. The father was a visitor to the household without any legal or recognized status in family relations." [22] This was the case for a significant number of slaves, although some had stable family conditions even while in slavery. Under the loose arrangement, respect and responsibility of one family member for another—so important in West African civilization—could not exist. The sexual and living arrangements that developed were foreign to African and European cultures, and maladaptive in America.

These patterns, so firmly established among so many slaves, were a crippling handicap in a society that left preparation for adult life so completely up to the individual family. It is so clear, in light of present-day evidence, that children who experience stable, supportive family life meet adult tasks better than children from unstable situations—be the children black, white or polka–dot.

White missionaries and schools made an effort to bring about constructive changes, but their functions could not touch many parts of black community life. Many blacks, excluded from basic American rights and privileges, were little influenced by some of the stated values and life styles of the system. Liberty, justice, and political participation were cruel and hypocritical jokes to blacks. Thus there were many who did not feel bound by the responsibilities that go with such opportunity and privilege. The only institution in a position to break such harmful patterns and repair some of the damage of slavery was the church. It had the right to tell people how to live "in order to enter the Kingdom of Heaven." It could censure "He who sins against his brother" or violated the word of God. In the Bible, the freedmen found a basis for a father-centered rather than a mother-centered family. It was the value-setting function of the black church that was still operating when the black Puritans in my home-town grumbled about "people carrying on over the baby [born out of wedlock] like it had a daddy."

A critical consideration in understanding many aspects of black American life even today is the early value-setting, direction-giving, judgmental role of the church and minister. The black minister, without the backing of a highly organized, long-standing, solidly institutionalized church, often obtained his authority by dint of a strong personality. Frazier suggests that the autocratic character of the black church and minister spilled over into other institutions of the black community, many of which are outgrowths of the church. The black school is often criticized for this characteristic.

Nonetheless, it was through the church that blacks pooled their money to buy their places of worship; formed mutual-aid societies to support one another in sickness and in death; and, occasionally, to buy real estate and establish businesses. Much private business among blacks, particularly in the South, developed from early church-sponsored programs—insurance firms, funeral homes, stores, etc. Between 1911 and 1932, blacks, mostly through churches—selling chicken dinners and giving gospel concerts—raised 17 per cent of the $28 million provided by the Julius Rosenwald Fund for the education of freedmen.[23]

While the black church did make some effort to go beyond the Bible, the Howard chaplain was correct in asserting that it did not go far enough as a substitute society. But it was not always safe to stray too far from saving souls. Being a "man of the cloth" did not protect a black man when he got in the way of whites. Recall the lynching in Mississippi of the black minister who was thought to have oil on his land. Moreover, for too many ministers it was profitable to discourage their flocks from being too concerned about the white man's world. There were some cases where it was in the interest of "God's work" that a congregation vote for a certain mayor or councilman, whether or not he was responsive to the needs of black people. Contributions by local politicians to the pastor's anniversary celebration were often quite large.

Nonetheless, the church served to launch the post-slavery black community toward stability, cohesion and participation in the total American social system. The church provided important organizational opportunities for blacks who were excluded from the activities of the larger society. The work of the trustees and deacons my father talked about was as close to the work of the city council or school board as most black men of his day could ever come. These leaders were accorded a comparable respect. That is why I was so shocked when I entered the steel mills and saw Deacon McKegney covered with dirt and grime, watching a white employee imitate blacks by dancing a jig. The white mind did not understand who these men were. It understood them as "just niggers"—these pillars of the black community.

Although their roles as stable churchmen, family men and citizens did not earn them respect and dignity in the white world, many blacks learned to operate organizations through the church and the businesses, fraternities and social groups that evolved from it. (This is the same function labor union movements served for many undisciplined, disorganized immigrants.)

The church also provided a place for the display of talents unwanted and unrecognized in the outside world—until blues, spirituals and jazz became desirable entertainment and cultural fare for whites.

The sense of fellowship in the old-time black church went beyond what one experienced in white churches. It is not possible to describe the great feeling of warmth, security, importance and belonging that I felt as a youngster when everybody crossed arms and took the hands of their neighbors to sing the benediction and respond to the lead of the minister: "May the Lord watch between me and thee, while we're absent, one from another." The minister understood that blacks in a hostile, white world needed psychological support. Thus, the sign in the vestibule of my church that read, "The finest people in all the world pass through these doors." The social clubs, fraternal organizations and fraternities that developed out of the church met these same needs.

This same aura of camaraderie and fellowship existed even in many bars and cabarets in the black community. They were more like private clubs than public bars.

The most maligned and misunderstood function of the black church was catharsis, yet catharsis was instrumental in helping many blacks hold on. Blacks could not rebel in large numbers, but their anger and frustration had to be dealt with in some way. Discharge in "a joyful noise unto the Lord" was the best way under the circumstances. Black intellectuals and other critics argue that this mechanism delayed militant action. Many of these critics underestimate the degree of the repression of blacks that existed in America.

The annihilation of American Indians suggests that aggressive action by blacks on a wide scale would have resulted in a similar fate for blacks. My uncle, who knew that his assistant principal had been beaten by a white county school superintendent in Alabama for demanding more school time for black children, understood the reality of the situation. And so he . . . we . . . sang and prayed and let it all out! And survived.

One understands, knowing the circumstances, why the pews

were almost torn from their moorings when the minister worked the audience up to an emotional pitch and then said, "He's a Rock in a weary land! He's a Shelter in a mighty storm! . . . He brought the children of Israel out of bondage and He'll take care of *you!*" The crying that followed the shouting was much like that which I have observed in patients after they have worked through great conflict.

Black religious music, like the message of the sermon, was a way to hold on and to overcome great stress. It is understandable that the anthem of the black movement became "We Shall Overcome." The lyrics of many songs expressed a gamut of emotions.

The feeling of loneliness, despair and hopelessness in a hostile land:

> *Nobody knows the trouble I've seen.*

Or:

> *Way down yonder by myself*
> *And I couldn't hear nobody pray.*

The feeling of persecution and violation of the self:

> *Were you there when they crucified my Lord?*
> *Were you there when they nailed him to the tree?*
> *Were you there when they pierced him in the side?*
> *Oh! . . . Sometimes it causes me to tremble, tremble, tremble,*
> *Were you there when they crucified my Lord?*

If you have ever been in a black Baptist church and watched people who grew up before 1940 sing this song, you would know who was being crucified, in addition to Christ. In the singing and the sorrow, the congregation, along with the Lord, moved beyond the misery of this world.

Religion as moral training and value setting:

> *I'm work-in' on the build-in' for my Lord,*
> *If I were a sinner, I tell you what I would do,*
> *I'd throw away my sinful ways and work on the build-in' too.*
> *I'd throw away my dancin' shoes and work on the build-in' too.*
> *I'd throw away my gamblin' dice and work on the build-in' too.*

As an indication of worth and value in spite of what people thought about you:

> *If you cannot preach like Peter,*
> *If you cannot pray like Paul,*
> *You can tell the love of Jesus,*
> *And say, "He died for all."*

Holding on, better world a-coming:

> *O stand the storm,*
> *It won't be long,*
> *We'll anchor by and by*
>
> *O Breth'ren, stand the storm,*
> *It won't be long,*
> *We'll anchor by and by.*

Or:

> *Keep on plowing and don't you tire,*
> *Every rung goes higher and higher,*
> *Keep your hands on the plow,*
> *Hold on!*

Not all the songs were created by the black man. Nor was all the religion. It is what the black man did with the available music and religion that made them his own. He leaned on them, exploited them, changed them, did them over in his own image to meet the needs that grew out of his condition . . . his suffering . . . his soul. The deep emotion, the indescribable but ever so palpable feeling that marked the funeral services for Dr. Martin Luther King, Jr., is what I am talking about. The white mind, with no desire to understand the mechanism that dealt with potentially overwhelming oppression, looked at the black church and said, "Savage emotionalism." Looking at history like it is raises the question of whether the real savage was not the white.

It is true that not all blacks were in slavery, and that those who were not had a different experience, sometimes more traumatic than slavery but usually less so. It is also true that there was a wide spectrum of experiences and of the consequent adaptations made by blacks of slave origin. In some of these the church played no part at all. But to understand the experience of a group, the course taken by the masses is as important, perhaps more important, than that taken by the leaders and by the exceptions. It was the black church that enabled the masses of blacks to hold on until at last the tide began to turn.

The tide has turned. In 1955, I had trouble getting into the predominantly white University of Indiana School of Medicine. In 1972, Indiana is actively recruiting black students. While little appears to have improved for the blacks who are still "standing in the storm," this turn of events reflects the remarkably rapid social change that has occurred in thirteen years without massive bloodshed. Even as the black slaves sang, "Keep on plowing and don't you tire," the dawn of a new day was in the making.

The task of the blacks as freedmen was to make America's social system respond to their needs. Almost every ethnic and religious group had the same task on arriving in this country and a certain amount of group unity was required to gain the prerequisite political, economic and social control. However, none but the blacks faced a society so thoroughly hostile and rejecting, and no other group came to the task so traumatized and divided. Black division was not superficial or ideological; it was, and still is, rooted in the loss of African culture, and in the kinds of adaptation blacks had to make to slavery—and to a marginal existence in the century that followed abolition.

Blacks, who had to identify with their master to obtain a degree of self-esteem, tended to accept the master's view of themselves as an inferior and inadequate people. Slaves who lived in close contact with the master copied his style and considered themselves better than those who were more distanced and different. House slaves looked down on field hands; the slaves of important and wealthy masters considered themselves better than those of poor masters; "mixed bloods" sought social distance from "pure blacks"; those who advocated revolt and sabotage despised those who accepted their lot. Finally, all freedmen considered themselves better than slaves, while some slaves considered themselves better than the struggling freedmen. The forces for division after slavery were therefore many and strong. The forces for cohesion were almost nonexistent. The freedmen had only one thing in common—massive oppression. When people are powerless and divided, oppression does not unify them; it only divides them more deeply.

The black church was the sole unifying force. But, given its peculiar role as a substitute society, it was more subject to the tensions and divisions generated by extra-religious life than was its white counterpart. These divisions limited the development of group unity and perpetuated intragroup conflict, jealousy and mistrust. Moreover, the loose-to-nonexistent local, state and national affiliations of the churches, as well as of other black institutions, made unified economic, political and social action difficult. The black community was well-organized—perhaps over-organized—but only in small parochial units, often centered around churches and later around larger civil-rights and social organizations that were frequently antagonistic toward each other.

Under such conditions, blacks could gain positions of prestige mainly through relationships with powerful whites rather than from a base of black support. As a result, a black man was often more interested in being the first and only Negro in a position of nominal power and prestige than in utilizing his access to the powerful to bring greater opportunity to the black masses. He did not try to be the black man in the mayor's office checking to make sure that a fair share of the rewarding financial contracts went to the "brothers." There was no influential black man in any predominantly white medical school protesting because black students were not being admitted. There was nobody at City Hall to raise hell because the garbage was always collected in the white neighborhoods before it was in the black.

Facing extreme racism with too much group division and too little power, blacks had a long row to hoe. Division and powerlessness in the face of rejection and oppression breeds disrespect for the self and for others like the self. This is a major reason for so much jealousy between blacks and for the acts of violence by blacks against other blacks. But blacks eventually turned the straw of opportunity into the gold of solid achievement. Blacks from the organizing environment of the church (and many from not so thoroughly organized backgrounds) began to achieve along lines that would enable them to influence society. With every generation, the number of blacks able to cope grew larger, challenging the widespread notion that blacks were inherently inadequate and inferior.

The blacks who were brought out of the backwoods by the flooding Mississippi soon learned that there was an alternative to serfdom. The least traumatized among them used this knowledge. World War I brought blacks to Chicago and took a few to Paris. World War II opened the floodgates and brought large numbers north and west, to a higher level of economic opportunity and security. Unskilled black laborers and domestics sacrificed and saved to send their children to college—telescoping the "three-generation leap" of the white ethnics. More and more black parents could give economic security to their families in spite of wall-to-wall discrimination and denial—in some cases because of it.

It is not by chance that so many black achievers come from the black-church leadership group. The importance of this background is reflected in the 1966 findings of a compensatory-education program for which I was a consultant. Of 125 black students from ten Southeastern states picked for the program on the basis of academic promise, 95 per cent had parents who were regular church-goers, deeply involved as organizers and leaders in the church community.

When the myths about blacks were weakened, the wall of segregation and the denial of opportunity began to crumble. The negative black self-image began to move toward the positive. Black youngsters watched Jackie Robinson play ball and noticed that he played pretty well. Soon they were chuckling at the fact that seven of the top ten National League batters were black. A black student recently suggested that America might bolster its Olympic winter sports team by dropping off some skis and skates in Harlem. A generation of black youngsters has watched a whole line of black superstars emerge in every sport—Willie Mays, Jimmy Brown, Muhammad Ali, Bill Russell, Arthur Ashe. Entertainment has followed a similar pattern. At an understandably slower rate, an impressive group of blacks began to emerge in politics, education, literature and science. The message was changing. It now reads: blacks can achieve.

Black men have always fought and died for justice. The recent deaths of black-movement leaders, including Malcolm X, Medgar Evers and Martin Luther King, Jr., has had a tremendous impact on black youth in particular. These deaths jarred the black mind. Black youth will never stand for repression again.

It is worth mentioning here that there have always been blacks who never completely bought the notion of white adequacy vs. black inadequacy. Some observers have overstated the prevalence of black self-hatred. From the rebellious slave to Mrs. Rosa Parks, whose refusal to take a "colored" seat sparked the Montgomery bus boycott, many blacks have, at one time or another, rejected the notion of white superiority and its right to privilege. Black arrogance, based on notions of black moral, physical and intellectual superiority, is evident wherever black folks meet. The theory that blacks are *inherently* more moral than whites has its eloquent defenders.

As black pride expanded, Dr. Martin Luther King, Jr., was able to marshal domestics and laborers into an active resistance force. And the first successful, large-scale, black resistance came from the organized and disciplined masses of the black church. Black protests and appeals until then had been through courts and statehouses, all packed with racists. But the profoundly religious black community would have had trouble proceeding in any other way. Even Dr. King had to present a moral justification for civil disobedience before he could move the black community toward aggressive self-assertion. To the white mind, the problems of blacks were their own fault, and anything but a nonviolent movement would have been crushed. Only a people inured to hardship and injustice could have sustained the abuse long enough to demonstrate to the country and to the world that the defect was not in the oppressed but in the oppressors.

Some of the black churchmen stopped saying, "Turn the other cheek" or "Hold on for a reward in Heaven." Black Americans were better educated and they had watched black Africa emerge from colonialism. In those early days of the movement, William Holmes Borders, the activist Atlanta minister, preached a sermon that electrified the Howard University chapel. It was entitled, "I Am Somebody." Blacks were beginning to believe it. Black youth had less tolerance for the inconsistency between what white America preached and what it practiced. For the first time, most blacks began to feel that they were entitled to every opportunity available to other Americans. An angry chorus of "Why?" began to challenge every insult, every denial, every abuse, and every attempt to refuse a black man his right to oppose injustice aggressively. Thus, it is understandable that the cry of Black Power arose when James Meredith was gunned down in his 1966 march through Mississippi. Black pride demanded Black Power to counter white intransigence.

Black Power meant many things to many people: blacks are many different kinds of people with but one problem in common —being black in a white-controlled and racist country. But, from black street-corner men to housewives to intellectuals, they were all beginning to feel a new-found pride in being black. Most blacks have learned the hard way that no amount of achievement or success can make life comfortable in a racist society. I learned it on that bus in Atlanta in 1962. The sit-in generation learned that brutality, death and violence were the risks taken by every black man who attempted to exercise his constitutional rights, whether he was a college student or a garbage collector. Young black adults who have grown up since the mass media partially checked the hand of the violent repressor do not even ask "Why injustice?" They simply react to it. White resistance to constructive and rapid change was one of the chief nutrients of the Black Power movement. At best, society was prepared to acknowledge that there were some injustices toward blacks, but it was not prepared to correct them or to compensate for the effects of injustice in the past. A segment of our society is still prepared to crush the black movement. But blacks are moving on.

What we observe today is an energized black community groping for a way to force society to change. Some write, some talk, some sing and some dramatize the problem. Others organize programs to meet the long-neglected needs of black folks and still others simply react when a black man is arrested, ignored, slighted or even looked at in a peculiar fashion. Some of the reactions are extreme and violent. But the outrage and anger that blacks feel is not a product of the moment but of 350 years. It is directed not only at the white man but at the self for having tolerated the intolerable. Finally, it is not anger alone, but anger mixed with anxiety. Where do we go from here? That is an anxiety-provoking question!

Blacks had to go the long and rocky route but they have now

come to the place all other ethnic groups reached before moving as a large body into the mainstream of American life. But blacks reach it at a time when there is a danger that the stream is polluted. It is a time when opportunities formerly available to large numbers of disadvantaged people no longer exist. Jobs for the unskilled are fewer. The frontier has disappeared. The larger society's fundamental institutions—formal education, a "competitive" economic system, the family—all are being challenged. But, assuming the system's survival, many blacks have by now lost faith in white America's ability ever to relinquish the advantages of racism voluntarily.

It is clear to blacks that a "meat-and-bread freedom" is the best kind of freedom. And it is clear that we can have dignity and pride as human beings only when we can have dignity and pride as blacks. The new black mind is being born. Blacks are rejecting the notion that black is bad; that black is weak; that black is stupid; that black is immoral; that black is ugly. Indeed, many blacks truly believe that black is beautiful.

The effort to bring about the kind of change that will enable blacks to be comfortable with blackness is as responsible for the unrest in the black community as is the economic situation. The white mind, which more often than not conceptualizes a problem around instrumental needs—jobs, voting, education—is missing the point entirely. The new black mind is not just a black copy of the white mind—not even of the enlightened white mind. It is something unique in history, and something that history has not prepared the white mind to deal with. It is not interested solely in "getting ahead." The new black mind is more interested in bringing about changes that enable people to accept whatever they are —black, white or polka-dot. As humane blacks and whites stand divided by the legacy of the past, the nation is drifting dangerously close to a point of no return.

# Divided
# We
# Stand

A "black people" is being born. Only now is the black community becoming an ethnic group comparable to the others in America. Most blacks no longer want to escape their blackness. We no longer need to be doctors, lawyers or Indian chiefs before we feel entitled to all the rights and privileges of every other American—although a few of us think we have to be African chiefs. But before blacks can make effective use of their cultural heritage and establish a positive racial identity as a basis for group pride and power, the black experience will have to be glorified, institutionalized and transmitted in book, song, art, rhetoric, costume, and so on. Only then will it be available as an adaptive mechanism that people can use. Meanwhile the socio-economic train of the late twentieth century is pulling out of the station and some people are afraid that many blacks taking a cultural bath are going to miss it.

The train is leaving at a time when American values, traditions, customs, government and styles are under severe and well-publicized challenge. Getting on the train means contact with whites whom blacks know best as masters and oppressors. Some blacks are not sure they want to catch that train, but most blacks realize there is no other train to catch. If the black community has turned its gaze inward, its intention is not to resign from the American system but to gain strength so that the system can be made to work for blacks as well as whites.

/ The value of the self-awareness that the black power movement has produced is unquestionable. /The director of a compensatory education program for black youngsters from the Southeast reported that the new black awareness had produced a dramatic improvement in the achievement scores of his students, although their local schools and teachers had not changed at all. /Black pride became the motivating force prompting many students to remain in school or to return to school and make the most of the experience. /This, in turn, has permitted them to develop the skills and confidence that are necessary to make it. Others, with a new sense of group pride, moved to make their universities, labor unions, aldermen, and storekeepers more responsive to the needs of all blacks. Black pride has encouraged blacks who have moved into the world of power and decision-making to remain loyal to their people. Black Power has made it possible for blacks within the Establishment to concern themselves with black-community interests, with less fear of losing their jobs.

The movement toward black awareness, pride and power is not primarily separatist or anti-white. /In fact, it is a humanist movement. It is a statement that blacks are human beings; that we demand to be treated as such; that we demand the opportunity to rear our families in a humane way and to live in a humane society. / In this sense, black awareness transcends the issue of race. And that is as it must be, because the needs of the black community are massive, and meeting them will require a coalition with like-minded whites.

To bring about the kind of change that will reduce black and white conflict and take America successfully to and through the twenty-first century, a powerful humanist coalition must emerge— a coalition composed of education and health lobbies, consumer advocates, environmentalists, minorities, women, the young, liberals and humanistic conservatives. Political and social action— in integrated groups, in separate groups, in temporary and sustained coalitions—is needed to force the leaders of the country to respond realistically to the needs of all its citizens.

The future of America depends on the quality of the development of its young. The cost of the health, education and income programs that will be necessary to insure adequate development of all youngsters is astronomical. In 1968, the average cost of educating a child in a public school in America was $623—$976 in Alaska, $346 in Mississippi. The black community can't go it alone. It must try to wring from the larger society—in spite of the level of its racism—the money, programs and personnel that will make a "meat and bread freedom" possible for the present and the future generations of black youngsters. To do this, blacks must become an influential part of a complex political, economic and educational establishment that determines who gets what in the way of programs that promote individual, family and community development. The black task will be particularly difficult in that the community must not only secure a proportional share, as figured on a current basis, but reparations enough to compensate for past inequities.

Increased black awareness should make it possible for blacks to work with whites, when it is in the black interest to do so, in spite of their legitimate anger and distrust. Paradoxically, the blacks who are especially hostile to whites put themselves in a position of subservience to white initiative by ignoring the distinction between black self-determination on the one hand and automatic opposition to whites on the other. They do not act positively, as blacks; they simply react negatively to whites. It does not matter to them whether a given proposal or action benefits the black community; if a white hand was in it, they reject it.

They are like the freedman who knew none of the political candidates running for office. When asked how he picked a man to vote for, he answered that he watched who "Ole Boss" (the former slavemaster) voted for and picked the other candidate. There was a certain survival-logic in this, but the record shows that "Ole Boss" was more often supportive of black rights than was the opposition candidate. The point is that many blacks and many whites have needs in common. Blanket opposition on racial grounds may mean voting against one's own best interests.

The oppositional stance, in spite of the self-assertion it appears to reflect, is often a dependency reaction that consumes much of the psychic and intellectual energy needed to develop independent functioning. Rallying blacks against an issue simply because whites support it is an abuse of the black movement. Nothing more completely reflects this than the issue of family planning.

A black social scientist told me that he was unalterably opposed to family planning because he had once heard a white banker defend the program on the grounds that the country should "stop having so many of those black degenerates." Others hold that family planning and population control are white code words for genocide. These are reactions to a white position that constitute oppositional programming. They glaringly reflect continuing white control of the black mind. Self-determination is reflected in a position taken independently, asking not what the white man is up to, or what *he* wants, but only what is in the best interest of black people, as determined by black people. The question should be, "Would family planning be of value to the black community?"

Power is not a function of numbers alone. Other groups in America, with fewer members but holding the aces of expertise, strategic position and money, are much more powerful than blacks. To have real power, blacks must gain expertise and position and at least enough influence to have a voice in determining the direction of the flow of ideas and money. In this complex age, those aces fall to the guys with a good education.

Studies clearly demonstrate that, on the average, youngsters from families with two to four children, spaced at least eighteen months apart, perform better in school than those from large families. Children of young and immature parents, children without fathers at home, and children whose parents have had little education are also more likely than others to perform poorly in school. In fact, just a casual glance at the schools will show that a disproportionately large number of the under-achieving and disruptive children come from large families or difficult family situations. Future black power depends not so much on the absolute number of black babies now being born as on the relative number that grow up without stultifying handicaps. Blacks who do not take these realities into consideration, but oppose family planning in unthinking reaction to "the Man," are promoting not black power but black powerlessness. In Nigeria there is no such problem. The government cooperates with family-planning agencies in the interest of human and economic development.

Another abuse of blackness is the rejection reflected in the expression "Give America back to the white folks." A momentary and false sense of power is behind this—the feeling that "I am black and beautiful and I don't need you."

This view of America as the property and the rightful inher-
itance of the white man is something that whites have worked
hard to make blacks accept. Consider the white liberal's question
to a well-educated, middle-income black: "What kind of problems do *you* have in our white middle-class society?" *Time* carried an article entitled "Working in the White Man's World."
Whites who think of America as their exclusive possession consider fair play and change as things that they have the right to
grant or withhold at will. This mind set was reflected recently in
the attitude of a white coed at the University of Mississippi who
said to complaining blacks, "If you don't like it here, why don't
you leave and go up North?" A black coed, angry but not confused, shot back, "This is as much my state as it is yours, and as
much my university. And I have as much right to get things
changed the way I want as you have to get them changed the way
you want."

The concept of America as the white man's patrimony is rooted
in the old rationalization for slavery—the notion that blacks are
fundamentally different, less good, less competent, less entitled
to the world's bounty. The black mind was conditioned to accept
this notion. Consider the ex-slave who said, "I don't dabble in
white folks' business, and that white-folks' voting is their business."

The affairs of America as a whole have never been the black
ball game. Black institutions and groups where participants had a
sense of belonging, ownership and control became the things
to get involved in. The church, the Women's Improvement Club,
the black Masonic lodge, the Regal Theatre in Chicago, the Savoy
Ballroom in New York City—these were the places where blacks
"turned on," got excited, gave of themselves. Recall that some of
my black classmates who were quite withdrawn in school were
lively and active participants in church activities; unable to read
for their white teachers but reading and mastering chapter and
verse at the Baptist Young People's Training Union Bible drill.
Recall the soloist at the storefront church whose response to the
enthusiasm of his audience was, "One thing I like about this
church is that if you have any speck of talent you can use it and
the people will love you and respect you for it." But that was in

the small and restricted part of life where it was safe for blacks to feel competent.

The courts, the schools, the city councils, the steel mills, downtown and uptown, all belonged to "the Man." They were places to go to earn meager pay, to be judged, to pay fines. The lack of black investment in "the Man's system" is one part of the problem of under-participation in politics. Blacks working in institutions beyond the "black community" are often viewed as belonging to "the Man"—custodians without power. The drive for local control of schools has been one attempt to give the community some power and thus an investment in institutions that mold the lives of its children.

The relegation of America to the status of the white man's possession may bring temporary relief from the constant bombardment by racist messages, deliberate and inadvertent, large and small. I understand the impulse and share the pain. But withdrawal is no solution. It is like taking an aspirin to relieve the pain of a broken bone. Only healing will really work and healing will require power and that will require coalition. After all, nobody promised anybody a rose garden—or a watermelon patch.

If blacks gave up their stake in American society they would relinquish what is rightfully theirs and fulfill the fondest dreams of white racists. More than 12 million black slaves helped establish the economic well-springs that have nourished every group in America. It is a well from which blacks have hardly had a sip. More than 12 million black children are entitled to the best care and training that American wealth and ingenuity can provide. I have not heard of one alternative—Pan Africanism, separate states, or anything else—that speaks to this undeniable obligation.

To talk and dream of revolution and a new system are luxuries black folks can hardly afford. In fact, if the present system is not forced to prepare this generation of black children to cope with science and technology, blacks will be at the bottom and will remain powerless in whatever government and economic system may develop in the future.

Oh yes, there is a top and a bottom in every system. People who set out to organize "the People" against the Establishment often deny that they see themselves as an elitist group in a potential alternative establishment. In fact, status and power are sometimes their major interests. It is tragic that many revolutionists are no more humane than the leaders of the Establishment they condemn.

Accompanying the concept of a white man's America is the notion that all whites are the unyielding enemy. This provides some blacks with a rationale for developing their own kind of racism— a low-level defensive and adaptive mechanism that has largely been available only to whites until now. (Black racism is still a cub when compared with the polar bear of white racism.) But any kind of racism is a trap, as many whites have learned. It interferes with the development of a more effective adaptive style, and delays the formation of the humanist coalition of blacks and whites that alone can hope to make any progress toward healing the racial rift.

A Black Muslim minister once said that most people are unaware that the Muslims encourage the legitimate but repressed anger of blacks toward whites only as a first step in helping them to gain a better self-image. From that point on, they encourage self-discipline, self-control and responsibility to self, family and community. The Muslims count on these traits to bring a man success in life and to reinforce his personal and group pride. The minister pointed to the Muslims' schools and their open-door policy toward whites in their business enterprises as evidence of their method in practice.

An economically under-developed group within a nation or within the world of nations has no choice. It cannot turn away except to make preparations to return—with more ability to influence the total system. It must utilize the money, expertise and experience of others—even sometime enemies—along with its own emerging resources. The rapid rise of Japan to an economic superpower in less than two generations is a case in point. Outside help is needed because advanced scientific and technological societies require complex bureaucratic systems to function. Bureaucracies in business, government and education are by nature giant apprentice systems. A man or a woman learns to operate in them by working with and for other people with greater experience.

Successful new businesses and ventures of all kinds are launched most often by people with experience gained working for someone else. In spite of this, almost 50 per cent of all new businesses fail. Politicians are often elected on a second or third try as a result of what they learned when they lost. Although blacks are eager to demonstrate adequacy without white help, the reality of America is that whites, for the most part, have had experiences at powerful, decision-making levels, and blacks have not. If blacks are to acquire that expertise, it must be in a manner similar to the cooperative relationship Japan established with America.

Obviously it is easier for the Japanese or any independent nation that has a separate and positive racial or ethnic identity. The black community is a sub-group influenced by the attitudes, decisions and actions of a national whole. Although I have come to view the fact that the seat next to me on the airplane is always either vacant or the last one to be filled as evidence of racism and to dismiss it as the white man's problem, it still takes energy to deal with its implications. I must still work to maintain my self-esteem. That is why I am sometimes not in the mood to talk with white folks in the airport limousine on the way home. That is why many blacks would rather go it alone than pay the psychological tax.

Blacks have been trying to gain position and power in the total society for over a century, in spite of the pain. Some are tired. Some want to be spared the mental anguish of being the victim of daily racism on jobs with whites. Some suspect that the values and practices of the system that work to keep blacks at the bottom of the heap—from the schoolroom to Wall Street—are unalterable. Some view the white system and white people as fundamentally immoral. Thus some blacks want to claim a fundamentally different psyche—more moral, more capable of emotion, feeling and love than whites.

The trap again. Some blacks come to associate things like getting an education, working for advancement, or becoming a part of a bureaucratic system as adopting "the Man's" way. They consider blacks who aspire to these things as sellouts and "house niggers." Black college students worry about losing what is black while being trained for life and work in the total society. They get so hung up about "soul loss" that they cannot study. So they miss their chance to make an impact on America.

These concerns perpetuate black-against-black conflict. Some Negro students hide their ambivalence about low-income blacks by busying themselves with "black talk" on the predominantly white campus, while they make no effort to help the black children around the block who cannot read. The low-income black community senses the real feeling and turns against the middle-income black community. The guidance of a middle-income black woman with rare skills was rejected by a needy, low-income Negro group because one member said, "She doesn't even speak to me on the street." Neither really knew each other. Plots by blacks to assassinate black leaders with whom they disagree have been reported.

The origin of such conflict is obvious. The disrespect for self and projection of bad feelings onto others like the self is behind much black-against-black conflict. The outcome is tragic. But only a relatively united black community can operate effectively in a coalition without the suspicions and jealousies that turn blacks against blacks, or permit blacks to be manipulated by white opportunists.

There is nothing more certain than that the future of all blacks depends on the ability of some of them to influence the major forces determining economic and social policy in America. Andrew Brimmer, the only black man on the Federal Reserve Board, recently recommended incentives to investment in low-income areas. This may do more to achieve black power in the long run than all the protest action of the past decade. Yet, a bright black youngster I worked with wanted to drop college algebra because all of his friends said algebra was "white stuff." (Of course, I am not unaware of the fact that a black member of the Federal Reserve Board may in part owe his presence there to the protest of the past decade.)

Part of the problem is that what is black, what is white and what is human get distorted in the struggle to make black beautiful in a society that regards black as ugly. But people the world over are fundamentally the same. All people have the same basic human drives, which are channeled and elaborated by their different experiences. All people are involved in the business of finding security and a sense of adequacy and meaning in a world that can be threatening. All customs, traditions, and attitudes are adaptive and defensive mechanisms to deal with threat, fear and uncertainty. The differences in styles and traditions simply reflect the varied ways people respond to the challenge that merely being human presents. Using a microscope to combat disease does not reflect a greater native intelligence than making an offering to the gods or the evil spirits, nor does the latter reflect a higher spiritual endowment.

Heightening black awareness is a completely understandable, effective and legitimate way to deal with the damaging effects of racism. Black awareness is the recognition of the strength and determination of people to survive and thrive under extreme hardship. But black is Africa *and* America. It is the study and appreciation of all the adaptive tools blacks have used—from African-influenced songs to church-deacon boards, to men who held two jobs, to disciplined black folks singing, "We Shall Overcome" to the fiery oratory of Malcolm X. It is the blues of Bessie Smith and the "Joy" of Oscar Brown, Jr., the jazz of John Coltrane and the opera of Leontyne Price. Black is the lively atmosphere of the street and the bar on Saturday night, and the same atmosphere in the choir on Sunday morning. (But, given black variety, black can be a very restrained choir too.) Black is electrician, ditch-digger, and doctor. It is the glorification of all these things to give blacks a sense of self-esteem comparable to what whites derive from glorifying the pioneers blazing a trail to the West and George Washington crossing the Delaware.

Black is, most of all, the utilization of the positive sense of one's self and one's group to permit humane relationships between people. Black is a quest for the establishment of a decent society. To make the movement for black awareness, pride and power more or less than this is a damaging distortion. It is "telling it like it ain't" which some blacks claim is "a white thing." If it does not prepare black people for full participation in the economic and social system of the 1970s and beyond, it cannot increase black power. If it draws on anti-white hostility, it is not a movement toward establishing a humane society. But does this mean that there are no differences between black folks and white folks?

There is evidence that certain defensive and adaptive patterns are utilized with different frequency by each group because different demands are made upon them. Blacks must be more cautious, find more discharge outlets, compensate for more feelings of rejection, develop more mechanisms for "making it" than whites. Their ways of using the English language are more or less different, but neither is common to all blacks or all whites. A black colleague is more likely to say "See you later, man," than a white. I'm much more likely to play Isaac Hayes's "Hot Buttered Soul" album on my stereo than Rachmaninoff's Piano Concerto in C Minor. (But—my brother prefers Rachmaninoff.) My black colleague is more likely to be proficient in dancing the frug than my white colleague. But none of these differences justify the denial of opportunity to blacks.

Ironically, the similarities in styles and habits between white and black are less different among Southerners and range from the love of collard greens and pot liquor to a tendency to say, "Well I declare!" I heard two ladies talking on a plane and turned around to see who those sisters were. They were whites from Georgia! But these things are not fundamental. Neither are some other patterns sometimes lumped together as "the black style."

The mother-dominated family, or the manchild, or the sharing of services like babysitting, transportation and child and sick care are often romanticized by black and white students of black community life but they are not basically black. They are often an adjustment to poverty and not necessarily a preferred way of life. For everyone benefiting from an act of beauty that romanticists find in the ghetto, there is someone like Walter Stoner's girlfriend, hit in the head with an iron by her mother. There is Walter, the "manchild," being taught to survive while longing for protection and concern from a father who cannot afford to care because he cannot be a man. There is Tim Sands in my hometown telling jokes to keep from crying.

One black professor has described the danger of getting trapped in what he calls the "porkchop nationalism bag"—pork chops being a favored meal of blacks who could not afford steak. His point is that some of what we see, glorify and romanticize in the black community is the result of deprivation imposed by forces outside the community; it is not always evidence of self-determination. Sometimes it is not humane behavior. Some conditions in the black community are the consequences of an unsuccessful fight against overwhelming odds. Yet, in the effort to be different in some deep and fundamental way, every aspect of black life—particularly ghetto life—is being given the black seal of approval. To my dismay, one black student, a heroin addict, told me that heroin usage was part of black culture. He retreated when I asked him if snatching pocketbooks and terrorizing young and old, black and white, to get the money for the habit did not suggest that black addicts were victims of a destructive process that had nothing to do with culture.

Whites in search of "meaning," "truth" and "honesty" tend to romanticize acts of frustration in the black community that have nothing romantic about them. The attitude and style of such whites often make it difficult for blacks to work cooperatively with them.

Three kinds of whites who work with blacks present special problems—the rescuer, the masochist and the pseudo-ally. The rescuer holds thinly concealed feelings of superiority. He assumes that blacks are in trouble because they are inferior. Thus, he comes with a "white plan" and ignores previous black adaptive efforts, direction, or needs. He is satisfied when he is leading blacks but has trouble taking black direction. A young white lawyer worked on a plan to sue the state in the name of a black neighborhood group without their knowledge or permission. When the blacks rejected his plan he wanted to take his marbles and go home. This was one of the problems that led to the expulsion of whites from the protest movement. Government social policy is often developed by such rescuers and thus fails to take into account what the black community has already done to solve problems before the "help" arrived. Judging by the rescuer's mode of operation, it is sometimes not clear whether his intent is to rescue, or to carry out a "mission control." Many rescue efforts have only reinforced the status quo. Welfare programs in the 1930s and 1940s completely ignored the critical role of the black church as an adaptive mechanism and contributed to its decline in the 1950s and 1960s. Properly fostered, the black church could have become a more powerful stabilizing agent than it had been in the past, and an effective political and economic force.

The white masochist is a pathetic yet dangerous figure. He too has "nasty" feelings of superiority but feels guilty about them and seeks punishment in the form of abuse by blacks. He often carries submissive, acquiescent and even obsequious behavior to obscene extremes. A black militant has called this kind of masochist a "white nigger." He applauds anything a black person thinks, says or does. Initially this reaction is viewed by blacks as support. But is this not the attitude of some neurotic parents toward their children? Eventually blacks come to realize this and become angry, resentful and abusive toward him, which is what the masochist is seeking. One black speaker addressing a white suburban group talked "without rattling his sword." A disappointed woman in the audience interrupted with, "When are you going to get mad at us?" As one black community worker put it, "You wear yourself out hitting a paper bag." That is exactly what such a relationship is, subconsciously, designed to do—divert energy from real tasks to meaningless flagellation. In the meantime, it effects little significant change.

The guilt-ridden white, with or without a masochistic compulsion, interferes with the development of black power. Guilt-ridden whites are pawns in the hands of black jive cats, who trade on the so-called radical chic. But in the end the blacks lose. Dependency and lack of opportunity create a disproportionately large number of jive cats who learn how to deceive and to exploit the powerful through sham, subterfuge and verbal facility. They know how to pull the guilt strings to get what they want for themselves. They often pretend to an interest in the black community when their real interest is largely selfish. They often have good ideas but little ability or discipline to carry out a long-range project. That is quite all right with the person of power who has no wish to share it. The failure of undisciplined or undedicated blacks in any role becomes "the Man's" justification for withholding opportunities from all blacks. White-controlled government agencies and businesses find it only too easy to cancel programs favorable to blacks by making policy changes "necessitated" by the failure of some jive cat Negro. Sometimes it is hard to avoid suspecting that the jive cat was picked in the first place because he was sure to fail.

Two students in a compensatory education program for low—

income high school youngsters called "Upward Bound" were called into a conference because they had been reported for poor class attendance. The students explained that they didn't attend the Social Issues class because it was taught by a white teacher. So the guilt-ridden whites, wanting to "do what's right," brought in a black teacher. The students still did not attend the class. Had the staff not been so guilt-ridden they would have noted in the first place that the students were not attending their other classes either. They were hiding behind the issue of race. That is jive behavior that whites who are not "drowning in guilt" can detect as easily as blacks can.

A black patient told his psychiatrist that he stole from whitey and felt justified because of the exploitation of blacks in America. The black therapist remarked that he who stole from whitey often also stole from blacky. He also indicated his suspicion that his patient was a jive cat. At the next session the patient acknowledged that he had stolen from his father on occasions. He also acknowledged that his failure in two "irrelevant" white colleges and in a black trade school had more to do with his own lack of discipline than with the schools' lack of relevance, a fact that should have been evident since the trade school was his own career choice. But prior to his confrontation with another black, his rationalizations had been taken at face value by guilt–ridden whites.

Students who demand stereophonic music components, free liquor bars and first-class air travel for pre-enrollment interviews from guilt-ridden white college officials while they refuse to tutor black grade school children are abusing blackness. "Ain't no revolution in the first-class cabin." Those who abuse blackness and ignore self-development as an instrument of group development, coalition and power are not black. It is said on the street that they are "pimping the movement."

The need to deal firmly with self-indulgent jive cats is one reason some blacks working with the "hard core" unemployed prefer all-black programs. As the head of an apprentice program for construction workers put it, "I don't want any bleeding-heart whites in here, because sometimes I have to give the brothers a soul sermon and tell them where it's at." Guilt-ridden whites avoid such confrontations. In fact, their guilt actually invites "jive" behavior.

Certainly most blacks are dedicated to the task of making it possible for more black people to advance. In fact, black college students of the sit-in era provided the spark that ignited this nation's movement toward a more just society. Black student action remains effective. I am unhappy only with the abuse of blackness.

Fooling "the Man" is fun, gratifying, a way to release anger. Recall the spirit of James David Corrother's poem, "An Indignation Dinner":

> . . . An' we eat a full an' plenty,
> big an' little, great an' small,
> Not beca'se we was dishonest,
> but indignant, Sah. Dat's all.

The literature of slavery is full of examples of clever ways to rip off "the Man." They were justified when effort did not bring appropriate rewards, but not when real opportunity is almost within reach. The task is great and the time is short, too short for self-indulgent, jive behavior.

Fooling or exploiting whites in the short run hurts blacks in the long run. Blacks will provide much of the health, education and other developmental services for other blacks. It is the blacks who must provide the expertise and the power of strategic positions to help other blacks break out of the double-jeopardy bind of racism and poverty. The black men who reject discipline, personal development and dedication to learning and service will condemn other black men to the same second-best experience that white men forced on the black population.

Bringing about change in this complex society requires the discipline of organization and the discipline to sustain effort in the face of entrenched resistance. Discipline does not develop out of relationships that permit and even promote sham, subterfuge, and jive behavior. One of the first moves of all revolutionaries is to develop discipline among the undisciplined peasant and working–class youth. The second move is to deal with jivers. Some of the brightest young blacks in America are lost to constructive black efforts, many of them through narcotic and alcohol addiction. Addicts do not bring revolutions—violent or nonviolent, social or cultural. Anyone who claims he is "working for the people" while strung out on drugs, robbing elderly ladies and stealing community program funds to feed his habit is a jiver, despite the tendency of white pseudo-allies to regard him as a martyr figure who is utterly fascinating to watch. From a distance, of course.

This kind of ally is the most unforgivable of white helpers. He is often a failure in his own life who plays on his whiteness to gain acceptance in predominantly black groups or programs. He often exploits legitimate black anger to throw his own rock at the white power structure without concern for the consequences to the black. Two white social scientists on the West Coast encouraged black youngsters to go downtown in protest and "get the Establishment  . . ." The students took them literally, threw fire bombs downtown and went to jail. The protest changed nothing, but the black students now had police records. Back on campus, the professors continued to pick up their comfortable salary checks. Recall that blacks with a record for loitering have more difficulty getting jobs than some whites arrested for rape and robbery.

Even when the pseudo-ally is not directly exploitative, he is troublesome to blacks. He often views black needs from the framework of his own needs and experiences. In a school where a disproportionate number of children have not had adequate socialization and are hence undisciplined, he often imposes a program without sufficient structure. His investment in this approach may be rooted in reaction to his own overstructured middle-income upbringing. A drama teacher marveled at the spontaneity she found in black students but lacked herself. Much of what she was really looking at was mere impulsivity. After weeks of effort without being able to bring off a finished production, she all but called them a bunch of wild animals and quit. This kind of ally does not ask himself whether his program is in tune with the developmental needs of the youngsters with whom he is working. His intentions may be good, but the children lose. This is self-indulgence at the expense of blacks.

The pseudo-ally often leaves in a huff when blacks decide to structure programs to meet their needs as they see them. When they suit the ally's purpose, blacks are okay, but when they do not, they are called militant, Uncle Toms, ignorant, or poorly informed. One such ally who lost control of a multimillion-dollar program walked out saying, "You niggers won't even know how to spend six million dollars."

Underdeveloped communities do, of course, need people with the full range of talents necessary to cope in the total society. They need teachers, health personnel, industrial developers, and so forth. They need the most talented and sensitive people they can find. Complicating the matter is the fact that they are in competition with middle-income suburban communities that maintain their lead in competence and advantage by acquiring the best personnel available. And, while some of the most effective and dedicated personnel are blacks who have overcome racism and poverty, others are white. The effectiveness of black power will depend on the development of talented black people; that will require working with the best "people developers" available, whether black or white. It will also require legislation and financing by those in power, black and white alike.

Another major obstacle to the development of a coalition is the anger of youth with the Establishment. While many critics flail away at our educational system, the fact remains that it has produced a large number of very bright, very creative and independent-thinking young people. Duplicity, hypocrisy, incongruity and denial of the existence of problems does not sit well with them. This becomes a stumbling block for many of the very brightest and most honest young Americans.

The country is still largely controlled by people who are quite comfortable with the inconsistencies between social and moral principles and practice. In fact, the seniority system in the United States Congress makes it possible for excessive power to be in the hands of men who made their peace with these very inconsistencies not one but two generations ago—at a time when the disparity between expressed American values and practice was easily rationalized. Such men have a hard time understanding why youth—growing up without the defenses of extreme denial and rationalization—are so upset. The blatant level of incongruity and duplicity produces anger in youth and is seen by them as an insult to their intelligence.

A black student from Mississippi pointed out that Americans should be outraged by the fact that Senator James Eastland is the Chairman of the Senate Judiciary Committee when the record shows that he has not spoken one word in his entire career against the abuse of fundamental rights in his own state, one that has persistently denied blacks the rights guaranteed to them under the United States Constitution; that, in fact, he is powerful *because* blacks have been illegally denied their rights; that he and others whose power is based on the denial of opportunity to blacks are able to bargain with the President of the United States on issues of race versus support for other programs. A white student asked me if it was really possible to improve America without violent revolution, when the President of the United States defends his nominee for the Supreme Court against a charge of signing a restrictive covenant, on the grounds that many people in Washington are doing the same.

The problem here is more severe than meets the eye. As the adolescent struggles for maturity, one of the things he tends to do is downgrade his parents and other authority figures, reject their values, exaggerate their faults and criticize their style. In time, the adolescent should find that they are not really so bad. He eventually discovers that he himself is more competent than he had imagined and thus has less need to attack others or downgrade adults. Adolescents then begin to identify with and become like important surrounding adults. (They rarely become *just* like surrounding adults and this is one of the important ways that societal change takes place.) This process is complicated when the adults are not good models.

Adding to the complications in our era is the decline in formal moral training. The church is less influential and many of the young turn to public figures as models of morality, fair play and justice. But they find too many leaders at every level as corrupt as they had suspected; they find too many societal practices archaic by the rules of logic youth are being taught to value; they find the style and customs of adult society impractical and unjust. Young people who discover that their parents are not able to guide, protect and care for them are often anxious and fearful on the inside while putting on a tough and belligerent front. There is a similar feeling of anxiety in adolescents and young adults, still struggling with their personal development, when they realize that if America is to be a land of justice and opportunity, they—not their parents—must make it happen.

Most public officials have failed to realize their tremendous importance in establishing the moral tone and quality of interaction of their communities and nation; that, in fact, they—the leaders—have become, along with parents, significant and relevant authority figures. The appointment of a Supreme Court justice is more than a political act to achieve a practical political end. It is an act of great symbolic and psychological significance. It reinforces or weakens humane values. It increases or reduces one's willingness to lay aside self-serving, exploitative behavior according to whether or not there is protection for the individual in the intelligence and integrity of the men who safeguard justice.

Information sources—schools, television, newspapers—are "telling it like it is" more and more every day. Television, in particular, has put public officials at every level in a high-visibility fishbowl. They could get by with more in the days when few people traveled beyond their own regions, when you could take a radio report or leave it and doubted the reports in your hometown newspaper. Now the television camera takes you to the scene and shows you the hero or villain at work. And too often the villain turns out to be one of our traditional models of morality—the mayor, the policeman, the President. The result among our youth is anger, rebellion, disillusionment and alienation.

Social scientists have been quick to call recent student unrest a manifestation of adolescent rebellion. Others have been even more unkind and proposed that much of the unrest is the product of the students' troubled mental functioning—paranoia, hysteria, and so on. But it is all too clear that a large number of students, even many who have not been involved in violent or peaceful protest, and who are quite healthy, are simply dissatisfied with the prevailing social policies. It is odd that psychiatric labels are never pasted on men of power who fail to face up to current problems though they are obvious examples of defective reality testing.

On the other hand, it does not help to romanticize youth. Adolescence, by its very nature, permits attitude change at a rate that is impossible for older people. But it is irresponsible to drink from the fountain of youth with your eyes closed. A twenty-year-old has about a four- to five-year perspective on the world. Even with these limits some young people reflect a maturity beyond that of many older people. But youth tends to formulate simplistic action approaches in the face of complex problems. That just complicates the problems. The complex nature of man and society demands careful assessment and sophisticated strategies for change rather than the superficial actions youth is inclined to take.

I recall one meeting of social scientists that a group of students took over to tell us how terrible the world was. Few people are more knowledgeable about the need for change and more helpless in effecting change than social scientists in America. (The students might have acted more relevantly if they had chosen as their targets the hardhats working nearby.) In the course of the discussion one young demonstrator, after hearing a few details about the complexity of the problems, threw up her arms and said, "It doesn't matter what the facts are. That's what's wrong with you people. You just want to talk facts and reality. Reality is what you *feel.* You've just got to feel and love." Her emotion and her outstretched arms reminded me of Sunday morning in my Baptist Church—all shouting and no organization and no program for sustained action. A number of protest groups appear to have simply recreated my Baptist Church.

Several adults in the audience thought we were cruel to confront those "beautiful young people" with complexity. That is a patronizing attitude. The purpose of dialogue is to engage in an honest exchange that improves mutual understanding.

Confronted with the way it is and idealizing the way it should be, the young face the fact that they have neither the tools nor the access to machinery to change or greatly influence the course of the society. Small wonder that many have developed the phoenix mentality of revolution—tear the society down and something beautiful will develop from its ashes. But violent unrest is more likely to bring severe repression than revolution. The metaphor that better reflects the probable outcome of extreme unrest and violence is "ashes to ashes." The climate for revolution here does not run very deep. In the cool light of reality, America is not the true capitalistic, free-enterprise system comprising a vast number of peasants and a few extremely rich people that would-be revolutionaries envision. In a hotel simultaneously hosting conventions of steel workers, doctors and bankers, I could not tell who was who. The cars, the clothes, and the golf bags all looked the same. A majority of Americans are living at an income level that makes family stability and security a real possibility.

This country has not been a true capitalistic system for a long time. A truly capitalistic government does not give away billions of dollars for price-support programs for farmers. Nor does it manipulate the economy with wage and price freezes. The Social Security Program, Medicare, the public education system and even the welfare system—poor as it is—all reflect a gradual move over time toward more concern for human needs.

Where the rights and hopes of many people are guarded and espoused by organizations of their own making—unions, for instance—most are not about to give up a fair level of security in the hand for a promised ideal of security in the bush. The man with a family, a television set, a car, a job, hope, social security and no money in the bank is more likely to resist revolution than students, academicians, and people enjoying a higher level of social, psychological and economic security. That is why student-worker and student-minority group alliances have not been very successful. White radical students who attempted to disrupt a black school in the East were met by parents who wanted to make sure their youngsters got an education and a chance. If you listen closely to the demands of various welfare-rights groups you will not hear, "Man the barricades," but, "We demand a reasonable income!"

Most blacks understand that in an outright attempt at violent revolution, blacks would suffer first and most, with no assurance that things would be better in the end. White students burned down a branch of the Bank of America in California and police retreated to avoid hurting any of them. One policeman used a sling-shot to help repel the predominantly white student group. The slaughter of black students in South Carolina and Mississippi brought forth no public outrage comparable to that produced by the Kent State incident. There is no question in my mind about where the heavy hand of repression would strike first and hardest.

More important, humane legislation and behavior are much more likely to evolve from existing relationships and structures than from the ashes of an old order. Human beings have the potential for love, cooperation and fair play. We also have the potential for violence, exploitation and abuse. The latter is instinctual and always available. The former must grow out of person-to-person and person-to-institution relationships that foster it. When these relationships are not well established or when they break down, the worst in man comes out. Lynching in America and the Nazi concentration camps are two striking examples of this fact. The history of tragic violence and injustice after conquest and revolution is as inhumane as the record of Establishment repression. Overturn an existing order, anywhere in the world, before creating a belief, value, and reward system that promotes humane values and every existing inhumanity will be intensified.

The frustration and reaction orientation of many—both blacks and whites—particularly the young, are justified and understandable. But nothing would be more pleasing to the people about to lose illegal and immoral power than to be able to use the threat of violent revolution as an excuse for repression. Nothing would frighten them more than for the humanist forces to develop a powerful coalition that could turn the country around.

Going farther down the repressive road would garner spoiled fruit for this nation. It has already shaken and disillusioned many young people reared on "liberty and justice for all." It would weaken the moral, the political, and eventually the economic position of America in a world three-fourths dark-skinned and largely poor, many of whose inhabitants consciously or unconsciously identify with the poor and black in this country. Repression would also divert the nation from facing up to the demands of the scientific and technological age—perhaps beyond the point where recovery is possible.

Revolutionary activity consumes the time and energy of some youth, but not many. It pulls some people away from effective action within the established social order, but not most. It confuses the issues somewhat, but not much. It provides bogeymen for repressive forces needing to assert a clear and present danger, but not often. The real tragedy is that some of the nation's brightest, most sensitive and creative young people see little chance to make the society more responsive to human needs by any method and have "dropped out."

The formerly activist wife of a young physician told me that she still voted in general elections out of habit, but would not encourage anybody else to bother. One student said to me, "Both political parties are hopeless; nonviolence doesn't work; violence doesn't work. To hell with it. I'll smoke my pot and forget it!" There are indications that psychic depression is running higher in college youth than ever before. In fact a few psychiatrists are predicting that the decade of the seventies will be the "Age of Depression"—and they are not talking of economics.

Unfortunately, life goes on. The powerful do not "drop out." The fact that many blacks in the North took to the streets in the last decade rather than to the ballot boxes did not stop Congress from passing legislation that put money, power and control into the hands of state governments, North and South, all traditionally antagonistic to the cities and unsympathetic toward the black community. Young adults who are "too pure to vote" still have to go to war and carry out the policies of officials they did not defeat at the local polls. Indeed, all the backtracking on humane social policy now taking place is possible largely because the "idealists" have given up, dropped out, left the ball game to the establishment power brokers.

The belief that one can drop out of this or any other social system is a kind of happy myth—or maybe an unhappy myth. Hippie communes can exist because they can use the goods and services produced by the larger society. "System" medical supplies were brought to an alternative life style rock festival in a "system" ambulance and across "system" roads, and the sick were evacuated in a "system" helicopter and treated by "system" doctors in "system" hospitals. When one realizes that "the price of tea in China" influences the value of the Russian ruble and the American dollar, affects Chrysler's sales and work force, determines employment levels and, eventually, affects the quality of home life in Keokuk, Iowa, it is all too clear that there is "no hiding place down here," as unlettered black slaves put it many years ago.

Unfortunately, the urgency of the need for coalition is not appreciated. Daniel P. Moynihan, the former domestic affairs adviser to President Nixon, saw a "deterioration of the fabric of Negro society," but his narrow focus prevented him from seeing that the deterioration is in the total fabric of American life—reflected first in vulnerable minority groups, but increasingly in the white majority too. The evidence is in the high level of fear and insecurity that permeate the land; a crime rate rising faster in the suburbs than in the cities; suspicion and distrust of our leaders; anger, alienation, apathy, confusion and unhappiness even among the middle-income young—the chief beneficiaries of America's horn of plenty.

The threat is as great as that posed by the great Depression or the attack on Pearl Harbor. Yet there is a general feeling that we are in a temporary stall, that all will be resolved in time. That is blind denial. We are still living with the unresolved problems of 1619, 1865, 1915 and the 1930s. Time solves nothing. Time that heals wounds also puts wrinkles in a pretty face. Time can make things worse as well as better.

Meanwhile, as the elements of the possible humanist coalition remain divided, the nation is backtracking on gains conceded during the 1960s, and at the levels where it counts most—in government, in business and in industry.

The evidence of backtracking is spectacular. The primary value of the Supreme Court decision on school segregation was not its contribution to education, but its embodiment of the doctrine that the government of the United States of America is in opposition to the theory of white supremacy. The climate of racism rises and falls with the attitude of government leaders toward the implementation of this policy. Only the Supreme Court decision kept the federal administration from backtracking on school desegregation in 1969. Backtracking is presently reflected in President Nixon's 1972 stand on bussing.

Until northern congressmen balked, the federal administration was prepared then to turn the poverty program over to the state and local governments where it would have been destroyed. It lives today, with tenuous reprieve. The Nixon administration and many congressmen also wanted to weaken the protection of black voting rights. In Mississippi the climate is still such that you can write to the State House and get racist literature. I wrote the Mississippi State House:

January 21, 1970

Office of Information
State Office Building
Jackson, Mississippi

To Whom It May Concern:

I am deeply concerned about the amount of racial mixing going on in this country. I would appreciate any literature you have or references to literature which might be used to combat it. Thank you.

Sincerely yours,

James P. Comer, M.D.

I received the following:

Citizens Councils of America
254 East Griffith Street
Jackson, Mississippi    39202

February 19, 1970

Dear Dr. Comer:

Your letter of January 21 addressed to the Office of Information, State Office Building, has been forwarded to us for reply.

We are enclosing a recommended reading list, plus the January and February issue of *The Citizen*.

Please look over the list of available literature in the February issue and let us know if you would like any additional information.

Thank you for your interest.

Sincerely yours . . .

Surely black voting rights are not safe in this climate. Some blacks who attempted to vote for Charles Evers, a black candidate for Governor of Mississippi, were intimidated and abused in 1971.

The trend toward block grants to the states (in what has been called creative federalism) for critical expenditures such as health, education and welfare, without federal supervision, is evidence of backtracking. Recall that there is already an example of local control of federal money in the Department of Agriculture—and a frightening example it is. In 1969, of the more than 4,000 people serving on federal agricultural county committees, determining who will reap the benefits of government programs, there were only two blacks. Yet, more than 20 per cent of the South's population is black and more than 50 per cent of the total black population is located in the South. The North is not so different. A study of New York state programs revealed that aid per capita favored suburbs at a 2.6 to 1 ratio; health, 2 to 1; highways, 8.1; etc. Blacks, for the most part, do not live in the suburbs.

There has been a flagrant and systematic exclusion of blacks at decision-making levels in all aspects of state and local government in the South, and a significant exclusion in many areas of the North. Communicable diseases—once brought largely under control through federal programs—are increasing among poor children in communities where local officials decide where to put the health dollar. State regulatory boards in Indiana denied the city of Gary the right to purchase two helicopters and a new school—approved by the people of Gary. These were unprecedented actions. The mayor of Gary is black. The population is heavily black.

Other data suggest that black Americans have good reason to distrust state and local governments that have no federal supervision and where the federal government has no power of intervention. The action of the Georgia Board of Regents regarding former Secretary of State Dean Rusk's proposed teaching position at the University of Georgia was a flagrant example of why there is distrust. It was well known that the appointment was questioned and opposed because of Rusk's liberal political philosophy and the fact that his daughter married a black man. It is cause for alarm when the overseers of education are concerned about the political viewpoints of a man who has served in one of the highest offices in the land and can hardly be accused of malice toward the American government. Concern about the private life of his daughter is the height of irrelevance and arrogance. The question of whether he is a good teacher was never raised.

A disturbing chain of events made the backtracking possible. Southern and conservative congressmen, and some state and local government and business leaders, shrewdly prevented a massive federal government response when black frustration spilled into the streets in 1967 and 1968. Adamant white leaders understood that if they could prevent the government from making basic institutional changes and from investing large sums of money in relevant programs while the iron was hot, it would cool. Recall the cries, "We must not reward violence. We must not act hastily," etc. When the black cup blew off its lid and ran over, and critical changes still did not occur, healthy black anger and hope turned into malignant anger, accompanied by desperation, rhetoric and action. The response from whites, threatened, uncertain and confused, was backlash. Black anger and white backlash spiraled upward together. It is in this climate that institutional backtracking has been taking place. Fortunately, times have changed, and it is not so easy now to backtrack on promises to black people or poor people as it was in the past.

Black political power since 1965 has put more than twenty-five black mayors into office across the country, mostly since 1967. Black membership in city councils and state legislatures has shown a marked increase, and the United States Congress has moved from five blacks in 1965 to fourteen in 1971. More gains at the local, state and national level are predicted in the near future. Many of the new officials were elected by black community groups, antagonistic to or independent of powerful political machines.

In spite of these signs of progress, the black mayors have expressed fears that black aspirations may be squashed by severe repression within the next twenty years. Mayor Richard Hatcher of Gary, Indiana, commented in 1970, "The status of black people in the United States twenty years from now will be at a desperately low level unless the nation awakens to the need of dramatic change and takes sweeping action in reordering its priorities." (Mayor Hatcher, who was a college classmate of mine, has always tended to be an optimist rather than an alarmist.) The appraisal of this thoughtful, capable mayor, face-to-face with the critical problems of the age, cannot be taken lightly. I believe that his pessimism and that of others on the front line are well founded.

Like many black leaders, Mayor Hatcher understands that the

key to black power lies in a shift of large numbers of blacks from the lowest and least influential socio-economic level to a more in- fluential position. Such a shift would be fine, but unnecessary, in a society that adequately addresses itself to the needs of people, whether or not they have power and influence. But, you can ex- pect such rational behavior in less than a handful of current so- cieties.

But wait a minute, isn't the fact that there are black mayors in major cities a basis for optimism rather than pessimism? Increas- ing black political power is certainly a basis for hope. But in this age of advanced science and technology, political power, while very important, must share the stage with education, experience, and expertise as levers of power and influence. Money still reigns as the important source of power. The black population is in trouble on every one of these scores.

A sobering consideration is that, even if blacks were exercising full social power—political and economic—and had experience and expertise, and the power that comes with holding strategic positions, the black population would remain a minority. A minor- ity group is politically effective only when it is able to exercise its full power as a part of an influential coalition with other groups. Standing alone and against the majority can produce heroes, mar- tyrs, psychic release and thrills, but not a "meat-and-bread" free- dom.

Healthy black and white relationships do exist and their num- ber can be enlarged. There are some very effective white teachers in black schools. Cooperative efforts between experienced white businessmen and inexperienced blacks have been successful in a number of places. Black and white political alliances have helped to elect need-oriented public officials in a number of cities. These healthy alliances are made of the same stuff all healthy relation- ships are made of: give and take, sensitivity, mutual demands for trust and respect, and mutual responsibility of a quality that earns trust and respect.

But we live in a society that makes trust and respect difficult. Our social system produces too much uncertainty, fear and anxiety. This is due largely to the fact that America has a de- fect in its executive or leadership structure, and in its ethical or moral structure, similar to ego and superego defects or weaknesses in an individual. In fact, the behavior of too much of the leadership group resembles neurotic patterns in individuals—fleeing from responsibility, failing to face up to reality, self-destructiveness. I think of the problem as a national ego and superego defect.

# Beyond
# Black
# and
# White

Black and white conflict is very real and very painful. In 1971 a black baseball player was the victim of brutality at the hands of white policemen. A white woman out Christmas shopping was severely beaten by a black teenager for no other reason than that she was white. A college in Illinois decided not to play the national anthem before a ball game because black students threatened to protest unless the black national anthem, "Lift Every Voice and Sing," was also played. A black parent asked me, "What should I tell my child when the kids call him 'nigger'?" A white parent asked me, "What should I tell my child when black kids beat him up?"

Schools across the country reflect racial tension. The military services are seething with it. The jails remain racial powder-kegs. Yet many whites feel that any favorable response to black protest means that blacks are gettting preferential treatment. The father of a white youngster who was sent home from school for fighting charged that his son would not have been sent home if he had been black. Blacks, aware of a history of gross injustice, are angered by such attitudes and the conflict is deepened.

Because the problem is omnipresent, we have trouble looking beyond black and white.

Black and white conflict is a by-product of a more basic problem: the failure of this society to develop a social system that enables all people to meet their basic human needs at a reasonable level. Until this is done, we will not be able to move beyond black and white.

The underlying problem is related to a sudden acceleration of human history which at one and the same time enabled man to solve many problems and created new ones that he had never faced before and was ill-prepared to solve. Several legacies of our past—the principles of the Protestant Reformation, the destitution in Europe that drove out the oppressed, slavery, immigration and an expansionist psychology in America—prevented this nation from moving quickly enough to adjust to the changing society.

The horse and buggy of 1900 was only a slight advancement over the discovery of the wheel. Between 1900 and 1970—only a second on the clock of human history—man flashed from the age of the horse and buggy, through the automobile, the airplane and the jet ages to the age of space ships. Advances in science and technology had as dramatic an impact on all other aspects of life as they had on transportation, with vast biological, social and psychological effects and implications.

Prior to 1800 man sought security in police power, relatives, tradition and religion. He viewed himself as the victim or the beneficiary of external power, with only limited control over his own destiny. With control from the outside, the emergence of the notion that poverty was a punishment for sin and wealth a sign of God's blessing was understandable. The right to power of those blessed by God was taken for granted. Conflict resolution was often cruel. Social organization was often unjust. But life was relatively simple, basic needs could often be met through independent effort, and expectations and aspirations were low. While there were discontent and unrest, they did not generally flow from a widespread notion that it was possible for everyone to live a decent life.

Then suddenly man could fly. Fewer people died from epidemic diseases. Radio and television showed the deprived how the average man lived. Improved technology produced an abundance of food, goods and services in reduced time. Human expectations soared. Yet, each technological advance made it more difficult for the individual to meet his basic needs through his own independent effort. Just as "dishwater gives back no images," sidewalks give back no turnips. Vast and complex production and distribution systems are necessary for the survival of man in an urban environment.

Each stage of scientific and technological development required greater social and skill development of children. Such development in children requires stability and support from families, schools and other developmental institutions in the society. A job or an income sufficient to meet the basic needs of the family is the major ingredient of family stability. Children from these circumstances are better able to acquire the skills necessary to cope in this complex age.

But a job or income is not enough. Adults must feel that they are preparing their children for full and fair participation in their society. They must feel that they belong, are valued and have something to contribute to the society. Their experiences tell them whether this is or is not the case. If they are treated fairly at the polls, in the courts, in the employment office, in the classroom and in the media, it is clear that the society believes that they belong, are valued and have something to contribute. Human beings react to a sense of rejection and valuelessness in ways that are harmful to themselves, their children and their society.

Apathy, depression, drugs, alcoholism and other troublesome behavior are the result. Increasingly the reaction is against the society—the apparent rejecter. Overt reactions such as bombings, threats and alienation receive all the attention. But passive reaction is the greatest threat to society. Respect for law and order stems largely from constructive inputs made by parents to children throughout their development and not from sophisticated crime-fighting equipment, street lights, policemen and strict courts. Parents in passive reaction to a sense of rejection often make understandable but troublesome inputs.

Despairing over rising crime rates, Eric Sevareid, the television news analyst, explained that his potential career in crime was brought to an end when a parent took him to the woodshed after an unsuccessful candy heist at the local store. That is probably the way all of our potential careers in crime and other undesirable social behavior come to a screeching halt. But it is not the paddling that does it. The clear expression of disapproval by important supportive people—in his case a parent and probably the local store owner—did the trick. It isn't even necessary to use the paddle or the woodshed. Important adults are the child's source of self-esteem and security. Their approval is more important than a Tootsie Roll. Eventually the child internalizes their attitudes and values. Success in many other areas of life weakens the impulse to grab your reward wherever you can. It is through the same set of circumstances that children learn to contribute their fair share whenever they can and not take something for nothing —exploitative dependency, the root of welfare dependency and exploitation of all kinds.

What happens to a child who experiences rejection from parents or is not valued by parents, teachers and other important adults? The child fights back or seeks attention in the only way he or she knows how—through physical and verbal abuse, by doing the opposite of what the parent wants, by hurting important but hostile adults in any way possible. Stealing a Tootsie Roll, getting caught and getting a spanking can be a way of getting attention or making a protest. Indeed, stealing can be a way of feeling competent and capable of handling oneself. Some of these youngsters, through compensatory ways, will manage to develop fairly well. Others will turn to crime or develop serious personality problems.

What happens to the child whose parents feel they are cheated and rejected by the society and in turn reject the values of the society in defense of their self-esteem? What happens when they view those who control the society as the enemy? These attitudes are often passed on to their children, and for them it is open season on the society just as for the society it is open season on them. There is no social contract, or perhaps there is a negative contract, as a result of this relationship: "You show no responsibility to me, and I will show no responsibility to you."

What happens to a child who does not have a local candy store owned by a neighbor or a family friend? Who is this person who owns the supermarket downtown with all the goodies out on a counter? He is from enemy territory. So what if he does disapprove?

Scientifically and technologically complex societies require a high degree of individual competence and skill, cooperation and personal control. As a result of his family, school and life experience, Walter Stoner received little of what it takes to cope in a complex society. A disproportionate number of people in each wave of immigrants had the same experience. The black American experience is the extreme statement of this problem.

The lesson of the black experience is that human beings, given the smallest opportunity, will strive to meet their basic needs. When this opportunity is blocked, a healthy individual or group will fight. To avoid excessive conflict, society must facilitate the effort of all people to meet their needs, must facilitate their effort to cope.

Other scientifically and technologically complex societies made a systematic effort to make it possible for people to meet their needs at a higher level in the early part of the twentieth century. Health-care delivery systems in many European countries reach far more people than our own. A number of countries have family income allowances and subsidies. Child-care programs are much more extensive in many countries far less affluent than our own. New towns and other housing programs taking the pressure off the large cities are much farther along in most large European cities. Our rail transportation system is a poor cousin to those in the technologically advanced countries around the world.

Industrial jobs and new towns took people away from work on the farm down the road, but well-managed mass transportation systems made it possible for them to get to available jobs. Comprehensive child-care programs enabled people to work without leaving their children unattended. Small families are best suited to this age but they increase relationship pressures on adults. Child-care programs brought necessary relief to such parents, working or not, and enabled them to be better parents. Such programs give children from small families, in danger of developing selfish and individualistic tendencies, an opportunity to learn cooperation. Child-care programs can help children from troubled families develop the full range of skills necessary to cope in modern society. They provide constructive activities for teenagers, freed from the factory and the farm by child labor laws, who are now faced with boredom until eighteen to twenty-five years of age when they can finally acquire family and work responsibilities.

Allowances and subsidies provide for the needs of orphans and the handicapped of all kinds. They minimize the movement of poor people from one place to another in search of a marginal existence. These programs prevent families from falling below an income level that will support a humane way of living.

Comprehensive health-care and education programs reduce the possibility that a child's development will be interrupted by the illness, injury, or failure of a parent. They prevent malnutrition, retardation and a number of preventable diseases that in the long run cost the society more than the cost of preventive health care.

The availability of such services sends a message. They say to every individual: we care—your neighbors, your leaders, your doctors, your teachers. They say to every member of society: you belong, you are valued, you have something to contribute to the society. This decreases the suspiciousness and barriers between service personnel—teachers, doctors, social workers—and clients, between people and institutions. Because such programs and services are given grudgingly in this country, rather than from the conviction that people are entitled to them, this level of trust is never achieved.

Institutions and policies of an advanced scientific and technological age must enable people to have the same kind of security they had when the protection against danger came from religion, ritual, and relationships with their family, tribe, religious leaders, the family doctor and the townsfolk. The insecurity created by scientifically advanced societies that break up emotional roots with no guarantee that health, education and other services will be available is already high and is going to increase in the future. Families are smaller and mobility is greater. Therefore, the likelihood of separation of family members as adults is greater. I have four sisters and brothers. My two children will just have each other in a society where there are few societal messages that say, "We care about every one of our citizens."

The anxiety and fear we feel as a nation results from a very clear message that if you can't pay for your every need, look out. The penalty is more than doing without. You are despised and looked down upon. The myth holds that anybody who works hard can be rich and stand alone. Being needy strikes terror in the hearts of most Americans. That is why we need people below us. That is why some children on welfare wear $35 shoes. "I am somebody of value. I am. I am!"

Indeed, even if you can pay for your every need, look out. The reaction of the anxious, frightened and unsuccessful affect all of us. The low-level adaptive mechanism of racism is a result of anxiety and fear and affects all of us. Angry, alienated youth is a result and affects all of us. Strike after strike for security that can't be bought is a result and affects all of us. Rising crime is another result and affects all of us. The more anxious and frightened we are as a nation or as a group of people within a nation, the less tolerant we are of differences, of change, of any threat or potential threat. We are likely to pick on or scapegoat the most vulnerable people around us. Thus we are up in arms about welfare cheating of $500 million by 5 per cent of the recipients across the nation and less concerned about $1 billion in Medicare cheating by physicians in New York state. An elderly white welfare recipient leaned on his cane and complained about cuts in welfare benefits for himself while charging that blacks who receive welfare didn't want to work. In this state of anxiety, fear and scapegoating, we are all fair game for those who would use the social disequilibrium to advance their personal, political and economic interest and fortunes.

The United States attempted to develop policies to head off this burgeoning fear and anxiety, just as most other scientific and technologically advanced societies did. In fact, much reform in human-need legislation is in the legislative hopper right now. It is true that it was easier to develop such policies in smaller, more homogeneous societies. But our size and heterogeneity are not the major causes of our failure. We are trapped and delayed by our inappropriate legacies.

Most early Americans were refugees from destitution and deprivation in Europe. Destitution and deprivation do not produce many people greatly concerned about the rights and needs of other people. It often produces suspicious, distrustful people, grabbing themselves from poverty and insecurity. a period of vast and rapid business and acquisition of great wealth without suf- eds of other people was sanctioned by a t Reformation—poverty is a sign of sin od's blessing. In addition, we had scapegoats—waves of vulnerable immigrants and slaves. Slavery, even more than the abuse of Indians and immigrants, permitted the society to play ostrich.

The basic rationalization for American slavery—that there was a different and inferior kind of man—gave support to the notion that some others are destined to wealth, power and privilege. The effect of slavery on blacks and whites produced rationalizations and stereotypes that maintained primitive notions about the nature of man, his environment and human needs long after they had been discredited in other countries undergoing scientific and technological development.

"He who works hard enough can be rich." "Show me a poor man and I'll show you a lazy man." "They don't want to do any better." "What is good for General Motors is good for the country." "Nature is man's handmaiden." "The height of a woman's ambition is a full vagina."

Realistic observations should have eradicated these notions. Facing the fact that men, not God, passed the legislation that all but gave away the wealth of this country should have undermined them. The fact that illness, changing technology and business fortunes in a region cause poverty should have had a devastating effect on such notions. The fact that people who have worked the hardest remain poor gives a message to the contrary. The fact that highways take too few people where mass transit systems need to take many more should have told us that the interests of General Motors are not always the best interests of the country. Polluted water and dirty air speak to the same point. Angry minorities and women discredit the notion that "they don't want to do any better." Yet some congressmen are still passing welfare legislation based on a myth—most people on welfare are lazy and don't want to work, while many on welfare are standing in lines applying for jobs that do not exist. These old rationalizations were so convincing that I myself was sold—until I met a few Walter Stoners.

We are not getting realistic legislation because a powerful few have been able to play off group against group to advance their own selfish, personal, political and economic interests without developing rational social policies. Governor Wallace of Alabama regained his office in 1970 by warning whites unprotected by modern social programs to beware of "the bloc vote"—understood by many as "the black vote"—endangering your jobs, your neighborhood, and your daughters. But the last time there was black power in Alabama—Reconstruction power—social legislation was passed that helped prepare the white South for the twentieth century—public education, railroad building, public work programs, and so on. Wallace is presently "bussing" toward the Presidency in 1972.

We have now reached the danger point. We do not have the social programs which take the extreme fear and insecurity out of modern living. The people who have been scapegoated are angry. More fortunate but still relatively powerless whites are frustrated, confused and feeling falsely blamed. The level of trust between various interest groups in America is extremely low. Many leaders still view political victory or economic gain by any means necessary as more honorable and American than supporting essential social policies that may lead to political defeat or less immediate financial profit.

The parallel between individual and societal psychological functioning is very striking. The functions of the executive or leadership group—government, business, industry, labor, education, communication systems, and so on—are like those of the ego. The functions of the superego parallel those of religion, the judicial system, and other bulwarks of ethics and morality within the society. The societal id is our irrational pursuit of personal gain without concern for the needs of others.

National leaders must reconcile their own needs and desires and those of their class with the needs of all the people, the environment and the society. They cannot overuse the defenses of denial, rationalization, projection and so on. Compare the black experience as it is and as the white mind views it and it is quite clear that the same overuse of defenses that lead to individual neurosis and psychosis have operated on our whole society.

Because of the vulnerability of ex-slaves, the society was free to overuse damaging defenses and adaptive methods. As a result the national ego did not adequately mature. The arrest is at a level close to that of the three- to six-year-old child or the opportunistic stage of ego development. Jane Loevinger described this stage as one in which "interpersonal relations are manipulative and exploitive . . . Conscience pre-occupation is with control and advantage, domination, deception, getting the better of and so on. Life is a zero-sum game; what you win I lose." [1] These traits characterize many concerns and struggles in American life today.

The mature ego is tolerant of the attitudes and problems of others, and capable of dealing with their personal inconsistencies, shortcomings and conflicts. It is capable of the reconciliation of conflicts between desires, duties, and needs. A mature national ego could say, "It would be nice to put a man on the moon, but it does not make much sense with so much needless suffering on earth." It could say, "Blacks, Orientals, and whites are different in some respects, but isn't that nice?" It could appreciate the essential sameness of man's needs and the beauty of man and life. It could forge social policy that would enable its citizens to live humanely and to contribute toward the general welfare as well. Instead, the national ego and super-ego has worked in the service of the national id—the pursuit of personal gain without concern for the needs of others.

Theoretically, the legislative, judicial and executive systems check and balance one another. The interest of labor, the interest of business and industry, the interest of blacks, whites, women, old folks, young folks, country folks, city folks and various other folks —mediated through government—should do the same thing. If this arrangement worked, the needs of all people would be met. This would result in good national ego and superego functioning. The national id would be under control. It has not happened.

Blacks were robbed of political power. The judicial system didn't work for blacks. Not one chief executive before President Franklin Roosevelt took a stand for black rights or needs. Business, industry and labor turned their backs. Educational systems, science and the mass media should have served the nation's policy makers as the intellectual system serves the ego of an individual, searching for truth, anticipating the consequences of various policies. They did not. In fact, they were used to rationalize the abuse of blacks. Organized religion found whatever rationalization it needed to cop out.

Some of the most powerful congressmen in the United States

today inherited their power from politicians who helped to disen-
franchise their black constituents and maintained that power by
exacerbating the atmosphere of antagonism toward blacks. The
inheritors, for political survival, play the same game. Thus, staffs
of programs such as the Child Development Group of Mississippi's
self-help Headstart program are harassed by their senators, the
very persons who should be protecting and fostering them.

The seniority system in Congress gives the worst offenders the
most power. In the 90th Congress, the senators from the deep
South had an average tenure of nineteen years and those from urban northern industrialized areas had an average tenure of eleven
years. Conservative senators, the allies of Southerners, had served
an average of fifteen years.

In 1967 and 1968, six of the most powerful white congressmen [2] from heavily black and poverty-stricken Southern districts
opposed a bill that would have permitted the government to sign
forty-year contracts with private, nonprofit housing sponsors to
pay an additional $10 million a year in rent supplements for low-
income families; opposed $75 million for urban renewal in Model
Cities projects; opposed increasing the housing allotment for
Model Cities programs from $237 million to $537 million; all,
except the late Mendel Rivers, initially opposed a rat-control-and-
extermination bill; George Andrews, Thomas Abernathy and Albert Watson opposed the passage of the food-stamp bill authorizing appropriations of $195 million for fiscal 1968; opposed
passage of the Elementary and Secondary Education Act of 1967
authorizing $3.5 billion dollars for programs in 1968; opposed
passage of the Economic Opportunity Act amendment of 1967
authorizing $1.6 billion dollars for anti-poverty programs for
fiscal 1968.[3]

The distressing record is not rational considering the fact that
the per capita personal income and the average expenditure per
pupil for education in South Carolina, Alabama and Mississippi
ranked them forty-seventh, forty-eighth and fiftieth among all the
states in 1967. Arkansas was forty-ninth. From the congressmen's
voting patterns one would think that their constituents lived on
New York City's lower Park Avenue rather than in the bowels of
poverty.

The same voting pattern shows up for the most powerful senators from the deep South. Senators Allen Ellender and Russell Long from Louisiana were the exceptions. They supported elementary and secondary education acts benefiting the disadvantaged, Headstart, rent supplements and Model Cities programs.

The coalition of unrepresentative Southerners and conservatives from the North and West blocks legislation necessary to provide adequate social, psychological and intellectual development for millions of American children, black and white. It allows Department of Agriculture programs, designed to aid depressed areas, to be used to maintain white supremacy in the South; and it thwarts urban programs, watering them down, reducing budgets and devising delays.

The Congress, particularly its key committee chairmen, influences the President, federal agencies, state and local governments, business and industry and the mass media. A *Wall Street Journal* report on the work of the late Representative Mendel Rivers, from South Carolina, illustrated the relationship:

> In his present role as chairman of the House Armed Services Committee, in fact, Mr. Rivers has become the center of fierce controversy as perhaps the most vocal and most powerful advocate of what has come to be known as the military-industrial complex . . .
>
> Big defense contractors also have flocked to the district. In just the four years since Mr. Rivers became chairman of the Armed Services Committee plants have been built in the district by General Electric Company, Avco Corporation, J. P. Stevens and Company, McDonald Douglas Corporation and Lockheed Aircraft Corporation. United Aircraft announced earlier this year it had chosen Charleston as the site of a new helicopter plant . . .
>
> There is no question that the influence of Mr. Rivers is responsible for many of the defense installations. In some cases, Pentagon officials or corporate executives built facilities in the Charleston area on their own initiative in what clearly seemed to be attempts to win the Congressman's favor.
>
> But in many instances Mr. Rivers aggressively sought the installations. Of the Lockheed factory, for example, Mr. Rivers says with a smile: "I asked them to put a lil' ol' plant

here." In the mid-nineteen fifties when Navy Officials were seeking Congressional approval and funds for Polaris submarines, Mr. Rivers didn't become a supporter until he was told that a Polaris base probably would be built here [Charleston, South Carolina area.] [4]

When I worked in the Department of Health, Education and Welfare, I learned that congressmen, particularly Deep-South congressmen, keep an eye on the activities of HEW in a way that sometimes amounts to harassment. Great-Society programs developed by the Johnson administration threatened the power base of Southerners, Northern machine-democrats, and conservative Republicans. Consequently, there is now pressure to place federal administrators and congressional appointees on committees to review and oversee the planning and funding of social-science research.[5] (Social programs that give power and opportunity to previously denied people often grow out of social-science research and investigation.)

State and local governments and local leaders who have political ambitions must pay homage to powerful congressmen. It is a cooperative relationship. It costs money to be in politics; political organization at the state and local level is required to get elected and to remain in office. Business, industry, labor, state and local officials provide the money and organization for congressmen and, in return, they receive the favors and contracts that they need. There is no such direct obligation for the development of social programs.

It is no secret that oil families have contributed heavily to the campaigns of presidential and congressional candidates who favor the oil-depletion allowances that rob the treasury of millions of dollars in taxes. Expensive favors offered and accepted by our "watch dogs" in Congress are common and hardly innocuous. A recent newspaper article reported that Sears, Roebuck & Company, the nation's largest retail store, Kerr-McGee Corporation (oil) and other firms provided Representative Wilbur Mills, chairman of the House Ways and Means Committee, with free plane rides to speaking engagements.[6] If Chairman Mills was not so close to business and industry, there would be no question about his motives in helping to delay a proposal for public financing of election campaigns that would remove an advantage that people with money now have.

As a result of these relationships, the checks on power are nullified and the scales do not balance. The national ego does not work to reconcile the conflicting desires and needs of all; it works in the service of the national id.

The role of the mass media in this power complex is crucial. In an individual, the ego, supported by information it has received from perceptual centers and learning, serves as an observer of the id and the superego. Good observation facilities good mediation between the id and superego. In a society, the media should act as the window on our world. Thomas Jefferson viewed public education and the mass media as protection against an unruly national id and a negligent national superego—in other terms, of course. He wrote a planter, Paul Carrington, in 1787:

> The people are the only censors of their governors . . . They may be led astray for a moment, but will soon correct themselves . . . The way to prevent these irregular interpositions of the people, is to give them full information of their affairs through the channel of the public papers, and to contrive that those papers should penetrate the whole mass of the people.[7]

Today, radio, television, documentary films and the printed word carry the awesome burden of providing the information necessary to prevent the abuse of privileges by those who govern. But the mass media are themselves big business and a significant component of the nation's power structure at the national and local level. The editors of the *Atlantic* magazine commented, "Ownership of media for fun, profit and significant power is increasingly characterized by Very Big Business." [8] In 1968, the advertising revenue for the television industry was $3.4 billion and is rising steadily. So good are the pickings that a San Diego television station was sold for $950,000 in 1950, for $10 million in 1965 and in 1969 was reportedly worth $20 million.[9] At the same time, the media's continued health and wealth depend on not pushing people with the power to regulate too far, on not challenging the status quo too blatantly.

Who appears on television and what is said or done depend on the attitude of the advertiser. The advertiser is too often interested in the welfare of his goods and services rather than truth, enlightenment, justice and fair play. Add to this the fact of interlocking political and financial relationships of the banker, newspaper publisher, television-station owner, industrialist, public official and merchant, which result from their sitting on each other's boards of directors, and the sentry function of the mass media is severely tested, if not negated.

In another discussion of the media, *Atlantic* editors stated: "There are a striking number of areas of the country where one media baron may not have a pure monopoly, but can have an equivalent impact through his preponderant interests." [10] Of "baron" E. K. Gaylord, they said:

> At ninety-six . . . [he] is a prototypical region press lord. His Oklahoma publishing company owns the state's most influential and profitable newspaper and TV properties (as well as television stations in Texas, Wisconsin and Florida), and is wont to employ them as weapons of war against legislation he dislikes (the Great Society's Model Cities Program) and politicians he opposes (Oklahoma's liberal former senator, Mike Monroney.) [11]

The guess is that Gaylord's worth is about $60 million. His gross intake in 1968 was an estimated $33 million. Across the country, families, churches and corporations (such as Hunt, Newhouse, Hearst, the Mormon Church, General Motors) with financial ties and relationships in multiple directions can greatly influence public opinion and social policy.

Government regulatory agencies are often not in a position to protect the public interest. In fact, the Federal Communications Commission has closed its eyes to the use of the public air to promote racism. In 1968, the F.C.C. renewed the license of Jackson, Mississippi's station WLBT TV by a vote of five to two, in spite of the fact that it was charged with deleting news references to the late Dr. Martin Luther King, Jr., promoting segregation, keeping blacks off the screen and otherwise abusing broadcast privileges. It took the action of U.S. Appeals Court Justice Warren Burger to suspend the station's license. Recently, the chairman of the F.C.C.

has occasionally been critical of broadcasters for carrying out their sentry function. Here we see the maze of conflicting interests turn the watchdog into the hawk.

As an arm of the executive branch of the government, the F.C.C. keeps a wary eye on the desires of the President. A *Wall Street Journal* article said of Chairman Dean Burch's response to Vice President Agnew's criticism of broadcasters, ". . . he was defending broadcast journalism to a Columbia University group only a few days before reacting favorably to Mr. Agnew's speech. An F.C.C. official agreed that there was a degree of inconsistency and concluded that Mr. Agnew's speech may have had the effect of solidifying a few positions." [12]

The national mass media have been more responsible than local media . . . fortunately. The television camera brought Bull Conner, the former Birmingham police chief, and his vicious dogs into the family room of Americans all over the country; Americans have watched student demonstrators being killed, gassed, beaten and verbally abused; they have seen the horrors of the Vietnam war "right down front"; people around the world have shared the deep sorrow of the families and followers of assassinated leaders; they have witnessed the great beauty and strength of black people and white people who "kept on keeping on" despite the brutalities and bloodshed. Now they are asking, "Where is our morality, our superego?" They have forced the national id to relent, to convert some id energy into ego energy. Many people and institutions once in unconcerned pursuit of personal gain acquired an interest in equitable reform.

However, there are still too many owners and decision-makers at local stations and on newspapers who tell it like they want it to be heard rather than like it is. Local news and entertainment media in the South and in areas where there are few blacks often present frankly racist views without opposition or challenge. Vice President Agnew has called for more objectivity in his damnings of the Eastern Establishment, but he has missed the mark. His complaints should be directed at local media, and not just at *The New York Times, The Washington Post,* and CBS. In Alabama, at a time when he launched one of his attacks on the national media, the Black Muslims were being harassed because they had bought a choice tract of land. When they called a news conference to explain their peaceful intentions, the local newsmen did not show. The ego eyes were closed.

Then there is the role of television in politics. Television has become a particularly effective medium in campaigning. The Citizen's Research Foundation of Princeton, N.J. reported that the total cost of political campaigns in 1968 was $300 million. This represents a 50 per cent increase over 1964 campaign costs. Fourteen contributions of $100,000 or more were listed and business interests of all types were among the heavy contributors.[13] Much of the increase reflects the cost of television time. In 1970, a prime-time 20-second television commercial in New Haven, Connecticut, cost $550 for gubernatorial and senatorial candidates and $470 for mayoral and House of Representatives candidates. Anyone who can afford to use this medium has a distinct advantage over those who cannot. Even before television, the high cost of running for public office helped to strengthen self-seeking political machines and political kingmakers, North, South, East and West, urban and rural.

Because so few people feel that they can alter their life condition through the political process, few try. In one of the most crucial and controversial presidential elections of all times, 1968, more than one of every three Americans of voting age did not bother to vote. In 1968, only one of every ten eligible voters in Sweden did not vote. In 1968, only one out of every three Mississippians voted in the presidential election. In Winston County, Mississippi, only 20 per cent of all voting-age blacks are even registered; far fewer vote. (There are 6,808 whites, 78.2 per cent registered, and 3,611 blacks of voting age in Winston.) Some of the most depressed and most needy people, because of threat of reprisal, economic and social conditions and depression, are the least involved in the political process or are the most easily exploited by the political pros. The resultant social conditions, from family disorganization to under-education and unemployment, become the source of continuing and growing social problems that affect us all.

I am not making an argument against business, industry, labor or government. Our social programs are possible because of the success of business and industry. I am not making an argument against capitalism or in support of socialism or communism. The merit of a system must be judged by its success in producing the kind of society that enables its members to cope and to contribute to the well-being of that society. The problem in America is not capitalism or democracy. The problem is irresponsible capitalism and selective democracy. A power imbalance leaves a majority of the people under-represented or unrepresented at the policy-making levels of our government, economic and communications system.

There is evidence that mixed economic and social systems best meet the full range of human needs. For example, Sweden has one of the most highly developed social-service programs in the world, yet business there is 95 per cent privately owned. Further, as I have noted, human rights and personal freedom are so highly valued in Sweden that dependent people of all categories—children, aged, sick—are well cared for; the schools and other developmental services are good; slums cannot be found, the streets are safe. Cars, television and good clothing are as common in Sweden as in the United States. In fact, Sweden has the highest standard of living in all of Europe.

Sweden is not much more socialistic than the United States. The critical difference is that the makers of social policy (their national ego) feel that their role is to make it possible for all people to meet their basic human needs. As a result, few people are alienated, angry, suspicious or insecure. They are not conditioned from birth to prepare to beat the system before the system beats them. A sense of community exists. As a result, there is less conflict on every level.

Trust and a sense of community can exist only when the leadership group works to reconcile conflicting desires and needs of all the people with those of the environment and the society; when all people have the conviction that the society respects their rights and operates in their behalf.

The task confronting Americans is to establish the power balance that will give us a mature national ego. This will require the emergence of a representative leadership group and the concomitant development of specific social programs that take excessive insecurity out of American life. Only then will there be less need for defenses that justify scapegoating and abuse of vulnerable groups. Both will require some basic reforms in our social system. Only a humanist coalition can bring these about.

When a problem is long-standing, complex and painful, everybody wants an immediate solution. Most people expect a dramatic solution. Concerned people want to be personally involved. "What can I do?" they ask.

When a bathtub is overflowing and the faucet is still on, there are a number of things you can do. You can wring your hands in despair or turn away. That's what complaining and copping out are all about. You can curse and abuse the person who left the faucet on. That is what so much anti-establishment action is all about. You can take a thimble and begin to dip water from the flooded floor. That is what so many programs to help the victims of inadequate social policy are all about. You can blow up the bathtub. That is what violence and instant and dramatic proposals are all about. You can turn off the water faucet, pull the plug, and then begin to dip water from the flooded floor.

The solution to black and white conflict and other fear- and anxiety-producing social problems will require turning off the water of those who are failing to produce a solution now. The action is not dramatic and resolution will not be immediate. But there is no faster feasible way.

The water is money. The single most important reform we can make is to take it out of politics. That would break the tie between government, big business, big labor and big industry. It would enable government to better serve as a mediator of conflicting needs and demands. Politicians would have to pay more attention to the social needs of the people.

In England, members of Parliament may not collect campaign funds; instead, they receive expenditures per capita for every eligible voter in their district. In Canada, free time is made available to candidates by the networks. While this would help, it would not benefit candidates to encourage more people to participate in the political process. The politician would be paid or could make their TV pitch with or without their participation. That is the problem inherent in legislation recently proposed by Congress. Because so many people have been closed out for so long, the political process must be structured to make it worthwhile for the candidate to seek or promote the maximum participation of people. The voter on public welfare would be important if his participation affected the amount of money a candidate would receive. This would be all the more important if regulations prevented candidates, individuals, or groups from contributing directly or indirectly to political campaigns.

A formula based on petition signatures and actual votes cast could be developed to provide campaign funds for candidates and incumbents at every level of government. This would make it prudent for politicians to involve more people in the established political processes and thereby reduce the number of people violently and nonviolently storming around them. E. K. Gaylord, the Oklahoma media baron, should have no more ability to influence the defeat of the liberal former Senator Mike Monroney than Mrs. Susie Brown, a welfare mother in that state. But through his media empire, he had the power.

When they are truly enfranchised, our citizens will gain economically, socially and psychologically. They will have a feeling of consequence . . . a feeling increasingly more difficult to come by in a society marked by impersonal and distant relationships. In subsidized elections, public officials would truly owe their allegiance to the people as opposed to the local political machine and others who could defray their campaign costs. The nation has a long precedent of promoting desirable ends through the effective mechanism of economic subsidies. Supporting people participation in government would appear to be as important and as consistent with the American way as is subsidizing the development of supersonic jets.

The second most important place for reform is in the U.S. Congress. Because social planning should be thirty years ahead of the needs of an age in a rapidly changing society, Congress should be made up of men capable of such planning and it should have rules that would foster progressive legislation. As it now stands, the men whose basic attitudes were formed in the period of a frankly racist, largely agricultural, sparsely populated America have the greatest power to shape the complex industrial, technological, largely urban, heavily populated country of today. They largely determine the kind of preparation the young will receive for the year 2000.

There is really no legitimate reason why the most effective representatives from either party should not be eligible to serve as committee chairmen as soon as they enter Congress. Permitting men to become powerful leaders because they happen to have good coronary blood vessels is a poor way to run a country. An open system would force the development of criteria that go beyond health for the selection of committee chairmen. Further, there ought to be a maximum time that a person can serve as a committee chairman. Chairmen serving a limited tenure would not become institutions, corrupting and being corrupted by business, industry and labor.

But the entire committee system is too political, and legislation too often reflects the stamp of the chairman and his interests rather than national interests. Highly trained and knowledgeable people in federal agencies such as the National Institute of Health and the Office of Education, the intelligence component of the national ego, sometimes provide less input relating to the shape of national legislation than committee staff people selected by a chairman. Sometimes committees' staffs are competent, but too often they are political-patronage beneficiaries. Even when able, a committee staff must respect the special-interest bias of the chairman.

One method for developing legislation that would reflect the national interest, rather than the power interest, is to establish a commission system. In recent years, Presidents Johnson and Nixon have appointed high-level commissions to study assassinations, crime, violence, and so forth. Although the commissions did some excellent work, they were studying the end result of a defective process . . . not the horse's meal or its digestive process but what it left in the barn.

Such commissions should come from the legislative rather than the executive branch, or they should work as a joint effort. Commissions appointed by the President with no input to the legislative bodies are window dressing. Other nations use commissions of inquiry to study matters of major importance and to help draft legislation that reflects the interest of all the people. In Sweden, commissions of inquiry may include members of parliament, including the opposition; representatives of major organizations affected by the problem at hand; and scientific and administrative experts. This decreases the possibility that sensitive issues will be used as political footballs so that the interests of a powerful few outweigh the interests of the less powerful and of the society as a whole. For example, welfare reform or income-maintenance legislation could be considered and drafted by congressmen, welfare-rights groups, social-science and welfare-administration experts, taxpayer groups and other affected people. There would be conflict, but confrontation around a vital task is one way for Americans to begin to give up our "powerful-take-all" psychology and move toward true democracy. This arrangement would provide checks and balance at a critical spot. It would give the national ego an excellent opportunity to manage the national id. While congressional committees are needed to move routine legislation quickly, major and controversial issues needing much research and planning should be handled by commissions.

In addition, significant reforms can be made in the structures and functions of the executive branches of government—regulatory boards, agencies and commissions which have vast power at the local, state and federal levels. Even at the local and state levels, such agencies have an impact on national conditions. Many policies established locally affect the lives of people who live in other places. Educational policy in North Carolina has had a very direct effect on Walter Stoner's life and on social conditions in Washington, D.C., and other northern cities. Regulatory agencies everywhere have a responsibility to develop policies consistent with the needs of the nation as well as with the desires of the people in their jurisdictions.

Not one penny of federal money should go to states or localities where blacks are a large percentage of the population but are not represented on important boards, agencies and commissions affecting individual and community development. There is no way, for example, to justify the absence of blacks on critical regulatory boards and agencies in such states as Alabama, Georgia, South Carolina, Illinois, and New York. Because the line between public and private money is so thin, every so-called private company or agency with a relationship to the government should be under the same obligation. There is nothing in the historical record that suggests that a power complex without black members will be responsive to the needs of blacks. The systematic exclusion of blacks from decision-making bodies is as illegal as the systematic exclusion of blacks and poor people from juries. The national ego and superego defects that engendered the white mind exist primarily because of the absence of blacks at critical decision-making positions in the power complex.

A basic error in minority-group strategy is to wait until policy is made and then react. Even trying to influence policy in the making is not enough if you are on the outside. On the inside, with a constituency with real power, you may not even have to be a majority to protect and advance the interest of the group you represent. Among people of power, decisions are more often made by consensus than by vote. Respect for the needs and rights of others is necessary under such conditions.

A final major reform must be in the communications or mass-media area. The ego function of "watching the world" can get lost when the masses of people are not represented among those who determine media policy. One remedy would be the election of local boards for each medium, reflecting the widest possible range of community people and interests. Financial subsidies might be used to insure participation by the poor. Such boards are particularly important where a radio or television station or newspaper is part of a far-flung conglomerate financial empire with little sense of responsibility to the local community. Effective representation of wide interests could be a requirement for licensure. This approach would help the ego eyes see better. It would help all Americans understand the real issues better.

But the eyes need help. Mass media programming is beginning to reflect more than top-of-the-head opinions from the man in the street and from public figures who have a vested interest in concealing the truth. It still has too few depth analyses of important problems. It still provides too little information about the level of basic services, opportunities and problems in a given community, particularly in a summary form. With the current event-by-event reporting, nobody ever has the overall picture needed for taking informed action.

There is a need for systematic monitoring of the gap between need and the availability of opportunities—for jobs, food, clothing, shelter, health care and so on. The media have a responsibility to transmit these data to the political arena. Otherwise politicians and other leaders can avoid or confuse the real issues to protect or promote personal interests.

These reforms could bring a sufficient number of people to the governmental economic-information complex who would give us leadership that respected the interests of all people; who would give us programs which would reduce the anxiety of all as well as the need to exploit or attack one group or another. They could transform our national psyche from materialism and opportunism to fair play and justice. With such leadership Americans could live, work and play with the conviction that their government functioned in their behalf; that they didn't have to "git while the gittin' is good" or "beat the system before the system beats us." A sense of national community could emerge. This is the climate that will produce safe streets and people who want to give their fair share rather than take—be it welfare payments, unfair tax deductions or unjustified subsidies.

Until Americans are certain that the leadership group or national ego operates in our behalf many programs and approaches necessary to create a sense of community will be resisted. The reaction of a significant segment of the black community to family-planning programs—particularly when it includes abortion—is a case in point. A leading black specialist in obstetrics and gynecology has said that if family planning and abortion are more than a white plot, the white power structure should show the same dedication to making it possible for blacks to have education and training comparable to that of whites as they have shown to providing family-planning programs for blacks.

But because the people have been so long misled in the service of the national id or personal gain, at the moment we are not the informed censors of our government that Thomas Jefferson had theorized we would become. The truth is that even with social system reforms, if every person in America of voting age voted today, some of the most corrupt, racist, selfish and opportunistic men in America would be retained in or elected to public office. Because many Americans have not had evidence that their society operates in their behalf, they have used less healthy psychological and social adaptive mechanisms: the rightness of whiteness, the exclusiveness of labor movement and "ethnic" politics are three prime examples. Many people have "made it," or gained opportunities and advantages for themselves, by belonging to groups that exploit one or all of these approaches. They identify with their leaders and thus experience a sense of power and security. They develop an irrational loyalty, whether their leaders are right or wrong, effective or ineffective. In fact, if the leaders are challenged from the outside, support from their own group often intensifies. Some politicians have been elected to office from jail, or while under federal indictment. That is why former Mayor Hugh Addonezio of Newark and the late Representative Adam Clayton Powell of New York remained powerful long after their indiscretions were revealed. Others such as George Wallace are elected in spite of a record of blatantly immoral racist acts.

"But one cannot change those people," says the liberal intellectual. Those people—gun-owning, flag-waving, beer-drinking, nigger-hating, Commie-hunting Middle Americans. Many who fit this description are in the $5,000- to $15,000-family-income group. About two-thirds of all white families have yearly incomes in this range. They are just making it, and they can fall from security with the slightest change in national conditions—inflation, a slowdown in the war effort, an end to job discrimination, cancellation of an industrial contract. Many Middle Americans "need" lazy people, welfare bums, degenerate hippies, blacks, Jews and that entire villainous crew they place themselves above. But the belief that most Middle Americans cannot face the real issues may reflect the liberal intellectual's own feelings of superiority rather than Middle America's rigidity.

A small-town, Midwestern official, whose constituents are largely Middle Americans, told me that if the people knew their real enemies, they would respond differently. He pointed out that some cities and towns are being robbed and raped by local businessmen and politicians, and, that the people do not know. He cited the practice of politicians and their associates, taking options on land at a low cost, bribing commissions to change the zoning regulations and selling the land for enormous personal gain. For his efforts to alert the people, banks have made it difficult for him to get loans for his business, contracts from other businesses have dwindled and his life has been threatened. This problem exists in many places throughout the country. The people who bribe public officials and threaten honest men are this nation's real chiselers, the real danger, not the people on public welfare. That the average man is beginning to see this and has no way to rectify the inequities further augments his frustration.

The Middle American's powerlessness leaves blacks and other traditional enemies open to his hostility . . . again. The white man's anger toward blacks and other minorities has been legitimized throughout history, whereas action against his "equals" or "superiors" has always carried the threat of reprisal. The Middle American can be convinced that change will be beneficial, not harmful, for him as well as for the blacks and the poor. Approximately two of every three students attending college under New York City's open-enrollment practice are the children of white blue-collar workers, although the plan was originally opposed by them as a plot to coddle unprepared blacks and Puerto Ricans. The Middle American is as tired of being a victim of a sluggish system as anybody else. With better information and with programs that reduce his insecurity, he can gradually be brought into the humanist coalition; he can become the censor of his government in a way that would foster the development of a mature national ego.

Programs to reduce the insecurity of all Americans are essential. Many people know that blacks and other minorities have been cheated. Some people know the level of corruption and collusion in and between business, government, labor; that the ego and superego are serving the id rather than mediating conflicting interests. Giving them more proof of these facts just when they are beginning to make economic ends meet simply forces them to turn off the input and turn up the defenses. That is why the black movement for reform has revived rationalizations that were in mothballs only five years ago. Now blacks can't learn again, as in the early 1930s blacks couldn't play football because of weak shins. Somebody should tell Bubba Smith now that he has no business on a football field.


The specific programs needed are no mystery. New housing, health care, job and income guarantees, child-care and retraining programs are but a few of them. But without a leadership group or national ego committed to creating a national sense of community, new programs can continue to divide blacks and whites, rich and poor, old and young, women and men, while benefiting only a few—relieving the insecurity of only a few. The humanist coalition everywhere in America must make certain that all our new social programs are designed to reduce the level of fear, anxiety and insecurity of all Americans.

To overcome the current fear, we need multiple islands of success—models of cooperation, fair play and mature leadership across the country—to establish the notion that a climate of community can exist. New towns and model cities provide an excellent opportunity to put bricks and mortar, programs, services and people with differing needs and interests together in such a way as to create a sense of community. Only a mature leadership group will appreciate the need to do this. It is more immediately profitable to erect suburban slums with inadequate services, and encourage people to flee the problems of the cities created by similar selfish id practices a generation or more before.

The new town of Columbia, Maryland, appears to be pointing the way. Columbia, financed by private business and designed to be a city of more than 100,000 by 1980, is built in neighborhood clusters of 800 to 1,200 families. Schools, recreation facilities and stores are within walking distance of each neighborhood. Almost anyone can afford to live there. If one qualifies for a low-income project, rent is as low as $99.50 per month. However, rents go up to $385 per month, and houses can be bought for some $15,000 to $50,000 (one custom-built house cost over $100,000). All the neighborhoods are racially integrated. There are thirty industries and more than one hundred businesses there now, with more to come. There is a pre-paid medical plan for Columbia residents at the Johns Hopkins Clinic already operating in the town. Almost every imaginable service is available. The spirit of community abounds. A reporter describing the town wrote, "Leaving Columbia in the evening you've still got a people-meeting-people glow." [14]

Building a highly planned new town is a great financial risk; as a result there are only a few in the country. To speed the development of new towns, communities functioning in the best spirit of democracy, the government could subsidize the development of new towns just as it subsidized the development of railroads. One hundred or more new towns by 1980 would do a great deal to spread the spirit of community across the country. Otherwise the isolated few will reflect the stress and strain around them and will eventually be beset with all the problems of the "outside world."

Most Americans cannot live in new cities or will not want to. Yet the principle and spirit of new towns can be transmitted to old towns, cities and suburbs. Suburban sprawl is costly on both economic and relationship grounds. Land use and financing policies that work to separate people of different races and classes should be checked by national guidelines and fiscal policies. New health, education, child-care, and income programs should come to old cities through leadership groups representative of all the people and financially supported by all the people. In that way they will not come to serve "id functions," the personal desires and ambitions of a few.

There are communities in this country where the races will not integrate because of the feelings of both blacks and whites. There are places where entrepreneurial efforts are inadvisable; business ownership by a few who are out to get rich in poverty-stricken communities is bound to lead to exploitation and retaliation. Community development in these areas in this age calls for economic and political approaches that will involve as many people as possible with as much ownership and investment as possible in the political and economic development of their communities, as quickly as possible. Poor people should be able to buy their apartments and homes with the rent they pay—even if it is subsidized. Cooperative management of homes, stores, credit unions, and other services should be developed. People who can feel a sense of ownership and control in their community are more likely to protect it, more likely to try to relate it to the larger community in a prideful way than to withdraw from or retaliate against the larger community.

Cooperative stores and services should not be viewed as a threat to private ownership. In many countries both operate successfully. Cooperatives and low-profit organizations that include local management are better suited for low-income, high-unemployment areas. In many such areas there is not enough profit to bother to start a business. Unrest and tension grow from the lack of goods and services. Government and big business should co-operate with funds and expertise to help local residents build and manage cooperative programs. Many people trained in such programs will be able to use these skills anywhere in the society and feel that they can function in the total society. Without such training many will be a burden on the society.

I am well aware of the fact that such approaches have often proved disappointing because some poor people cheat and steal and act in as irresponsible a manner as some rich people in a climate that encourages beating the system. Until a new national climate is created, this is to be expected.

Massive and systematic efforts should be made to find jobs for the jobless and to retrain persons displaced by technology or by the loss of industry in an area, to stop the wasteful drift from place to place of marginally employed and unemployed people, which is more disorganizing and traumatic to poor families than the middle-income movement for educational or job advancement. It is often against the will, without hope and in fear of new failure. There is little chance for a sense of continuity and community in classrooms and neighborhoods comprising inescapably mobile and insecure people.

Regardless of the kind of economic and political system or national climate a society develops there will always be people who are unable to function well. But I am intrigued by what happens to many rapists, child abusers, murderers and others when the pressure to "cut the mustard" is removed. In any prison setting you will find men with long criminal records peacefully tending the garden or managing some similar chore, without guards. This suggests that the society may be better off taking care of people who cannot take care of themselves than by labeling them criminals, deadbeats or worse.

In a climate of community and adequate developmental opportunities, the number of people who could not cope and had to be cared for would remain low. In a climate of community, the urge to live off of the system or exploit or harm others is reduced. Sweden, with its many social services, does not have a major problem with "lazy people who don't want to work." Swedes are reared with the philosophy that it is acceptable to receive, and that it is important to give according to the best of your ability.

They have trouble with people who come there to live as adults who have been reared on a beat-the-system philosophy.

Reforms and programs to reduce insecurity will help but it is late—perhaps too late. The generally improving racial attitudes we hold today should have been the rule in 1910. Social programs we are talking about today should have emerged in the 1930s, if we were to have been ready for the year 2000. We now prepare for life in the year 2000 still burdened by archaic social structures and remarkably primitive attitudes about people.

These attitudes will give under the pressure now being exerted by minorities, the young and women. Other relatively secure groups are supporting the development of leadership groups that work to reconcile the conflicting needs of all. The defenses of denial, rationalization, and projection are failing. The deterioration in the fabric of our society is becoming apparent. Our societal id is being exposed. It is becoming increasingly difficult to scapegoat any group to distract attention away from the real issues. As programs that reduce fear and anxiety emerge, the pace of conflict resolution will quicken. Certainly it will cost money. But getting the money is not the real question. The real question is whether we can make "the stitch in time"—before the fabric unravels completely.

We have the money; we simply spend it on the wrong things. A May, 1970 report by the American Orthopsychiatric Association tells a good part of the story:

### Expenditures for Human Services versus War Costs

Two billion dollars for a year's "War on Poverty" = one *month's cost* of the war in Vietnam.

One year's expenditures for food stamp and school lunch programs = cost of one *week* of war.

All our housing programs, including Model Cities, last year = cost of about one *month* of war.

Total cost of all federal educational programs last *year* = cost of about one *month* of war.

Total cost of all federal educational programs last year = cost of 10 *weeks'* fighting in Vietnam.

*One month's* tax dollars from New York City, now spent in Vietnam, would build new housing for 12,000 families.

*One hour's* tax money from New York City now ending up in Vietnam would run a high school for a whole *year*.[15]

Am I saying that the Black-Power and black-awareness efforts should be abandoned to establish a sense of national community? On the contrary. It is black awareness and self-appreciation that have enabled some blacks to cease a vain effort to be white, to re-examine society, goals and values. It is the fact of blackness that makes one aware of the fact that accomplishment and money are not enough. It is this re-examination that is forcing us toward an appreciation of the multi-racial, multi-ethnic nature of our country; toward the appreciation rather than fear of difference; toward a community of different people; toward the realization that we must have a representative, mature leadership capable of reconciling conflicting interests. The demand of every group for fair play and justice will bring either community or destruction. Only in a climate of community can we move beyond black and white.

As a child psychiatrist, I must draw from the wisdom of a nursery rhyme:

> There were two cats of Kilkenny
> Each thought there was one too many.
> So they fought and they fit
> And they scratched and they bit
> Until there wasn't any.

# Footnotes

Footnotes to Chapter II

1. Erik Erikson, *Childhood and Society,* 2nd ed. (New York: Norton, 1963), p. 260.

2. For further discussion of minimal psychopathology, see Milton J. E. Senn and Albert J. Solnit, *Problems in Child Behavior and Development* (Philadelphia: Lea & Febiger, 1968).

3. *Children Problems and Services in Child Welfare Programs* (Washington, D.C.: Welfare Administration, Children's Bureau, 1963), pp. 1–13.

4. Alan K. Campbell, "Inequities of School Finance," *Saturday Review,* January 11, 1969, p. 44.

5. For further discussion of race and intelligence, see Walter F. Bodmer and Luigi Luca Cavalli-Sforza, "Intelligence and Race," *Scientific American,* October, 1970, pp. 19–29; and Arthur R. Jensen, "How Much Can We Boost IQ and Scholastic Achievement?" *Harvard Educational Review,* Winter, 1969, pp. 1–123.

6. By the Staff of The Wall Street Journal, *Here Comes Tomorrow!: Living and Working in the Year 2000* (New Jersey: Dow Jones Books), 1966, pp. 1, 7, 14, 15, 16, 21, 26, 168.

7. U.S. Department of Labor, Bureau of Labor Statistics, "Occupational Employment Patterns for 1960 and 1975," Bulletin #1599 (Washington, D.C., 1968), pp. 3, 13.

8. Data on Swedish social services obtained from Mrs. Maud Helling, First Secretary, National Swedish Social Welfare Board, and Mrs. Thyra Brandter, Secretary, Social Committee of the City of Stockholm.

## Footnotes to Chapter III

1. Peggy Streit, "Why They Fight for the P.A.T.," *The New York Times Magazine*, September 20, 1964, pp. 20–21, 122, 124–125.

2. *Newsweek*, "The Troubled American," October 6, 1969, pp. 31, 36, 52, 57.

3. For further discussion of subsidies in American life, see William Raspberry, "Uncle Sam's Handouts Aren't Only for the Poor," *Washington Post*, July 15, 1968, p. B1.

4. Gustavus Meyers, *History of the Great American Fortunes* (New York: Random House, The Modern Library, 1907), p. 49.

5. *Congress and the Nation, 1954–1964: A Review of Government and Politics in Post War Years* (Washington, D.C.: Congressional Quarterly Service, 1965), pp. 1027–45; and U.S. Senate Committee on the Judiciary, "Homestead Act Centennial," Hearings, 87th Congress, 1st Session (1961), p. 2.

6. *Ibid.*, U.S. Senate Committee on the Judiciary, p. 2.

7. *Op. cit., Congress and the Nation*, p. 1031.

8. *Ibid.*, pp. 553–554; Joint Economic Committee Print, "Subsidy and Subsidy-Effect Programs of the U.S. Government," 89th Congress, 1st Session (1965), pp. 9, 59.

9. Matthew Josephson, *The Robber Barons: The Great American Capitalists* (New York: Harcourt Brace Jovanovich, A Harvest Book, 1962), pp. 23–24.

10. Joseph M. L. Schafer, *The Origin of the System of Land Grants for Education*, Bulletin of the University of Wisconsin, #63, History Series Vol. 1, #1 (Madison, Wisconsin, 1902), p. 40.

11. Federal Security Agency, Office of Education, *Land Grant Colleges and Universities*, Bulletin 1952, #21 (Washington, D.C., 1952), p. 12; and Edward Danforth Eddy, Jr., *Colleges for Our Land and Time: The Land Grant Idea in American Education* (New York: Harper & Brothers, 1957), pp. 257–258.

12. *Ibid.*, Federal Security Agency, p. 12.

13. "1964–1965 Voluntary Support of America's Colleges and Universities" (New York: Council for Financial Aid to Education, Inc., 1967), pp. 3, 21–59.

14. Earl J. McGrath, *The Predominantly Negro Colleges and Universities in Transition* (New York: Columbia University Teacher's College for the Institute of Higher Education, 1965), pp. 154–169.

15. *Historical Statistics of the United States, Colonial Times to 1957* (Washington, D.C.: U.S. Bureau of the Census, 1960), pp. 213–214.

16. *Ibid.*, p. 214; and U.S. Department of Labor, Bureau of Labor Statistics, "The Negroes in the United States, Their Economic and Social Situation," Bulletin #1511, June, 1966 (Washington, D.C., 1966), p. 194.

17. John Hope Franklin, *Reconstruction after the Civil War* (Chicago: University of Chicago Press, 1961), p. 108.

18. David Blose and Ambrose Caliver, "Statistics of the Education of Negroes, 1929–30; 1931–32," U.S. Department of Interior, Office of Education, Bulletin #13 (Washington, D.C., 1936), p. 16.

19. James P. Comer, Martin Harrow and Sam Johnson, "Summer Study-Skills Program: A Case for Structure," *The Journal of Negro Education*, Winter, 1969, pp. 38–45.

20. Jackie Robinson, *Baseball Has Done It*, edited by Charles Dexter (Philadelphia: J. B. Lippincott, 1964), p. 18.

21. Sterling D. Spero and Abram L. Harris, *The Black Worker: The Negro and the Labor Movement* (New York: Atheneum, 1968), pp. 23–24.

22. *Ibid.*, p. 15.

23. Arthur M. Ross, "The Negro in the American Economy," in *Employment, Race and Poverty,* Arthur Ross and Herbert Hill, eds. (New York: Harcourt Brace Jovanovich, A Harbinger Book, 1967), p. 7.

24. Josephson, *op. cit.*, p. 21.

25. Marcus Lee Hansen, *The Immigrant in American History* (Cambridge: Harvard University Press, 1940), pp. 60–68, 72–76.

26. B. A. Botkin, ed., *Lay My Burden Down. A Folk History of Slavery* (Chicago: University of Chicago Press, Phoenix Books, 1958), pp. 222, 226, 229–230, 231, 241, 242, 247.

27. James S. Allen, *Reconstruction: The Battle for Democracy, 1865–1876* (New York: New World, 1963), p. 72.

28. C. Vann Woodward, *The Strange Career of Jim Crow*, 2d rev. ed. (New York: Oxford University Press, 1966), p. 19.

29. Dudley Taylor Cornish, *The Sable Arm: Negro Troops in the Union Army, 1861–1865* (New York: Norton, 1966), foreword.

30. Spero and Harris, *op. cit.*, p. 8.

31. *Historical Statistics of the United States, Colonial Times to 1957, op. cit.*, pp. 11–12.

32. E. Franklin Frazier, *The Negro in the United States*, rev. ed. (New York: Macmillan, 1957), pp. 166, 572; Ross and Hill, *op. cit.*, p. 4.

33. Franklin, *op. cit.*, p. 52.

34. *Ibid.*, p. 52.

35. Donald Comer, *Braxton Bragg Comer (1848–1927): An Alabamian Whose Avondale Mills Opened New Paths for Southern Progress* (New York: The Newcomer Society of England, American Branch, 1947), pp. 10–11.

36. Franklin, *op. cit.*, pp. 146, 147, 148, 149.

37. Lerone Bennett, Jr., *Black Power U.S.A.: The Human Side of Reconstruction, 1867–1877* (Chicago: Johnson Publishing Co., 1967), pp. 331–332.

38. *Congressional Record—House*, January 29, 1901 (Washington, D.C.), p. 163.

39. *Ibid.*, p. 1635.

40. *Ibid.*, p. 1635.

41. Langston Hughes, *Fight for Freedom: The Story of the NAACP* (New York: Norton, 1962), p. 78.

42. *Ibid.*, p. 19.

43. *Ibid.*, pp. 76–77.

44. *Ibid.*, p. 85.

45. Frazier, *op. cit.*, pp. 191–192, 208.

46. Southern Regional Council, "A Study of Negro Farmers in South Carolina," SRC: 23 December, 1962 (Atlanta, Georgia).

47. *Ibid.,* p. 20.

48. U.S. Bureau of the Census, U.S. Bureau of Labor Statistics, "Recent Trends in Social and Economic Conditions of Negroes in the United States" (Washington, D.C.: Government Printing Office, 1968), pp. 15–18.

49. Harold K. Schulz, "The CDGM Story," *Christianity and Crisis,* January 23, 1967, pp. 315–320.

50. U.S. Bureau of the Census, *Pocket Data Book, USA 1969* (Washington, D.C.: Government Printing Office, 1969), pp. 108, 174, 212–213.

## Footnotes to Chapter IV

1. *Washington Post,* April 4, 1968, pp. A1, A11.

2. Arna Bontemps, ed., *Great Slave Narratives* (Boston: Beacon Press, 1969), p. 306.

3. Barbara Patterson, et al., *The Price We Pay* (Atlanta: Southern Regional Council and New York: Anti-Defamation League, 1964), p. 14; Lerone Bennett, Jr., *Before the Mayflower: A History of the Negro in America, 1916–1962* (Chicago: Johnson Publishing Co., 1962), pp. 352–362; U.S. Bureau of the Census, *Historical Statistics of the United States, Colonial Times to 1957* (Washington, D.C., 1960), p. 218; and Ralph Ginzburg, *100 Years of Lynchings* (New York: Lancer Books, 1962), p. 193.

4. Basil Davidson, *Black Mother: The Years of the African Slave Trade* (Boston: Little, Brown and Company, 1961), p. 5.

5. Basil Davidson, *Lost Cities of Africa* (Boston: Little, Brown and Company, 1959), pp. 78–79, 89–90.

6. Winthrop D. Jordan, *White over Black: American Attitudes Toward the Negro, 1550–1812* (Chapel Hill: University of North Carolina Press, 1968), pp. 24–25.

7. Maurice R. Davie, *Negroes in American Society* (New York: McGraw-Hill, 1949), p. 2.

8. William Graham Sumner, *Folkways—A Study of the Sociological Importance of Usages, Manners, Customs, Mores and Morals* (New York: Dover Publications, 1959), p. 294.

9. Daniel P. Mannix and Malcolm Cowley, *Black Cargoes: A History of the Atlantic Slave Trade, 1518–1865* (New York: Viking Press, 1962), p. 22.

10. Carter G. Woodson, *The Negro in Our History,* 5th ed. (Washington, D.C.: The Associated Publishers, 1928), p. 61.

11. John C. Calhoun, "Speech on the Reception of Abolition Petitions," in *Slavery Defended: Views of the Old South,* Eric L. McKitrick, ed. (Englewood Cliffs, N.J.: Prentice-Hall, 1963), p. 13.

12. William J. Grayson, "The Hireling and the Slave," *Ibid.,* pp. 63–64.

13. William Stanton, *The Leopard's Spots: Scientific Attitudes Toward Race in America, 1815–59* (Chicago: University of Chicago Press, 1960), p. 31.

14. *Ibid.,* pp. 50, 62.

15. *Ibid.,* p. 13.

16. John L. Thomas, ed., *Slavery Attacked: The Abolitionist Crusade* (Englewood Cliffs, N.J.: Prentice-Hall, A Spectrum Book, 1965), p. 173.

17. I. A. Newby, *Jim Crow's Defense: Anti-Negro Thought in America, 1900–1930* (Baton Rouge: Louisiana State University Press, 1968).

18. F. L. Olmsted, *The Slave States* (New York: G. P. Putnam & Sons, Capricorn Books, 1959), p. 95.

19. J. D. B. De Bow, "The Interest in Slavery of the Southern Non-Slave Holder," in McKitrick, *op. cit.,* p. 174.

20. Saul K. Padover, ed., *Thomas Jefferson on Democracy* (New York: New American Library, 1961), p. 99.

21. *Ibid.,* p. 101.

22. L. J. West, "The Psychobiology of Racial Violence," *Archives of General Psychiatry,* #16, June, 1967, pp. 646–647.

23. *Ibid.,* p. 647.

24. For further discussion of psychic associations relative to race, see Charles Pinderhughes, "Understanding Black Power, Its Processes and Proposals," *The American Journal of Psychiatry,* #11, May, 1969, pp. 1552–1557.

25. John Hersey, *The Algiers Motel Incident* (New York: Alfred A. Knopf, 1968).

26. Saul Padover, *op. cit.,* pp. 98–99.

27. Pauli Murray, ed., *States' Laws on Race and Color* (Cincinnati, Ohio: Women's Division of Christian Service, 1950), p. 31.

28. *Congressional Record—House,* January 29, 1901, p. 1638.

Footnotes to Chapter V

1. Waring Cuney, "No Images," in *The Poetry of the Negro, 1746–1949,* Langston Hughes and Arna Bontemps, eds. (New York: Doubleday, 1949), p. 145.

2. William J. Grayson, "The Hireling and the Slave," in *Slavery Defended: Views of the Old South,* Eric L. McKitrick, ed. (Englewood Cliffs, N.J.: Prentice-Hall, 1963), p. 63.

3. *Ibid.,* pp. 66–67.

4. Stanley M. Elkins, *Slavery: A Problem in American Institutional and Intellectual Life* (New York: Grosset & Dunlap, The Universal Library, 1963), p. 94.

5. Daniel Mannix and Malcolm Cowley, *Black Cargoes: A History of the Atlantic Slave Trade, 1518–1865* (New York: Viking Press, 1962), p. 20.

6. B. A. Botkin, ed., *Lay My Burden Down. A Folk History of Slavery* (Chicago: University of Chicago Press, A Phoenix Book, 1958), pp. 62–65.

7. *Ibid.,* pp. 70–72.

8. *Ibid.,* pp. 73, 75–76.

9. Frederick Law Olmsted, *The Slave States* (New York: G. P. Putnam & Sons, Capricorn Books, 1959), p. 41.

10. Josiah Henson, *An Autobiography of the Reverend Josiah Henson* (Cambridge, Mass.: Educational Services, Inc., 1965), p. 1.

11. Susan Dabney Smedes, *Memorials of a Southern Planter, Baltimore 1887* (Cambridge, Mass.: Educational Services, Inc., 1965), p. 3.

12. Josiah Henson, *op. cit.,* p. 4.

13. B. A. Botkin, *op. cit.*, p. 69.
14. Ralph Ginzburg, *100 Years of Lynchings* (New York: Lancer Books, 1962), pp. 90–91, 102.
15. *Ibid.*, p. 187.
16. *Ibid.*, pp. 141, 157, 235.
17. *Ibid.*, p. 36.
18. *Ibid.*, p. 179.
19. Elliot Liebow, *Tally's Corner: A Study of Negro Streetcorner Men* (Boston: Little, Brown and Company, 1967).
20. U.S. Department of Labor, Bureau of Labor Statistics, *The Negroes in the United States—Their Economic and Social Situation,* Bulletin #1511 (Washington, D.C., 1966), p. 179.
21. Hughes and Bontemps, *op. cit.*, pp. 22–23.
22. E. Franklin Frazier, *The Negro Church in America* (New York: Schocken Books, 1962), p. 31.
23. E. Franklin Frazier, *The Negro in the United States* (New York: Macmillan, 1957), p. 429.

### Footnotes to Chapter VII

1. Jane Loevinger, "Meaning and Measurement of Ego Development," *American Psychologist,* Vol. 21, No. 3 (Lancaster, Penn.: March, 1966), pp. 195–206.
2. Thomas Abernathy, Mississippi; Jamie Whitten, Mississippi; George Andrews, Alabama; John McMillin, South Carolina; Mendel Rivers, South Carolina; Albert Watson, South Carolina.
3. *Congressional Quarterly Weekly Report,* Vol. 25 (Washington, D.C.: Congressional Quarterly, Inc., 1967), pp. 220, 856, 910, 1044, 1332, 2362.
4. *Wall Street Journal,* June 17, 1969, p. 1.
5. For further discussion of this matter, see Bryce Nelson, "HEW: Finch Tries to Gain Control Over Department's Advisory Group," *Science,* May 16, 1969, pp. 813–814.
6. *New Haven Register,* June 4, 1971, p. 5.
7. Saul K. Padover, ed., *Thomas Jefferson on Democracy* (New York: New American Library, 1961), pp. 92–93.
8. "Being a Compilation of Data and Well-informed Conjecture Concerning Some but Not All Media Moguls, Together with Cartographical Depictions of Their Domains Obtained with Some Difficulty by the Editors," *Atlantic Monthly,* July, 1969, p. 83.
9. *Wall Street Journal,* June 30, 1969, p. 1.
10. "Being a Compilation of Data and Well-informed Conjecture Concerning Some but Not All Media Moguls, Together with Cartographical Depictions of Their Domains, Obtained with Some Difficulty by the Editors," *Atlantic Monthly,* July, 1969, p. 83.
11. "Travels in Medialand," *Atlantic Monthly,* July, 1969, p. 94.
12. *Wall Street Journal,* November 17, 1969, p. 6.
13. *New York Times,* June 20, 1971, p. 1.
14. Jeanne Lamb O'Neill, "Columbia, Gem of America's 'New Towns'," *American Home,* May, 1970, p. 142.
15. "Participation in a Campaign on Publicizing the Effects of a War Economy on Human Services," a memorandum, The American Orthopsychiatric Association (New York, May 14, 1970).

# Bibliography

## Chapter II

Aichhorn, August. *Wayward Youth*. New York: Viking Press, 1963.

Bergen, Bernard J., and Thomas, Claudewell, eds. *Issues and Problems in Social Psychiatry: A Book of Readings*. Springfield, Illinois: Charles C. Thomas, 1966.

Bloom, Benjamin S. *Stability and Change in Human Characteristics*. New York: John Wiley and Sons, 1964.

Bowlby, John. *Maternal Care and Mental Health*. World Health Organization Monograph Series, no. 2. Switzerland, March, 1951.

Clausen, John A. *Socialization and Society*. Boston: Little, Brown and Company, 1968.

Comer, James P. "Technology and the Inner-City School." In *To Improve Learning: An Evaluation of Instructional Technology*, vol. 2, Sidney G. Tickton, ed. with staff of the Academy for Educational Development. New York: R. R. Bowker, 1971.

Elmer, Elizabeth. *Children in Jeopardy: A Study of Abused Minors and Their Families*. Pittsburgh: University of Pittsburgh Press, 1967.

Elmer, Elizabeth, and Gregg, Grace S. "Developmental Characteristics of Abused Children." *Pediatrics* 40, Part I (October, 1967): 596–602.

Erikson, Erik. *Childhood and Society*. 2d ed. New York: Norton, 1963.

Fantini, Mario, and Weinstein, G. *The Disadvantaged: Challenge to Education.* New York: Harper & Row, 1968.

Freud, Anna. *The Writings of Anna Freud, Vol. V, 1956–1965.* New York: International Universities Press, Inc., 1969.

Hollingshead, August B., and Redlich, Frederick C. *Social Class and Mental Illness: A Community Study.* New York: John Wiley and Sons, 1958.

Kozol, Jonathan. *Death at an Early Age.* New York: Bantam Books, 1967.

Ladner, Joyce A. *Tomorrow's Tomorrow: The Black Woman.* Garden City, N.Y.: Doubleday, 1971.

Lidz, Theodore. *The Family and Human Adaptation.* New York: International Universities Press, 1963.

Lourie, Reginald S. "Personality Development and the Genesis of Neuroses." *Clinical Proceedings, Children's Hospital of the District of Columbia* 23 (June, 1967): 167–182.

Lustman, Seymour L. "Impulse Control, Structure, and the Synthetic Function." *Psychoanalysis—A General Psychology: Essays in Honor of Heinz Hartmann,* Loewenstein, R. M.; Newman, L. N.; Schur, M.; and Solnit, A. J., eds. New York: International Universities Press, 1966.

Redlich, Frederick C., and Freedman, Daniel K. *The Theory and Practice of Psychiatry.* New York: Basic Books, 1966.

Schorr, Alvin. *Poor Kids: A Report on Children and Poverty.* New York: Basic Books, 1966.

Schreiber, Daniel, ed. *Profile of the School Drop-out.* New York: Vintage Books, 1967, 1968.

Senn, Milton J. E., and Solnit, Albert J. *Problems in Child Behavior and Development.* Philadelphia: Lea & Febiger, 1968.

Solnit, Albert J. "Some Adaptive Functions of Aggressive Behavior." *Psychoanalysis—A General Psychology: Essays in Honor of Heinz Hartmann,* Loewenstein, R. M.; Newman, L. N.; Schur, M.; and Solnit, A. J., eds. New York: International Universities Press, 1966.

Solnit, Albert J., and Provence, Sally A., eds. *Modern Perspectives in Child Development.* New York: International Universities Press, 1963.

Toffler, Alvin, ed. *The Schoolhouse in the City.* New York: Frederick A. Praeger, 1968.

Wolff, Sula. *Children Under Stress.* London: Penguin, 1969.

## Chapter III

Allen, James S. *Reconstruction: The Battle for Democracy, 1865–1876.* New York: New World, 1963.

Aptheker, Herbert, ed. *A Documentary History of the Negro People in the United States, from Colonial Times Through the Civil War.* New York: Citadel Press, 1962.

————. *A Documentary History of the Negro People in the United States: II, From the Reconstruction Era to 1910.* New York: Citadel Press, 1964.

Bennett, Lerone, Jr. *Black Power U.S.A.: The Human Side of Reconstruction, 1867–1877.* Chicago: Johnson Publishing Co., 1967.

Botkin, B. A., ed. *Lay My Burden Down. A Folk History of Slavery.* Chicago: University of Chicago Press, Phoenix Books, 1958.

Cornish, Dudley Taylor. *The Sable Arm: Negro Troops in the Union Army, 1861–1865.* New York: Norton Library, 1966.

Donald, David H. *Charles Sumner and the Rights of Man.* New York: Knopf, 1970.

Franklin, John Hope. *Reconstruction after the Civil War.* Chicago: University of Chicago Press, 1961.

Frazier, E. Franklin. *The Negro in the United States.* rev. ed. New York: Macmillan, 1957.

Glazer, Nathan, and Moynihan, Daniel Patrick. *Beyond the Melting Pot: The Negroes, Puerto Ricans, Jews, Italians, and Irish of New York City.* Cambridge, Massachusetts: M.I.T. Press, 1963.

Hansen, Marcus Lee. *The Immigrant in American History.* Cambridge, Mass.: Harvard University Press, 1940.

Hughes, Langston. *Fight for Freedom. The Story of the NAACP.* New York: Norton, 1962.

Josephson, Matthew. *The Robber Barons: The Great American Capitalists.* New York: Harcourt Brace Jovanovich, Harvest Books, 1962.

McGrath, Earl J. *The Predominantly Negro Colleges and Universities in Transition.* New York: Columbia University Teacher's College for the Institute of Higher Education, 1965.

Meyers, Gustavus. *History of the Great American Fortunes.* New York: Random House, The Modern Library, 1907.

Phillips, Ulrich B. *American Negro Slavery.* Baton Rouge: Louisiana State University Press, 1966.

Pike, James S. *The Prostrate State: South Carolina Under Negro Government.* Robert F. Durden, ed. New York: Harper & Row, 1968.

Robinson, Jackie. *Baseball Has Done It.* Charles Dexter, ed. Philadelphia: J. B. Lippincott, 1964.

Rose, Willie Lee. *Rehearsal for Reconstruction: The Port Royal Experiment.* New York: Random House, 1964.

Ross, Arthur M. "The Negro in the American Economy." In *Employment, Race and Poverty,* Arthur Ross and Herbert Hill, eds. New York: Harcourt Brace Jovanovich, A Harbinger Book, 1967.

Schulz, Harold K. "The CDGM Story." *Christianity and Crisis* (January 23, 1967): 315–320.

Southern Regional Council. "A City Slum—Poor People and Problems." Atlanta, Georgia, April, 1966.

Southern Regional Council. "Hungry Children." Atlanta, Georgia, June, 1967.

Spero, Sterling D., and Harris, Abram L. *The Black Worker: The Negro and the Labor Movement.* New York: Atheneum, 1968.

Stampp, Kenneth M. *The Peculiar Institution: Slavery in the Ante-Bellum South.* New York: Random House, 1956.

Woodward, C. Vann. *The Strange Career of Jim Crow.* 2d rev. ed. New York: Oxford University Press, 1966.

## Chapter IV

Ackerman, Nathan W., and Jahoda, Marie. *Anti-Semitism and Emotional Disorder*. New York: Harper & Brothers, 1950.
Adorno, T. W., et al. *The Authoritarian Personality*. New York: John Wiley and Sons, 1964.
Allport, Gordon W. *The Nature of Prejudice*. Garden City, N.Y.: Doubleday, 1958.
Atkinson, James. *The Great Light: Luther and Reformation*. Grand Rapids, Mich.: W. B. Eerdmans, 1968.
Bainton, Roland. *The Reformation of the Sixteenth Century*. Boston: Beacon Press, 1952.
Bontemps, Arna, ed. *Great Slave Narratives*. Boston: Beacon Press, 1969.
Clark, Kenneth B. *Prejudice and Your Child*. Boston: Beacon Press, 1963.
Comas, Juan. *Racial Myths*. Paris: UNESCO, 1958.
Comer, James P. "Individual Development and Black Rebellion: Some Parallels." *Midway* 4 (Summer, 1968): 33–48.
Davidson, Basil. *Black Mother: The Years of the African Slave Trade*. Boston: Little, Brown and Company, 1961.
———. *Lost Cities of Africa*. Boston: Little, Brown and Company, 1970.
Davie, Maurice R. *Negroes in American Society*. New York: McGraw-Hill, 1949.
Doob, Leonard. *Communication in Africa; A Search for Boundaries*. New Haven: Yale University Press, 1961.
Dunn, L. C. *Race and Biology*. Paris: UNESCO, 1958.
Goldsby, Richard A. *Biology of Race and Races*. New York: Macmillan, 1971.
Goodman, Mary Ellen. *Race Awareness in Young Children*. New York: Macmillan, 1964.
Hersey, John. *The Algiers Motel Incident*. New York: Alfred A. Knopf, 1968.
Jahoda, Marie. *Race Relations and Mental Health*. Belgium: UNESCO, 1960.
Jordon, Winthrop D. *White over Black: American Attitudes Toward the Negro, 1550–1812*. Chapel Hill: University of North Carolina Press, 1968.
Karl, Adam. *The Roots of the Reformation*. Cecily Hastings, trans. New York: Sheed and Ward, 1957.
Klineberg, Otto. *Race and Psychology*. Paris: UNESCO, 1958.
Little, Kenneth L. *Race and Society*. Paris: UNESCO, 1958.
Mannix, Daniel P., and Cowley, Malcolm. *Black Cargoes: A History of the Atlantic Slave Trade, 1518–1865*. New York: Viking Press, 1962.
McKitrick, Eric L., ed. *Slavery Defended: Views of the Old South*. Englewood Cliffs, N.J.: Prentice-Hall, 1963.
Morant, G. M. *The Significance of Racial Differences*. Paris: UNESCO, 1958.
Murray, Pauli, ed. *States' Laws on Race and Color*. Cincinnati, Ohio: Women's Division of Christian Service, 1950.
Newby, I. A. *Jim Crow's Defense: Anti-Negro Thought in America, 1900–1930*. Baton Rouge: Louisiana State University Press, 1968.

Olmsted, F. L. *The Slave States.* New York: G. P. Putnam & Sons, Capricorn Books, 1959.

Padover, Saul K., ed. *Thomas Jefferson on Democracy.* New York: New American Library, 1961.

Poussaint, Alvin F. "Blacks and the Sexual Revolution," in *Ebony* (October, 1971): 112–120.

Simpson, George Eaton, and Yinger, Milton J. *Racial and Cultural Minorities: An Analysis of Prejudice and Discrimination.* New York: Harper & Row, 1965.

Stanton, William. *The Leopard's Spots: Scientific Attitudes Toward Race in America, 1815–59.* Chicago: University of Chicago Press, 1960.

Thomas, John L., ed. *Slavery Attacked: The Abolitionist Crusade.* Englewood Cliffs, N.J.: Prentice-Hall, 1965.

Woodson, Carter G. *The Negro in Our History.* 5th ed. Washington, D.C.: The Associated Publishers, 1928.

## Chapter V

Billingsley, Andrew. *Black Families in White America.* Englewood Cliffs, N.J.: Prentice-Hall, 1968.

Bryce-Laporte, Roy S. "The Slave Plantation: Background to Present Conditions of Urban Blacks." In *Race, Change and Urban Society,* Peter Orleans and William R. Ellis, eds. New York: Sage Publications, 1971.

Clark, Kenneth B. *Dark Ghetto: Dilemmas of Social Power.* New York: Harper & Row, 1965.

Cuney, Waring. "No Images." In *The Poetry of the Negro, 1746–1949,* Langston Hughes and Arna Bontemps, eds. New York: Doubleday, 1949.

Davidson, Basil. *The African Genius: An Introduction to African Cultural and Social History.* Boston: Little, Brown and Company, 1970.

Dover, Cedrick. *American Negro Art.* Connecticut: New York Graphic Society, 1970.

Drachler, Jacob, ed. *African Heritage: An Anthology of Black African Personality and Culture.* New York: Macmillan, 1969.

Dumond, Dwight Lowell. *Antislavery: The Crusade for Freedom in America.* Ann Arbor: University of Michigan Press, 1961.

Elkins, Stanley M. *Slavery: A Problem in American Institutional and Intellectual Life.* 2nd ed. Chicago: University of Chicago Press, 1968. brary, 1963.

Frazier, E. Franklin. *The Negro Church in America.* New York: Schocken Books, 1962.

Gibbs, James L., Jr., ed. *Peoples of Africa.* New York: Holt, Rinehart and Winston, Inc., 1965.

Ginzburg, Ralph. *100 Years of Lynchings.* New York: Lancer Books, 1962.

Greene, Lorenzo Johnston. *The Negro in Colonial New England.* New York: Atheneum, 1968.

Grier, William H., and Cobbs, Price M. *Black Rage.* New York: Basic Books, 1968.

Haselden, Kyle. *The Racial Problem in Christian Perspective.* New York: Harper & Row, 1964.

Herskovits, Melville J. *The Myth of the Negro Past*. Boston: Beacon Press, 1958.

Kardiner, Abraham, and Ovesey, Lionel. *The Mark of Oppression: Explorations in the Personality of the American Negro*. New York: World Publishing Company, 1951.

Leighton, Alexander H., and Lambo, T. Adeoye. *Psychiatric Disorder Among the Yoruba: A Report from the Cornell-Aro Mental Health Research Project in the Western Region, Nigeria*. Ithaca, N.Y.: Cornell University Press, 1963.

Lewis, Hylan. *Blackways of Kent*. Chapel Hill: University of North Carolina Press, 1955.

Liebow, Elliot. *Tally's Corner: A Study of Negro Streetcorner Men*. Boston: Little, Brown and Company, 1967.

Mead, Margaret. *Continuities in Cultural Evolution*. New Haven: Yale University Press, 1964.

Pettigrew, Thomas F. *A Profile of the Negro American*. Princeton, N.J.: D. Van Nostrand Reinhold Company, 1964.

Willie, Charles V. *The Family Life of Black People*. Columbus, Ohio: Charles E. Merrill Company, 1970.

Work, John W., ed. *American Negro Songs and Spirituals*. New York: Crown Publishers, 1940.

## Chapter VI

Allport, Gordon W. *Becoming: Basic Considerations for a Psychology of Personality*. New Haven, Conn.: Yale University Press, 1955.

Barbour, Floyd B., ed. *The Black Power Revolt*. Boston: Porter Sargent, 1969.

Blos, Peter. *On Adolescence: A Psychoanalytic Interpretation*. New York: The Free Press, 1962.

Broderick, Francis L., and Meier, August. *Negro Protest Thought in the Twentieth Century*. Indianapolis: Bobbs-Merrill, 1965.

Comer, James P. "The Social Power of the Negro." *Scientific American*. (April, 1967): 21–27.

Cruse, Harold. *Rebellion or Revolution?* New York: Morrow, 1968.

Havighurst, Robert J., and Taba, Hilda. *Adolescent Character and Personality*. New York: John Wiley and Sons, 1949.

Keniston, Kenneth. *The Uncommitted: Alienated Youth in American Society*. New York: Harcourt Brace Jovanovich, 1965.

Pelling, Henry. *American Labor*. Chicago: University of Chicago Press, 1960.

Reich, Charles A. *The Greening of America*. New York: Random House, 1970.

Wilson, James Q. *Negro Politics: The Search for Leadership*. New York: The Free Press, 1960.

## Chapter VII

Dahl, Robert A. *Who Governs?: Democracy and Power in an American City*. New Haven: Yale University Press, 1961.

Danelius, Hans. "Human Rights in Sweden." *Sweden Today*. Stockholm: The Swedish Institute, 1970.

Elder, C. M. *Government in Sweden: The Executive at Work*. New York: Pergamon Press, 1970.

Lindgren, Hans George. "Social Planning in Sweden." *Sweden Today*. Stockholm: The Swedish Institute, 1970.

Lundberg, Ferdinand. *The Rich and the Super Rich*. New York: Bantam Books, 1968.

Mills, C. Wright. *The Power Elite*. New York: Oxford University Press, 1959.

Ministry of Finance. *The Swedish Budget, 1970–71*. Stockholm, Sweden, 1970.

Mintz, Morton, and Cohen, Jerry S. *America, Inc.* New York: Dial Press, 1957.

Montagu, Ashley. *Man: His First Million Years*. New York: New American Library, 1957.

Murphy, Gardner. *Personality: A Biosocial Approach to Origins and Structure*. New York and London: Basic Books, Inc., 1966.

National Central Bureau of Statistics, Division of Judicial and Social Welfare Statistics. *The Cost and Financing of the Social Services in Sweden in 1968*. No. 20. Stockholm, Sweden, 1970.

Rose, Arnold M. *The Power Structure: Political Process in American Society*. New York: Oxford University Press, 1967.

Stern, Phillip M. *The Great Treasury Raid*. New York: Random House, 1964.

Stoodley, Bartlett H., ed. *Society and Self. A Reader in Social Psychology*. New York: The Free Press, 1962.

The Swedish Institute. *Facts About Sweden*. Stockholm, Sweden, 1969.

The Swedish Institute. "The Status of Women in Sweden. A Report to the United Nations, 1968." *Sweden Today,* Stockholm, Sweden, 1968.

The Swedish Institute for Cultural Relations with Foreign Countries. "Swedish Government in Action." *Fact Sheets on Sweden*. Stockholm, Sweden, 1969.

Tindall, George B., ed. *A Populist Reader: Selections from the Works of American Populist Leaders*. New York: Harper & Row, 1966.

# Index

Abernathy, Thomas, 231
Abortion, 244
Adams, James Truslow, 94–95
Addonizio, Hugh, 245
Adolescents. *See* Children; Colleges and college students
Advertisers, 235
Afikpo Ibo, the, 150, 151
Africa, 120–24, 126, 138, 148–54, 164. *See also* Slavery
Age-sets, 150–51ff.
Agnew, Spiro, 236
Agricultural Adjustment Administration, 105
Agricultural Stabilization and Conservation Service, 106
Agriculture (farming), 79, 104–6, 217. *See also* Land; Slavery

Agriculture, Department of, 105ff., 217
Alabama, 82, 95, 99, 103, 137, 167, 228–29, 231, 236–37, 242. *See also* specific places
Alaska, 194
Alcorn College, 79
*Algiers Motel Incident, The,* 134
Ali, Muhammad, 14, 116, 138
American Federation of Labor, 86
American Medical Association (AMA), 38
American Orthopsychiatric Association, 250
*Amos and Andy,* 170
Andrews, George, 231
Anson, Cap, 86

265